THE GOLDEN DOOR COOKS LIGHT & EASY

To Barbara and Sherwood

Bon Appitit
Good health!

Michel Stroot

THE GOLDEN DOOR COOKS LIGHT & EASY

Delicious Recipes from America's Premier Spa

BY CHEF MICHEL STROOT

Gibbs Smith, Publisher
Salt Lake City

12 11 10 09 08   9 8 7 6 5

Food Photographer: Beatriz Da Costa
Food Stylist: Anne Disrude
Prop Stylist: Lara Robby
Additional Photography: Glen Cormier, Nik Wheeler,
Joan Vanderschuit, John Durant

Published by
Gibbs Smith, Publisher
P.O. Box 667
Layton, Utah 84041

1-800-748-5439 orders
www.gibbs-smith.com

Designed by Kurt Wahlner
Printed and bound in Canada

Library of Congress Cataloging-in-Publication Data

Stroot, Michel.
   The Golden Door cooks light and easy / Michel Stroot—1st ed.
p. cm.
   ISBN 10: 1-58685-254-X ISBN 13: 978-1-58685-254-2
   1. Quick and easy cookery. 2. Low-calorie diet—Recipes.
3. Golden Door. I. Title.
TX833.5 .S77 2003
641.5'63—dc21
                                2002015657

To the memory of

ALEX SZEKELY

PRESIDENT, GOLDEN DOOR

CONTENTS

Michel Stroot, a chef you will get to know well in this book through his recipes and insights, is a man for all seasons—equally at home in the worlds of cooking, gardening, voluntarism and art (he is a wonderful sketcher and painter). He has the knack of making friends. I've often seen him smile like a shy kid when, upon entering the Golden Door's dining room at dinner, the guests rise to applaud him. He is the spa's "not-so-secret" lure, and is certainly one of the reasons many guests return over and over. I am no longer taken aback when I meet someone who has been to the Golden Door and they ask, "Is Michel, the miracle worker, still there?" I happily reply, "Yes!" and that, as any restaurant owner will tell you, is in itself a miracle.

This book is about enjoying, guilt-free, one of the greatest achievements of our age: the abundance, freshness, availability, wholesomeness and quality of an incredible variety of foods. No king or queen of ancient times could dine as well as we do today, nor could they even conceive of what we take for granted. Yet in the midst of all this abundance, we live in an era obsessed with fast and factory-processed foods.

I believe these are an anathema to long life. Michel champions the "slow food" cause, proving with every meal that food has always been about much more than calories, fat grams and color combinations. He sees food as the very fuel of life. Our spa guests agree, for they consider his weekly cooking class a "must not miss" event. Once they've spent a few hours with Michel as he demonstrates how to prepare life-giving, spirit-satisfying food, it may literally be years before most of them even contemplate walking into a fast food restaurant again.

Understanding and appreciating what food means to life, and sharing that knowledge with both skill and a twinkle in his eye, is Michel's *joie de vivre*—his labor of love. Even after twenty years, Michel says his job gets better all the time. It's not like going to work, he tells me with youthful enthusiasm, but rather like going out to play surrounded by his pots and pans. "I still wake up in the middle of the night dreaming of food," he says, and I believe him. I know he's always looking for new and exciting preparations and combinations.

One of the many things I admire about Michel is this rather special ability to grow, absorb and adapt the newest and best from amongst the flood of nutritional knowledge. It could easily overwhelm the less diligent chef, but Michel takes it in from all sources. He has traveled the world on sabbaticals and special cooking assignments. He volunteers his time and culinary efforts at innumerable fund-raisers. He listens to my opinions, something I appreciate because I am both a hands-on cook and an innkeeper who started in the spa business sixty-three years ago. Edmond Szekely and I founded Rancho La Puerta in Tecate, Baja California, Mexico, in a fertile mountain valley just over the border from San Diego County; from the beginning we relied on fresh fruits, grains and vegetables to form the basis of a hearty cuisine that satisfied the appetites of active guests.

When I started the smaller, more exclusive Golden Door almost two decades later, I knew that a large organic garden on the premises was a must. Yet it was still an era when

Elvis was on the car radio and the drive-in and drive-through hamburger stand craze was raging (I guess it still is, at least the drive-through part). Organic gardens seemed to be the last thing on Americans' minds, but from the beginning our guests were drawn to our gardens as if by magic. Their hunger was not just for food, but for comfort in knowing where it came from, how it was prepared, and how good it made them feel. Today Michel calls our organic garden his muse. He tells me he doesn't think he could live without his mornings out there, not far from the kitchen. "I'm renewed walking through it," he says, "and picking a leaf and crushing it to inhale the fragrance, or nibbling on a berry or a carrot still warm from the earth."

Now, thanks to the farmers market revolution in many cities and suburban areas, as well as the natural foods markets springing up everywhere, you too have access to the freshness Michel espouses. He wants you to remember that whatever you eat becomes as much a part of you as what you think and what you do. Its essence becomes your essence.

Your decisions about what you eat, and when, have a far-reaching ripple effect. Buying from local farmers keeps you close to the rhythms, seasons and even the soil of your home region. It also helps reduce the ridiculous amounts of energy we burn to transport foods all over the globe—again, buy seasonally and chances are good that the fruit you eat will have come from the valley over the hill rather than Chile or New Zealand. It will also be richer in vitamins and minerals, for it will have been picked riper, perhaps weeks riper. Our sole exception to this consciousness is the Golden Door's commitment to finding the freshest fish. At present, with fish such an important part of our weekly menus, we have to accept the fact that much fish comes via air transport from distant fishing grounds.

Use this book well. Use these recipes often. One seldom has time to cook every day, and I am no different. But try to keep what you learn about food in the forefront of your mind when you eat out. Simplicity and "in-season" are two key measurements. For those of us who have finished growing up, the key to not growing wide is half portions—split an entrée with a friend or save half for your lunch the next day.

Michel hopes your mantra will be a thought written by Thoreau: "A man may esteem himself happy when that which is his food is also his medicine." Keep in mind that your immune system is your very best friend. Tend to it carefully and it will be there for you. Abuse it and you will reap the consequences. Support it also by taking to heart the importance of movement, and welcome exercise as another vital path to a long healthy life.

Food is nature, is it not? Count nature as one of your best friends. Commune with her often. Breathe deeply of her peace. The rewards will be assured. You can begin this sensual, rewarding journey by turning the page.

DEBORAH SZEKELY
Founder, Golden Door

To Deborah Szekely, my deep and warm gratitude for helping me make this book a reality. Deborah has inspired and encouraged me and been my fair and astute critic during thirty wonderful and creative years that I have been at the Golden Door. Think of this—by the time I came to the Golden Door, Deborah already had thirty-three years of experience in meeting and exceeding spa guests' expectations, not only in the dining room but in all facets of the modern fitness-resort experience, which she pioneered at Rancho La Puerta starting in 1940. While I was writing this book, Deborah lost her son, Alex Szekely, long the president of the Golden Door and one of the founders of the International Spa Association (I/SPA). He was one of the kindest, friendliest men I have ever known, and the example of his indomitable spirit against all odds continues to inspire me and all of us in the spa world and beyond.

I am especially grateful to the enlightening and serene daily presence of Rachel Caldwell, general manager at the Golden Door, who has been a great supporter of my culinary trials and occasional tribulations. At my side in the kitchen, Jesus Gonzalez, Norberto Rojas, Dean Rucker, Claudio Sanjuan and Jennifer Sarkisian faithfully execute my recipes and bring their artistry to every plate. Their enthusiasm, hard work and good humor makes each day a pleasure. Debbie Cole, R.D., was most helpful with nutrition information. Out front, Martha Shissler, our dining room supervisor, offers her continuous support and friendship.

At home, my dear wife Irma, who has her own busy career, shares with me the joys of eating well and enjoying life in harmony. Sasha, my twenty-three-year-old daughter, is a bright young lady and a joy in my life; she has even included some of my recipes in her own parties, the ultimate compliment. My two sons, François and Pierre, of whom I am very proud, have witnessed Dad's evolution as a "spa chef" and have carried on our commitment to healthy eating.

Running a busy kitchen and writing a book cannot happen simultaneously without the help of many colleagues, who were as good at sharpening words and other elements of this book as a chef who cares for the edge of his or her favorite French knife: Christine Andes, Sue Annetts, Karen Berman (who edited and adapted, with delightful patience and perseverance, my recipes for home cooking), Mary-Elizabeth Gifford, Peter Jensen and Kelly

ACKNOWLEDGMENTS

Miller. I thank them for their dedication to the raison d'être of the Golden Door and cooking light. My editor, Madge Baird, has my gratitude, and the promise of a wonderful dinner, for her guidance and belief that light and healthful cooking can be complex in flavor but reasonably simple in execution.

Finally, I must thank all our guests, especially those who attended my weekly cooking class, as well as the many who have expressed their appreciation of new ideas and menus, offered their opinions, and made our dining room the most lively and engaging restaurant scene I can imagine. Their support continues to give me the energy and determination to look for new paths in my culinary journey.

Eating should be a happy experience. A nurturing experience. A respite from the day's cares and stresses that feeds both body and soul.

Too often in our hectic, harried lives, we find what feels like respite in a fast-food cheeseburger or a chocolate bar. But such indulgences are short-lived, relying as they do on too much fat, salt and sugar. No, the happy experience of eating that I'm referring to is one that can sustain us for the short and long term. One that tantalizes us with its aromas, dazzles us with its colors, and charms our taste buds with its sheer lusciousness—while, at the same time, bestowing on our bodies all the nutrients required for good health. I'm proud to say that guests have this kind of eating experience every day at the Golden Door, where I've been the chef for the past thirty years. Frankly, eating well here is easy. While guests concentrate their energies on the many activities of our fitness spa, my staff and I take responsibility for their meals and snacks.

At home, I know, it's a different story. There's an extra project at work, kids to be driven in different directions each afternoon, an ailing family member who needs looking after, a lawn to be mowed, a letter to be written—too often, preparing healthful, delicious meals can seem like a fantasy.

With this book, I want to help you make that fantasy into a reality—to bring a bit

INTRODUCTION

of spa life into your everyday life—at least, at mealtime. Part of the Golden Door experience is to discover new foods that are delicious and healthful. Indeed, most guests are surprised at the variety of foods we serve and at how good they taste. They learn to expect—and enjoy—something different each time they come to the table. There's no reason why your family and friends can't pick up this habit, too. Instead of your same old salad, try Frisée with Garden-Fresh Strawberries and Mango-Tahini Dressing. It's a salad as easy as its name: frisée lettuce, strawberries and, if you wish, scented geranium leaves and flowers, drizzled with a delicious low-fat dressing. (Once you taste it, you'll make it often.)

And please don't assume that spa food is only about salad. I promise you that eating healthfully from the recipes in this book will not mean going hungry. There's pizza here, and pasta, quesadillas, risottos, lobster and butternut squash ravioli—all the foods you love, adapted for the spa kitchen. Do you feel like cooking some comfort food on a Sunday afternoon? My Vegan Irish Stew will prove that you don't need to go out and buy a hunk of beef to create a soul-satisfying pot of stew. Is the weather enticing you to fire up the grill? My Grilled Salmon with Three Salsas will banish all thoughts of nitrate-laden hot dogs.

Of course, part of the spa experience is relaxing and being pampered. At home, you can't re-create an entire spa, but you can create an oasis for yourself, even if it's only in small doses. Linger over a cup of tea—but make it a special brew, like my Rose Hip and Cranberry Tea. It's as easy as adding some cranberry juice and honey when you steep a store-bought rose hip tea bag. I promise you that this small but flavorful addition will transform your tea break into a retreat.

And then there's dessert. Eliminating this course goes against the grain—after all, I was born in Belgium, the land of fine chocolate. In the spa kitchen, we do dessert, but we do it always in moderation, reducing the amount of fat and sweeteners, introducing alternative ingredients, but never sacrificing satisfaction. Try my Lemon Polenta Cake with Macerated Strawberries or my Golden Door Chocolate Chip Cookies, my Fruited Couscous with Mint or my Chocolate-Mocha Flan.

These are the kinds of things that can easily become part of any home cook's repertoire. I wrote this book in the hope that it will inspire you to take a few extra moments to nurture yourself and your loved ones with healthful, delicious food and drink, and skip those greasy overloaded plates of take-out food that so often pass for dinner. Fueled by good, tasty, easy-to-prepare food that you enjoy in the company of those you love, you can bring the spa life into your daily life.

I am fortunate to have the spa life as my daily work-life. My car all but drives itself as I head to work each day—I have made the trip so many times. Heading north from San Diego, I pass through an inland corridor of rugged hills. Immense granite boulders, shining silver in their morning robes of dew, stand amid avocado orchards covering steep hillsides. At a place with a lovely name, Deer Springs, I turn onto a winding two-lane road that plunges down a narrow canyon. In a few moments, I am at a large gate all but hidden in a row of tall pines. No name. No sign—only a Japanese-style monogram of a doorway sheltered by a curving roof.

The gate swings open. Cars are not a part of life here, so I park in a hidden area and take to the pathways. In this place, every walk is a meditation. Footbridges cross a thin thread of water winding through an oak grove. Inside a cluster of buildings clad in Japanese roof tiles, their rooflines curving upward, I walk beneath the eaves along one of many *engawas* (narrow decks) beside manicured landscapes where ancient traditions of scale and composition turn rocks into distant mountains and raked sand into seas. In one area, a waterfall tumbles off the hillside. In another, rainbow-colored koi glide lazily beneath water lilies. And I am home again.

Here I greet a new family each week. Some guests have returned more than fifty

times, while others will soon be new friends. My domain here is the kitchen, surrounded by my ranges, knives, pans and vast chopping-block counters. But it also lies outside in the sunshine, where I walk the rows of a three-acre organic vegetable-and-herb garden, pulling up a carrot, crushing marjoram between my fingertips, listening to the bees in the rosemary. What will be on the menu this week? The answer is in these rows, written by this warm soil. It will also come from my purveyors, the good men and women with standards like our own, who search for the freshest fish, free-range poultry, grains and other staples. My job is to bring out the flavors of their finds—flavors that honor the seasons. The dishes that emerge from my kitchen cannot rely on buttery sauces and well-marbled meats. It is a far cry from the foods that emerged from the kitchens of my youth, and though I look back fondly on those days, I am proud to see how my cooking has evolved.

My first memory of enjoying food was in my mother's kitchen on a cold winter evening in our home outside Brussels, Belgium. I remember my mother whisking creamy pancake batter, and as she poured the pancakes onto the hot griddle, they sizzled and filled the air with the aroma of butter and vanilla. My mother let me stand at the stove and flip the pancakes. Some of them went airborne as I wielded the spatula with a childish hand. It didn't matter to my dear mother, who heaped the finished pancakes onto a big platter and adorned them with jam she had made from tart spring rhubarb and succulent summer strawberries. How proud I was when we brought those pancakes to the table.

Nor will I ever forget my first encounter with oranges. British soldiers who were stationed near our village at the end of World War II handed out chocolate, fruit candy and other goodies. I was given a strange-looking piece of fruit. I did not know how to eat it, so I bit into it like an apple, to the amusement of the officer who had given it to me. The bitter peel made me grimace. But then I tasted the sweet inner juice—heaven! I quickly learned that I had to remove the peel so that I could enjoy the rest of this enchanting fruit.

At that time, farming was the main activity in our village; it was an occupation and a year-round source of food. I helped plant seeds for all kinds of vegetables, including the staple of northern European cuisine in those days—the potato. My favorite meal was *stoemp*, a stew of potatoes, carrots, leeks and any other vegetable that could fit into the large pot. Lamb or other meats were added to the pot, and after hours of simmering, the whole thing was mashed to produce a satisfying stew. It was the most delicious food possible—next to our excellent Belgian chocolate, that is.

When my mother and I went into town to shop, we would walk the avenues and read the menus posted outside the fashionable restaurants. It was all too fancy for a country boy like me, but when I chanced to peer into the kitchen, I was awestruck. There were cooks in their aprons, chopping, slicing and whizzing around; pots and pans clanking; sauces simmering; meats sputtering on the fire. It was an enticing thought, to work in such a kitchen. My mother wouldn't hear of it. She wanted me to work in an office. So, when I was a high school student, I dutifully got a job as a messenger in a local office. For me, it was deadly. When a new hotel and culinary school—the Centre d'Enseignements et de Recherches des Industries Alimentaires—opened in Brussels, I enrolled immediately. I loved school, and there, I learned everything about the food-service industry, from classical French cuisine to table service to accounting. I worked hard and graduated at the top of my class, all the while feeling that I was exactly where I was meant to be.

Since then, my vocation has taken me from Brussels to London, from there to Toronto and Vancouver, and finally to California, where I cooked in Monterey and Pebble Beach. Through all of these positions, my cooking was largely of the classical French school (although, like any good chef, I couldn't help picking up new ideas wherever I went). Then, in 1973, Deborah Szekely, founder of the Golden Door, invited me to be the chef at her spa. This new job forced me to rethink everything I had learned about cooking. And for that, I'm forever grateful.

When the Golden Door opened in 1958, the era of the destination spa in America began. From the beginning, a cornerstone of the spa's appeal was its fresh, colorful, flavorful food. Deborah Szekely had an artistic eye as well as a love of just-picked, organically raised fruits and vegetables. She knew from nearly twenty years of experience at her first spa—Rancho La Puerta, founded with her husband, Professor Edmond Szekely, in Tecate, Baja California, Mexico—that low-fat, simple-but-tasty meals could please guests as well as give them the energy they needed for active days spent hiking, stretching, strengthening and learning new ways of making the mind-body-spirit connection (with Tai Chi, meditation and yoga, for example). It wasn't a cuisine of denial or abstinence. For many guests, it was all about rediscovering the great flavors and freshness of childhoods spent on farms, in small towns, and even in great cities before the days of chain markets and restaurants. The big difference was the lack of butters and other animal fats common to classical cooking. It was, in a word, *light*.

I must admit that when I started at the Golden Door, I found myself thinking of all

the things I couldn't do. But then I started to read and to experiment—and the flood-gates opened. This was the perfect place to showcase California's bounty of fresh fruits and vegetables, seafood, and the region's wonderful melting pot of ethnic cuisines. Together, Deborah and I soon decided that Golden Door menus would have all the beauty and flavor of classical cuisine, but would be innovative and light, composed in accordance with the most advanced nutritional principles, in touch with the seasons, borrowing from all the cuisines of the globe—and, above all, it would be delicious. Today, guests at the Golden Door are often surprised by the zesty flavors and the variety they encounter at each meal.

Some time after I took over the Golden Door kitchen, Deborah's son, Alex, took the helm of the Golden Door. He provided me with constant support and encouragement. He believed in and valued innovation. Alex kept my cooking ever-young, and since we tragically lost him in 2002 at the age of 44, I have rededicated myself to his vision of a cuisine that is both delicious and good for you.

This book, the latest of several we have produced over the years, owes another real debt to the great variety of guests we have had at the Golden Door. When I meet them, either in my forays into the dining room each day or at the cooking class I offer every week, I see all kinds of people: working parents, single parents, international travelers, bon vivants, foodies, health-conscious types, dieters, home cooks, avid dinner-party host-esses, and businesswomen and men (we have a few men's weeks each year) with very full calendars back home. Cooking class at the Golden Door is popular, certainly because we have lots of fun and because we eat what we cook, but also because the guests want guidance and inspiration for the way they will cook when they return home. This book is for those guests and for the many readers who have not been to the Golden Door but who also want to improve the way they eat. I hope it will help people take greater pleasure in cooking and delight in eating nutritious food. I've learned a thing or two in my years at the Golden Door, and I am always thrilled to share what I know. Read—and cook!—and eat!—in good health.

MICHEL STROOT

A Few Words on How to Use This Book

About the Recipes

We no longer count calories at the Golden Door. Instead, we serve portions in line with guests' activity levels and personal likes. All, however, are based on a few simple principles. Each meal consists of 20 to 25 percent lean protein and 20 to 25 percent fat (from olive oil, vegetable oil, nut or seed oil). The rest is a combination of vegetables, fruit, dairy and whole grains. Beyond this basic formula, we focus on portion size as a way to control weight.

We use a concept developed by Debbie Cole, R.D., called The Smart Plate. The Smart Plate can be applied to virtually any meal. It works like this: Imagine a plate with a line drawn down the middle. Fill half with leafy greens and nonstarchy vegetables. Then draw a line through the other half to make quarters. Fill one quarter with lean protein. Fill the other quarter with a complex carbohydrate (such as rice, potato, bread, quinoa or other grain).

All the recipes in this book have been created according to these principles, with the goal of serving meals that are nutritionally balanced and portioned appropriately for good health. At home, keep in mind your own activity levels and metabolic tendencies, and size your portions accordingly. There's no single formula for everybody, but these principles are a good starting point.

About Oil in a Spray Bottle

Throughout this book, you will see that some of the recipes call for cooking oil in a spray bottle. We use spray bottles to mist oil onto pans and food. This enables you to use less oil, reducing total fat in the dish. I don't like to use the commercially available oil sprays because of the propellants in the spray containers. Keep two spray bottles close at hand. Fill one bottle with straight canola oil. Fill the other with a combination of one part olive oil to three parts canola oil. A healthful polyunsaturated oil that has no flavor, canola oil is good for cooking because of its high smoking point. (You can raise the heat and properly brown your food.) Olive oil adds its fabulous flavor, but has a lower smoking point; hence, the need to combine the two in cooking. In some dishes, you will want the rich olive oil flavor; in others, you can stick with the flavorless canola.

When an ingredient list reads "olive oil and canola oil in a spray bottle, or 1 teaspoon olive oil" and you find yourself without a spray bottle, spread the scant teaspoon of oil well.

Know, too, that misting doesn't work in all cases requiring oil. In some recipes, the ingredient lists call for olive oil (for salads) and dark sesame oil (to flavor Asian-inspired dishes). Whenever these instructions appear, follow the recipes as written.

About Golden Door Basics

At the end of this book you will find a chapter titled "Golden Door Basics." In a professional kitchen, certain recipes are considered foundation recipes—the basis for other more complex dishes. Until, say, the 1970s, in most fine-dining establishments these consisted of the same recipes—largely French—for stocks and sauces and such. Then came the food revolutions of the late-twentieth century, especially the influence of ethnic cuisines and an emphasis on healthful eating. Naturally, chefs began to add to their repertoire of foundation recipes. The "Golden Door Basics" chapter is a mix of foundation recipes, old and new, all in updated, healthful versions, of course. My basics include low-fat stocks that will help you create soups, stews and sauces; salad dressings, dipping sauces, salsas and tofu-based mayonnaise variations that you can mix and match with all kinds of dishes; luscious breads that you can use for sandwiches or serve in a basket on their own; and chips that can be served with dips or incorporated into formal appetizers and even desserts.

See page 11

See page 137

A sanctuary of serenity, joyous movement and delicious food awaits each spa guest behind these fabled golden doors.

See page 155

See page 132

A regimen combined of vigorous exercise, quiet moments and rejuvenating beauty treatments is essential for a refreshing week at Golden Door.

See page 40

GRILLED SALMON WITH THREE SALSAS

See page 116

Beauty and renewal lie at every turn, from sunrise on the mountain to the warmth of hot river stones and the soothing, timeless patterns of raked sand.

See page 57

See page 109

See page 86

See page 23

An ancient temple bell, its sonorous tones announcing dinner,
graces the dining room courtyard.

See page 172

See page 168

THE GOLDEN DOOR COOKS LIGHT & EASY

Dawn at the Golden Door. The air is still and heavy with moisture, for during the night a bank of cool fog has moved in off the ocean, threading its way up the canyon. You dress quickly in light clothing, lace up a pair of sturdy walking shoes, and take a windbreaker off its hanger. It may be chilly in the groves, especially near the bottom of the hill, but in one of those glorious moments that comes after a bit of sacrifice, you know that your group will step into streaming sunlight up on the ridge. A cluster of granite boulders waits there to serve as seats for the group's traditional mid-walk break.

Down in the kitchen, our staff is also up with the sun, slicing fruit from the orchard, baking muffins, perhaps making a whole-grain hot cereal or waffle batter. We know that some of us and our guests love breakfast more than any meal. After a good walk or hike to the top of the ridgeline, everyone will be hungry, even the most die-hard "I never need breakfast" soul who believes that a *grande* coffee during a commute is a meal in itself.

We give breakfast the feeling of importance and sanctuary that it deserves. Back from their walks, which usually last about an hour, guests return to their rooms to shower. We soon bring them a breakfast tray that includes hot tea, fruit, juice, yogurt and something substantial such as muffins, waffles or a small folded omelet. Simplicity is a theme, for even a hard-boiled egg with a little sea salt will taste fantastic after a good morning walk. The meal takes on a rhythm of its own, punctuated occasionally by the whir of a hummingbird above

BREAKFAST

each room's private deck. Alert and invigorated with oxygen from a thousand deep breaths, you can focus on a food's best natural attributes — textures, sweetness, acidity and combinations of flavors, both expected and surprising.

Food is fuel, of course, and we find that these simple meals of whole grains (rich in B-complex vitamins and indispensable trace elements), fruits and a little protein provide enough energy until lunchtime. Food also puts us in touch with our locality and its seasons. At the Golden Door, the appearance of spring's first strawberries marks the end of our mild winters. And food is nature itself: all of the muffins in this chapter are made with natural whole grains, including whole-wheat, semolina and oatmeal flours rather than the bleached white variety.

Do you have a morning walking habit at home? If not, try greeting the sun from the top of your favorite neighborhood hill or beach, or even the wet-grass reaches of your nearest ball field. That should be only the beginning.

Do you have a place at home set aside for your breakfast quietude? If not, consider starting a new habit of retiring to a corner of your garden far from any morning television news. A few plants on an apartment or condominium's deck will serve the same purpose. I realize that these recipes are the antithesis of the buffet-line excesses of a Sunday brunch, or the nostalgic heaven of perfectly prepared bacon and eggs and hash browns in your favorite diner. But fear not; they are every bit as satisfying.

SMOKED CHICKEN AND PEA SPROUT OMELET

MAKES 4 SERVINGS

The beauty of omelets is that the add-ins are completely open to interpretation. Use the basic ratio of 4 whole eggs to 8 egg whites to serve 4 people, and create combinations that please you. Here, a little smoked chicken and red onion, two ingredients with assertive flavors, are all you really need for a satisfying omelet. Pea sprouts are the flowering sprouts of snap peas or snow peas. Look for them at Asian markets, farmers markets or health food stores. If you can't find them, substitute sunflower sprouts or pea shoots.

Olive oil and canola oil in a spray bottle, or 2 teaspoons olive oil

1 medium red onion, thinly sliced

2 (4-ounce) skinless, boneless, smoked chicken breast halves, finely diced

2 cups pea sprouts, pea shoots or sunflower sprouts

$^1/_2$ teaspoon fresh thyme or lemon thyme leaves

4 eggs

8 egg whites

Spray or grease a nonstick pan with 1 teaspoon olive oil and set over medium heat. Add the red onion; sauté, stirring, until the onion is soft, brown and caramelized. Stir in the chicken; heat through. Remove from the heat and stir in the pea sprouts and thyme. Set aside.

Using an electric mixer or a fork, lightly beat the eggs and egg whites until thoroughly blended. Set aside.

Spray or grease an 8-inch nonstick pan with 1 teaspoon olive oil and set over medium heat. Pour in $^1/_4$ of the egg batter; cook for 2 to 3 minutes. Lift up the sides of the omelet to let the uncooked egg flow to the bottom of the pan. When the omelet is no longer liquid, scatter $^1/_4$ of the smoked chicken and pea-sprout mixture over the eggs; cook until the eggs are dry. If you wish, you can bake the omelet instead at 350 degrees F for 3 to 5 minutes to cook the eggs evenly.

Gently fold the omelet in half with a rubber spatula and keep warm. Repeat the process to make 3 more omelets with the remaining eggs and chicken and pea-sprout mixture. Serve immediately.

ASIAN OMELET

This fluffy omelet, fragrant with garlic and ginger, is fortified with soba noodles that are made with buckwheat flour. Drizzle with Ginger, Peanut and Cilantro Sauce and Dressing for a final, piquant flourish.

2 ounces soba noodles

2 teaspoons dark sesame oil

1 teaspoon minced garlic

4 large shiitake mushrooms, stems removed and thinly sliced

2 ribs celery, thinly sliced

4 ounces cooked crabmeat

6 scallions, thinly sliced

Olive oil and canola oil in a spray bottle, or 1 teaspoon olive oil

4 eggs

8 egg whites

Ginger, Peanut and Cilantro Sauce and Dressing (page 210)

Bring a small pot of water to a boil over medium-high heat. Add the soba noodles and simmer for 3 to 5 minutes, or until the noodles are just tender. Drain the noodles in a colander and run under cold water to stop the cooking process. Transfer to a bowl and set aside.

Heat the sesame oil in a nonstick pan set over medium heat. Add the garlic; sauté, stirring, for 1 to 2 minutes, or until soft. Stir in the sliced shiitake mushrooms and celery; sauté, stirring, for 3 to 5 minutes, or until the vegetables begin to soften. Remove from heat and stir into the soba noodles. Add the crabmeat and scallions and toss to combine well. Set aside.

Using an electric mixer or a fork, lightly beat the eggs and egg whites together until thoroughly blended. Set aside.

Spray or grease an 8-inch nonstick pan with olive oil and set over medium heat. Pour in $\frac{1}{4}$ of the egg batter and cook for 2 to 3 minutes. Lift up the sides of the omelet to let the uncooked egg flow to the bottom of the pan. When the omelet is no longer liquid, scatter $\frac{1}{4}$ of the soba-crabmeat mixture over the eggs; cook until the eggs are dry. If you wish, you can bake the omelet instead at 350 degrees F for 3 to 5 minutes to cook the eggs evenly.

Gently fold the omelet in half with a rubber spatula and keep warm. Repeat the process to make 3 more omelets with the remaining egg mixture and soba-crab filling. Drizzle each omelet with Ginger, Peanut and Cilantro Sauce and Dressing; serve immediately.

Tuscan Omelet

Anyone who has ever visited Tuscany knows the feeling: Just mention the word and it conjures thoughts of rusticity and remarkably fresh ingredients cooked simply—olives, juicy ripe tomatoes and just-from-the-garden basil. This omelet is an ode to that beautiful and bountiful place and to the healthfulness of its cuisine.

4 artichokes

1 lemon, cut in half

2 medium red potatoes

3/4 cup thinly sliced crimini mushrooms
   or oak mushrooms

2 tablespoons thinly sliced fresh basil

4 plum tomatoes, seeded and
   finely diced

Olive and canola oil in a spray bottle,
   or 2 teaspoons olive oil

4 eggs

8 egg whites

4 tablespoons grated Asiago cheese

Remove the stems and leaves from the artichokes and scoop out the feathery pulp that covers the hearts. Squeeze the juice of half a lemon over the hearts to prevent them from turning brown. Place the artichoke hearts into a pot of lightly salted water set over medium-high heat and bring to a simmer; simmer for 20 minutes, or until tender.

Meanwhile, place the potatoes into another pot of water set over medium-high heat and bring to a boil; boil for 20 minutes, or until the potatoes are tender and easily pierced by the tip of a sharp knife. Drain the potatoes, peel them and cut them into small dice.

When the artichoke hearts are done, remove them from the water with a slotted spoon, dice finely and transfer to a mixing bowl. Stir in the potatoes, mushrooms, basil and tomatoes.

Spray or grease a nonstick pan with 1 teaspoon olive oil and set over medium heat. Add the artichoke-potato mixture; sauté, stirring, for 3 to 5 minutes, or until the mushrooms are soft. Remove from the heat and set aside.

Using an electric mixer or a fork, lightly beat the eggs and egg whites together until thoroughly blended. Set aside.

Spray or grease an 8-inch nonstick pan with olive oil and set over medium heat. Pour in $\frac{1}{4}$ of the egg batter; cook for 2 to 3 minutes. Lift up the sides of the omelet to let the uncooked egg flow to the bottom of the pan. When the omelet is no longer liquid, scatter $\frac{1}{4}$ of the cooked artichoke-potato mixture over the eggs; cook until the eggs are dry. If you wish, you can bake the omelet instead at 350 degrees F for 3 to 5 minutes to cook the eggs evenly.

Sprinkle the eggs with 1 tablespoon of Asiago cheese and gently fold the omelet in half with a rubber spatula; keep warm. Repeat the process to make 3 more omelets with the remaining eggs and artichoke-potato mixture. Serve immediately.

THE ELEMENTS OF OMELETS

The elements of omelet-making might seem simple, but they are important. Start with eggs at room temperature. Use a pan that is six to seven inches in diameter and spray it with a mist of oil. Heat the pan, but don't make it too hot. Often "healthful" omelets are made from egg whites only; at the Golden Door, we use 2 egg whites and 1 whole egg for flavor, nutrition and texture. One yolk won't hurt you! When you pour the beaten eggs into the pan, stir with a spatula so that the omelet cooks evenly; lift the sides of the omelet to let the uncooked egg batter flow to the bottom of the pan. When the omelet is no longer liquid, add the filling and fold it over with the spatula. The outside of the omelet should be golden brown. Don't overcook or you'll wind up with a rubbery omelet.

BLUE CORN AND BUTTERMILK WAFFLES WITH SPICED PEAR BUTTER

MAKES 10 WAFFLES

Inspired by the waffles I ate with pure joy as a child in my native Belgium, I created this light, crisp version. Blue cornmeal gives them a wonderful crunch, while the buttermilk imparts a rich, tangy flavor. Made from fruit and spiced with cinnamon, Spiced Pear Butter makes for a sweet, gooey condiment. If you don't have a waffle iron, you can use this delicious batter to make pancakes.

For the pear butter:

$^{1}/_{2}$ lemon

3 medium pears, peeled, cored
    and diced

1 ripe banana, thinly sliced

$^{1}/_{2}$ cup unsweetened apple juice

$^{1}/_{2}$ stick cinnamon

1 tablespoon grated lemon zest

For the waffles:

1 cup blue cornmeal

1 $^{1}/_{2}$ cups sifted unbleached flour

2 teaspoons baking powder

$^{1}/_{2}$ teaspoon baking soda

2 cups low-fat buttermilk

2 tablespoons butter, melted

2 tablespoons canola oil

1 teaspoon pure vanilla extract

4 tablespoons honey

2 egg yolks

4 egg whites, at room temperature

1 tablespoon grated lemon zest

Canola oil in a spray bottle, or
    1 teaspoon canola oil

Maple syrup, optional

To prepare the pear butter, first acidulate the fruit to prevent it from browning: squeeze the juice of $^{1}/_{2}$ lemon over the pear and banana and toss to coat. Transfer to a saucepan set over medium-high heat. Pour the apple juice over the fruit and add the cinnamon stick. Simmer for 10 to 15 minutes, covered. Remove from the heat and let cool.

Remove the cinnamon stick and transfer the cooled fruit and cooking liquid to a blender or food processor fitted with a metal blade; process the fruit until smooth. Transfer to a storage container or serving bowl, stir in the lemon zest and set aside until ready to serve. *Makes 2 cups.*

To prepare the waffles, preheat a Belgian waffle iron or standard waffle iron. In a large mixing bowl, combine the blue cornmeal, flour, baking powder and baking soda. Set aside.

In a separate mixing bowl, combine the buttermilk, butter, canola oil, vanilla extract, honey and egg yolks; mix well.

With a spatula, make a small depression or "well" in the center of the dry ingredients and pour the buttermilk mixture into it. Stir gently but thoroughly, until well incorporated. Be careful not to overmix.

Using an electric mixer, beat the egg whites until they form soft peaks. Gently fold into the buttermilk batter until the whites are just barely blended in. Gently fold in the grated lemon zest.

Spray or grease the hot waffle iron with canola oil, pour in the batter until the iron is about $\frac{2}{3}$ full, and close the lid. Bake for 3 to 5 minutes, or until golden brown and crisp. Keep warm. Repeat the process with the remaining batter. Serve immediately with Spiced Pear Butter or maple syrup. Wrap any leftover waffles in plastic wrap and refrigerate. Reheat in a 325 degree F oven or toaster oven. Spiced Pear Butter will keep in the refrigerator, covered, for up to 5 days.

EYE OPENER

We always serve fresh seasonal fruit with breakfast. Blueberries, strawberries, peaches, apples—whatever you choose, the fruit will satisfy your craving for something sweet and give you energy to face the day.

GOLDEN DOOR BREAKFAST BURRITO WITH ROASTED SALSA MEXICANA

MAKES 6 SERVINGS

This breakfast burrito is one of the most popular offerings on the Golden Door menu. Roasting the salsa ingredients gives the dish an authentic Mexican flavor.

For the salsa:

2 tomatoes, quartered

$\frac{1}{2}$ red onion, coarsely chopped

2 tomatillos, papery skin removed and cut in half

1 jalapeño chili, cut in half lengthwise and seeded

1 clove garlic, cut in half

$\frac{1}{2}$ teaspoon olive oil

Salt and freshly ground black pepper to taste

Juice of $\frac{1}{2}$ lime

1 tablespoon chopped fresh cilantro

For the burrito:

Olive oil and canola oil in a spray bottle, or 2 teaspoons olive oil

2 tablespoons finely diced red onion

2 tablespoons seeded, finely diced Anaheim chili

$\frac{1}{2}$ cup sliced white or crimini mushrooms

2 tablespoons seeded, finely diced tomatoes

1 cup trimmed, thinly sliced spinach

Salt to taste

6 eggs

6 egg whites

$\frac{1}{4}$ cup crumbled feta cheese

6 (8-inch) whole-wheat tortillas

Fresh cilantro sprigs

To prepare the Roasted Salsa Mexicana, preheat the oven to 400 degrees F. Combine the tomatoes, onion, tomatillos, jalapeño and garlic in a small mixing bowl, add the olive oil, and a pinch of salt and black pepper; toss to coat. Place the oiled vegetables on a baking sheet; roast for 15 minutes, or until softened and lightly browned.

Transfer to a blender and pulse to a coarse consistency. Transfer to a mixing bowl and stir in the lime juice and cilantro. Season with salt and pepper to taste. *Makes $\frac{3}{4}$ cup.*

For the burrito, set a sauté pan over medium-high heat and spray or brush the hot pan with 1 teaspoon olive oil. Add the onion; sauté, stirring, for 2 to 3 minutes, or until softened. Add the mushrooms and chili; cook until the mushroom liquid is almost evaporated. Add the tomato and spinach; sauté, stirring, for 2 to 3 minutes, or until the spinach begins to wilt. Season with salt to taste; set aside.

Whisk the eggs and egg whites in a mixing bowl until thoroughly blended.

Heat a sauté pan and spray or brush with 1 teaspoon olive oil. Pour in the beaten eggs; cook, stirring, for about 1 to $1\frac{1}{2}$ minutes, or until the eggs reach a soft scramble stage. Fold the scrambled eggs and cooked vegetable mixture together. Scatter the feta cheese on top and season with salt to taste, if desired.

Preheat a grill or set a nonstick skillet brushed or sprayed with oil over medium heat. Heat the tortillas for 20 seconds per side.

Place the tortillas on a work surface and spoon $\frac{1}{2}$ cup of the egg mixture onto each. Drizzle about 2 tablespoons salsa over each, and roll the tortillas into $1\frac{1}{2}$-inch cylinders. Serve immediately, or cover with a clean kitchen towel and hold in a 200-degree oven for up to 20 minutes. To serve, slice each rolled tortilla in half diagonally and garnish with dollops of Roasted Salsa Mexicana and a little chopped cilantro. Roasted Salsa Mexicana can be kept in the refrigerator, covered, for up to 5 days.

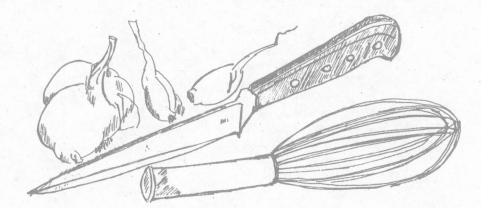

Rancho La Puerta Granola

MAKES 4 CUPS

This granola is prepared at Rancho la Puerta, our sister spa in Mexico. Enjoy it for breakfast with milk, but it's also great sprinkled on cottage cheese and fruit salad or eaten out of hand to soothe "sweet cravings."

2 cups old-fashioned rolled oats

$^1/_3$ cup sunflower seeds

$^1/_3$ cup sliced almonds

2 tablespoons oat bran

$^1/_2$ cup honey

$^1/_3$ cup pitted, chopped dates or dried currants

1 tablespoon ground cinnamon

Preheat the oven to 350 degrees F. Spread the oats and sunflower seeds on a baking sheet; toast in the oven for 10 to 12 minutes. Remove from the oven and use a spatula to toss (for even toasting). Bake for another 5 to 10 minutes, or until the oats are browned. (The oats will brown faster if they are spread thinly on the baking sheet.) Add the sliced almonds and oat bran; bake for another 5 minutes, or until golden brown.

Remove from the oven and drizzle the honey over the toasted granola, tossing with a spatula to coat. Bake for an additional 5 minutes. Remove from the oven and transfer to a large mixing bowl. Mix in the dates or currants. Toss to distribute evenly. Mix in the cinnamon.

Serve with milk or topped with plain or vanilla yogurt, or sprinkle over cottage cheese or fruit salad. Rancho La Puerta Granola can be kept in the refrigerator, covered, for up to 5 days.

Apple Spice Muffins

MAKES 12 MUFFINS

Yogurt adds lightness and moisture to these fragrant, hearty muffins. I make them for breakfast at the Golden Door, but they can also be served for supper with roasted pork or turkey, or enjoyed as a snack to satisfy your sweet tooth.

Vegetable oil in a spray bottle, or
1 teaspoon vegetable oil
1 1/2 cups old-fashioned rolled oats
1 teaspoon baking soda
2 teaspoons baking powder
1 teaspoon ground cinnamon
1/4 teaspoon grated nutmeg
1 1/4 cups whole-wheat flour

1 cup applesauce
1 Fuji or Gala apple, peeled, cored and diced
4 egg whites, lightly beaten
3/4 cup honey
3/4 cup raisins
1/2 cup nonfat plain yogurt

Preheat the oven to 350 degrees F. Spray or grease a 12-cup muffin tin with vegetable oil.

In a wide-based blender or a food processor fitted with a metal blade, process the rolled oats until they become a fine flour.

Sift the baking soda, baking powder, cinnamon and nutmeg into a large mixing bowl. Stir in the whole-wheat flour and oats.

Using a spatula, make a depression or "well" in the center of the dry ingredients and add the applesauce, diced apple, beaten egg whites, honey, raisins and yogurt. Stir gently but thoroughly, just until all the flour is incorporated into the batter. Pour the batter into the prepared muffin cups, filling them about 2/3 full.

Bake for 25 minutes, or until the tops of the muffins are lightly browned and a toothpick inserted into the center of a muffin comes out clean. Turn onto a wire rack; serve warm or let cool.

Jennifer's Soy-Flour Muffins

MAKES 12 MUFFINS

These miraculous muffins, created by Jennifer Sarkisian, my precious assistant, are dairy-free, wheat-free and fat-free. They were developed for guests who are vegan, have severe food allergies or are lactose intolerant.

Vegetable oil in a spray bottle, or
   1 teaspoon vegetable oil
$\frac{1}{2}$ cup dried cherries or cranberries
$\frac{1}{3}$ cup apple juice or water
1 $\frac{1}{2}$ cups soy flour
$\frac{1}{2}$ cup Plain Easy Quinoa (page 224)
$\frac{1}{2}$ cup chopped walnuts
2 teaspoons baking powder
$\frac{1}{2}$ teaspoon baking soda

1 teaspoon ground cinnamon
$\frac{1}{2}$ teaspoon kosher salt
1 cup soy milk
$\frac{1}{2}$ cup silken tofu
$\frac{1}{4}$ cup honey
1 teaspoon pure vanilla extract
1 tablespoon canola oil
1 ripe banana

Preheat the oven to 350 degrees F. Spray or grease a 12-cup nonstick muffin tin with vegetable oil.

Combine the dried cherries or cranberries and apple juice or water in a small bowl; soak for 10 minutes.

Combine the soy flour, cooked quinoa, walnuts, baking powder, baking soda, cinnamon and salt in a large bowl; stir to blend.

Place the soy milk, silken tofu, honey, vanilla, canola oil and banana into a blender or food processor fitted with a metal blade; process until smooth.

With a spatula, mix the soy milk–tofu batter into the dry ingredients. Add the soaked cherries or cranberries and the soaking liquid; mix to distribute evenly. Do not overmix.

Pour the batter into the prepared muffin cups, filling them about $\frac{2}{3}$ full. Bake for 35 to 40 minutes, or until the tops of the muffins are lightly browned and a toothpick inserted into the center of a muffin comes out clean. Turn onto a wire rack; serve warm or let cool.

ORANGE AND BUTTERNUT SQUASH MUFFINS

MAKES 12 MUFFINS

There's no doubt that fat carries flavor—not just in muffins, but in other baked goods and countless dishes as well. Since we're all trying to reduce our fat intake, one way to reduce the amount of fat in baking is to use flavorful ingredients that add moisture to the batter. Baked butternut squash and juicy oranges do the job here.

$\frac{1}{2}$ small butternut squash

Vegetable oil in a spray bottle, or 1 teaspoon vegetable oil

3 oranges

$\frac{2}{3}$ cup chopped pitted dates (16 to 18 dates)

2 tablespoons packed brown sugar

2 tablespoons canola oil

1 tablespoon honey

1 egg, lightly beaten

2 egg whites, lightly beaten

1 $\frac{1}{2}$ cups semolina flour

$\frac{1}{2}$ cup whole-wheat flour

2 teaspoons baking powder

1 teaspoon baking soda

$\frac{1}{4}$ teaspoon salt

1 teaspoon ground cinnamon

Preheat the oven to 350 degrees F. Place the butternut squash on a baking sheet; bake for 40 minutes, or until soft. Let cool, cut in half, and scoop out the seeds. (Reserve them for another use if you wish.) Scrape $\frac{3}{4}$ cup of the cooked squash into a mixing bowl.

Meanwhile, spray or grease a 12-cup nonstick muffin tin with vegetable oil; set aside.

Grate the oranges to make 2 teaspoons of zest. Peel the remaining oranges and separate the segments of all 3 oranges. Remove all pith. Cut the outer membrane from the orange segments. Chop the segments and add to the cooked squash. Mix in the orange zest, dates, brown sugar, oil, honey, and the beaten egg and egg whites.

In a separate mixing bowl, combine the semolina flour, whole-wheat flour, baking powder, baking soda, salt and cinnamon. Pour the butternut squash mixture into the dry ingredients; mix well.

Pour the batter into the prepared muffin cups, filling them about $\frac{2}{3}$ full. Bake for 30 to 35 minutes, or until the tops of the muffins are golden brown and a toothpick inserted into the center of a muffin comes out clean. Turn onto a wire rack; serve warm or let cool.

ORANGE QUINOA MUFFINS

MAKES 12 MUFFINS

Quinoa, oats and cornmeal replace flour in these wheat-free muffins, making them not only supermoist but also an excellent source of protein and other nutrients.

Vegetable oil in a spray bottle, or
   1 teaspoon vegetable oil
$^3/_4$ cup old-fashioned rolled oats
$^3/_4$ cup Plain Easy Quinoa (page 224)
1 $^1/_4$ cups cornmeal
2 teaspoons baking powder
$^1/_2$ teaspoon salt
2 teaspoons ground cinnamon
4 oranges

1 large ripe banana
$^1/_3$ cup apple juice
2 tablespoons packed brown sugar
1 tablespoon honey
2 tablespoons canola oil
1 egg
2 egg whites
$^2/_3$ cup chopped pitted dates

Preheat the oven to 350 degrees F. Spray or grease a 12-cup nonstick muffin tin with vegetable oil; set aside.

In a wide-based blender or food processor fitted with a metal blade, process the rolled oats into a fine flour. Add it to the cooked quinoa and mix in the cornmeal, baking powder, salt and cinnamon.

Grate the oranges to make 2 teaspoons zest. Peel the remaining oranges and separate the segments of all 4 oranges. Remove all pith. Cut the outer membrane from the orange segments. Chop $\frac{3}{4}$ cup of the orange segments and place into a large bowl.

In a blender or food processor fitted with a metal blade, process the banana with the apple juice, brown sugar, honey, oil, egg and egg whites. Pour into the bowl with the orange segments. Stir in the dates and orange zest and mix well. Pour the banana-orange batter into the dry ingredients and mix until well blended.

Pour the batter into the prepared muffin cups, filling them about $\frac{2}{3}$ full. Bake for 30 to 40 minutes, or until the tops of the muffins are golden brown and a toothpick inserted into the center of a muffin comes out clean. Turn onto a wire rack; serve warm or let cool.

THE SKINNY ON MUFFINS

Muffins, especially the giant-sized ones sold in many shops, have a reputation as diet saboteurs—full of fat and calories. At the Golden Door, we love muffins, and we lighten them up by using puréed fruits and veggies instead of loads of butter and oil. The results are wonderfully moist and tender. In our Apple Spice Muffins (page 11), we use applesauce. In our Orange and Butternut Squash Muffins (page 13), the butternut squash gives the muffin its rich texture and sweet, nutty flavor.

One of the most satisfying times for me at the Golden Door is the half hour or so before dinner. Even though I am busy in the kitchen, I know that the guests have begun to gather in a room located off the main dining area for the traditional "cocktail hour." They keenly anticipate the coming meal, both for the food and the dinner-table conversation, and this is my chance to give them a taste of surprises to come.

Appetizers play an important role before any dinner, even a casual one: they satisfy immediate hunger pangs; they set the stage artistically for the meal to come, especially if they are lively and imaginative in colors, tastes, textures and presentation; and they even liven up the conversation, for who can say that they have never exclaimed or thought with delight, "Oh, what is this?" when tempted by a passing tray of hors d'oeuvres.

By definition, appetizers are any small portions of hot or cold food that are passed around or placed out before a meal, or served as a first course. We all know them by a wide variety of names: canapés, spreads, dips, hors d'oeuvres, nibbles, relishes, cocktails (such as a seafood or fruit cocktail). We also know that most traditional appetizers are a high-calorie sneak attack on any resolutions to eat lightly—and the meal has not yet begun! Loaded with mayonnaise, cheeses, butter, salt, preserved and other rich meats, they teeter atop small, trans-fat-laden platforms such as salty crackers or pastry crusts. The word *canapé* means "couch," and if the couch doesn't spoil your healthful resolutions, then what's on it will.

APPETIZERS

At the Golden Door, we enjoy the challenge of creating many variations of low-fat appetizers, proving that one can survive without serving a wedge of Brie *à point*. I long ago welcomed the meaning of *hors d'oeuvre* ("outside the main work") as an opportunity for low-fat creativity rather than restrictions. As guests sip mock-cocktail drinks of fresh fruit juices infused with crushed mint, lavender and other aromatic herbs, they often gravitate to a basket laden with fresh vegetables (crudités) and fruits—the selection is different each night depending on what is perfectly ripe in the garden.

Some are quickly blanched in boiling water and shocked in ice water before serving; this is a desirable first step for asparagus, broccoli, cauliflower, green beans and snow peas. Blanching makes certain vegetables easier to digest. It also sets their vivid color and brings them to a pleasing level of crunch.

I set out creamy, flavorful dips such as Asparagus Guacamole or Artichoke and Basil Dip. We occasionally offer chips, and you will discover that they can be easily cut from flour or corn tortillas, lightly seasoned, and baked to provide plenty of crunch and dipping power without the fat.

I urge you to take pleasure in this part of your day. These appetizers—combined with what Deborah Szekely calls the secret ingredient: joy—will make your cocktail hour at home as special as ours here at the Golden Door.

RICOTTA-HERB CROSTINI

MAKES 6 SERVINGS

Here is the hors d'oeuvre to make when you find yourself having an impromptu gathering—it couldn't be easier. I prefer English cucumbers to the waxy-skinned variety. I often pipe the herbed cheese on top of the bread for guests at the Golden Door, but at home I prefer to be informal and spread it on with a butter knife.

$^1/_2$ cup part-skim ricotta cheese

2 teaspoons creamed horseradish

2 tablespoons chopped fresh basil

2 tablespoons chopped fresh parsley

1 teaspoon chopped fresh thyme leaves

24 slices Garlic-Herb Baguette
    (page 216), toasted

1 English cucumber, peeled and
    finely diced

Fresh thyme sprigs for garnish

Place the ricotta cheese, creamed horseradish, basil, parsley and thyme into a blender or food processor fitted with a metal blade; process until smooth. Spread a little of the herbed ricotta on a toasted baguette round and top with the diced cucumber. Place 4 crostini on an appetizer plate and garnish with fresh thyme sprigs. Repeat the process to assemble 5 more plates; serve.

Beet Tartare on Garlic-Herb Baguette

MAKES 6 SERVINGS

The ingredients that give the French classic steak tartare its characteristic flavor are just as easily tossed with roasted chopped beets for an earthy, low-fat appetizer. Serve it as we do at the Golden Door, with Garlic-Herb Baguette, or go for the best-quality store-bought baguette you can find, or use Belgian endive leaves. The tartare can be made a day or two in advance and refrigerated.

Olive and canola oil in a spray bottle, or 1 teaspoon olive oil

3 small beets, trimmed

2 tablespoons capers, drained and chopped

2 tablespoons finely chopped cornichon pickles

$^1/_4$ cup minced red onion

$^1/_2$ cup finely chopped fresh parsley

1 tablespoon finely chopped fresh tarragon

$^1/_2$ teaspoon freshly ground black pepper

1 tablespoon olive oil

2 tablespoons whole-grain mustard

Garlic-Herb Baguette (page 216) sliced into 24 rounds, or 24 Belgian endive leaves, washed and patted dry

Fresh parsley sprigs for garnish

Preheat the oven to 350 degrees F. Spray or grease a roasting pan with olive oil. Place the beets into it; bake for 1 to 1$^1/_2$ hours, or until the beets are fork-tender. Remove from the oven and cool.

Peel the cooled beets, cut them into $^1/_8$-inch cubes and transfer to a mixing bowl. Add the capers, cornichons, red onion, parsley, tarragon, black pepper, olive oil and mustard; mix well. Cover and refrigerate for 1 hour to let the flavors marry. Bring to room temperature. Spoon onto Garlic-Herb Baguette slices or Belgian endive leaves. Place 4 filled baguette rounds onto an appetizer plate and garnish with parsley sprigs. Repeat the process to assemble 5 more plates; serve.

Cabbage Hand Rolls with Gingered Wild Rice

MAKES 6 SERVINGS

Steamed cabbage is an excellent wrapper for all manner of savory fillings, including this unusual, yet delicious, combination of East-West flavors. Wild rice and cranberries are tossed in a ginger-sesame paste and topped with buttery sunflower sprouts.

$^1/_2$ cup uncooked wild rice

1 cup Chicken Stock (page 200) or Vegetable Broth (page 201) or water

1 bay leaf

$^1/_4$ cup dehydrated cranberries

$^1/_4$ cup chopped pickled ginger

$^1/_3$ cup chopped scallions, including tops

2 teaspoons dark sesame oil

1 tablespoon mirin (sweet rice wine)

1 teaspoon Vietnamese chili paste

12 large leaves Savoy cabbage (about 1 head)

1 cup sunflower sprouts or bean sprouts

Combine the wild rice, stock or broth or water, and bay leaf in a small pot set over medium-high heat. Simmer, partially covered, for 40 to 45 minutes, or until the rice is tender. Remove the bay leaf. Transfer to a mixing bowl and let cool. Stir in the cranberries, ginger, scallions, sesame oil, mirin and chili paste; mix well. Cover and refrigerate until ready to use.

Bring a large pot of water to a boil. Meanwhile, prepare a large bowl of ice water. When the water is boiling rapidly, immerse the cabbage leaves in it for 1 to 2 minutes, or until softened. Then, using tongs or a slotted spoon, plunge them into the ice water for 30 seconds to stop the cooking process. Place them on a paper towel or clean, dry towel and pat dry. Cut the leaves in half and remove the center ribs.

Place a half leaf on a work surface, spoon about 1 tablespoon of the wild rice filling into the center, and top with a small pinch of sunflower sprouts. Gently fold the edges of the leaf over the rice and sprouts; roll into a cone-shaped hand roll. Repeat the process to make 24 rolls with the remaining cabbage leaves, wild rice filling and sprouts, reserving some of the sprouts for garnish. Place 4 rolls onto an appetizer plate and garnish with some sprouts. Repeat the process to assemble 5 more plates; serve.

CARROT-DILL POTATO PANCAKES

MAKES 6 SERVINGS

These pancakes are among the most popular offerings at the Golden Door cocktail hour, especially during Men's Week, when many of the guests show up and eat them before they ever make it out of the kitchen. Serve them with sour cream and fresh chives, or for a more elegant presentation, spoon a little beluga caviar or smoked salmon on top.

1 egg	$^1/_2$ cup finely diced onion
2 egg whites	1 tablespoon chopped fresh dill
$^3/_4$ cup 1 percent low-fat milk	1 small potato
2 teaspoons canola oil	1 small carrot
$^1/_2$ cup sifted whole-wheat flour	Vegetable oil in a spray bottle, or
$^1/_3$ cup sifted unbleached flour	1 teaspoon vegetable oil
$^1/_2$ teaspoon kosher salt	$^1/_2$ cup nonfat sour cream
$^1/_2$ teaspoon baking powder	3 tablespoons minced fresh chives

Pour the egg, egg whites, milk and canola oil into a blender or food processor fitted with a metal blade; pulse to combine. Add the flours, salt and baking powder; process until smooth. Transfer to a mixing bowl; stir in the onion and dill. Let the batter stand for at least 1 hour, but no longer than 2 hours.

Just before you are ready to cook, peel and grate the potato and carrot. Use your hands to squeeze the excess liquid from the grated vegetables; stir them into the batter.

Spray or grease a nonstick pan with vegetable oil and set over medium-high heat. Spoon 1 tablespoon of the batter into the hot pan and cook for 2 to 3 minutes on each side, or until the pancakes are golden brown. Repeat with the remaining batter, making sure not to let the pancakes overlap when you turn them. (Work in batches if necessary, or if you can manage it, you can work with two pans at a time.) Keep the finished pancakes warm until you are ready to serve. Place 8 pancakes onto an appetizer plate. Garnish with a dollop of sour cream. Repeat the process to assemble 5 more plates. Sprinkle each with chives; serve immediately.

INDIVIDUAL BLACK BEAN TOSTADAS

MAKES 6 SERVINGS

Suggesting that you make your own corn chips may seem like a lot to ask, but the purchased low-fat variety just can't compare to these, which are made from fresh corn tortillas, brushed with egg white and baked to a golden brown. If you're pressed for time, store-bought low-sodium corn chips (baked, not fried) and canned black beans (15-ounce can) will produce a tasty and very respectable appetizer.

3 cups water

³/₄ cup black beans, soaked for 2 hours or overnight and rinsed

Vegetable oil in a spray bottle, or 1 teaspoon vegetable oil

1 teaspoon crushed chili-pepper flakes

6 corn tortillas

1 egg white, lightly beaten

Salt to taste

Freshly ground black pepper to taste

2 cups finely chopped or shredded Romaine lettuce

2 cups Salsa Mexicana (page 212)

¹/₂ medium avocado, cut into 36 thin slices

1 cup finely shredded Cheddar cheese (about 2 ounces)

Pour the water into a small pot, add the black beans and chili-pepper flakes, and set over medium-high heat; bring to a simmer. Simmer for 1 hour, or until the beans are tender, adding more water if necessary. Drain the beans, reserving the liquid.

Preheat the oven to 375 degrees F. Spray or grease a baking sheet with vegetable oil and set aside.

Meanwhile, brush the corn tortillas on both sides with the beaten egg white. Cut each tortilla into 6 triangles and arrange the pieces on the prepared baking sheet in a single layer; bake for 10 minutes. Using a spatula, loosen and turn the chips; bake for a few more minutes, or until they are golden brown. Remove from the oven and let cool.

Transfer the beans with half of the reserved liquid to a blender or food processor fitted with a metal blade; process until smooth and creamy. Season with salt and black pepper, if desired.

To serve, place 6 toasted tortilla triangles on an appetizer plate. (You can reassemble them in a circle or arrange them in a decorative pattern on the plate.) Spread about 1 tablespoon of the black bean purée onto each triangle. Top each with a little shredded lettuce, 1 teaspoon of the salsa and an avocado slice. Sprinkle with a little Cheddar cheese. Repeat the process to assemble 5 more plates and serve.

EGGPLANT CAVIAR WITH PURPLE POTATOES

MAKES 6 SERVINGS

Black sesame seeds give this eggplant caviar a look that approximates the real thing. Pairing the slate-colored eggplant with purple potatoes produces an appetizer that looks as good as it tastes. The eggplant can also be served as a dip for crudités or with tortilla chips.

1 large eggplant

Canola oil in a spray bottle,
or 1 teaspoon canola oil

5 medium purple potatoes (about 2 pounds)

$\frac{1}{2}$ cup finely chopped fresh parsley

1 tablespoon finely chopped capers, drained

1 tablespoon olive oil

2 teaspoons balsamic vinegar

2 teaspoons fresh lemon juice

1 teaspoon minced garlic

$\frac{1}{2}$ teaspoon ground cumin

$\frac{1}{2}$ teaspoon freshly ground black pepper

$\frac{1}{2}$ teaspoon salt, or to taste

$1\frac{1}{2}$ tablespoons sesame seeds, preferably black

Vegetable oil in a spray bottle,
or 1 teaspoon vegetable oil

Fresh chervil sprigs for garnish

Preheat the oven to 350 degrees F. Spray or brush the eggplant with canola oil, pierce with a fork and place into a shallow baking dish. Roast for about 1 hour, or until soft, turning once.

Meanwhile, place the potatoes into a medium-size pot with enough water to cover, and bring to a boil. Boil for about 15 minutes, or until fork-tender but still firm. Remove from the heat, drain and let cool. Slice the cooled potatoes, with skins on, into $\frac{1}{4}$-inch rounds; set aside.

When the eggplant is done, cut it in half lengthwise and let it cool. Scrape the eggplant pulp away from the peel, and place the pulp into a blender or food processor fitted with a metal blade. Add the parsley, capers, olive oil, balsamic vinegar, lemon juice, garlic, cumin, black pepper and salt; pulse to a coarse consistency, then transfer to a mixing bowl.

Set a small, dry nonstick pan over medium heat. Add the sesame seeds and toast lightly, stirring often, for 2 to 3 minutes. Stir the toasted seeds into the eggplant mixture.

Spray or grease a separate nonstick pan with vegetable oil and set over medium-high heat. Place the potatoes into the pan in a single layer and sear for 2 minutes on each side, or until light brown. Remove and let cool.

To serve, place about 5 or 6 potato slices onto an appetizer plate. Top each with 2 teaspoons of the eggplant caviar and garnish with sprigs of chervil. Assemble 5 more plates; serve.

Napa Cabbage and Crabmeat Salad with Wasabi–Sour Cream Sauce

MAKES 6 SERVINGS

Rather than serving crab dip, that full-fat cocktail party standard, toss juicy chunks of crabmeat with tender napa cabbage in a light sesame dressing and spoon it into a Golden Door favorite: cradle-shaped Savory Five-Spice Tuiles. (When I make these at home, I serve the salad on endive leaves.) The accompanying Wasabi–Sour Cream Sauce gives the cabbage and sweet crabmeat a little zing. Just remember that wasabi (Japanese horseradish) has a distinctive sinus-clearing characteristic that can be overpowering, so use it sparingly. The sauce is also delicious with Cabbage Hand Rolls with Gingered Wild Rice (page 20) or any seafood.

For the sauce:
1 ½ tablespoons wasabi powder
1 ½ tablespoons water
¾ cup nonfat sour cream
2 teaspoons honey

For the salad:
2 cups shredded napa cabbage
2 tablespoons mirin (sweet rice wine)
2 tablespoons seasoned (sweet) rice wine vinegar
1 teaspoon dark sesame oil, optional
8 ounces cooked crabmeat
1 tablespoon grated orange zest
30 Savory Five-Spice Tuiles (page 221) or 30 endive leaves

To make the sauce, combine the wasabi powder and water in a small bowl; mix to make a paste. Add the sour cream and honey; whisk until smooth. Refrigerate until ready to serve. *Makes 1 cup.*

To make the salad, combine the cabbage, mirin, rice wine vinegar, sesame oil (if using), crabmeat and orange zest in a mixing bowl. Mix well, cover and refrigerate for 30 minutes.

Fill the tuiles with the salad; arrange 5 on an appetizer plate. Repeat the process to assemble 5 more plates. Drizzle each filled tuile with about 1 tablespoon of the Wasabi–Sour Cream Sauce; serve. Or, if you are using endive leaves, place 5 on an appetizer plate in a "daisy petal" arrangement. Spoon some salad into each leaf. Repeat the process to assemble 5 more plates. Drizzle each filled leaf with about 1 tablespoon of the Wasabi–Sour Cream Sauce; serve. Wasabi–Sour Cream Sauce can be kept in the refrigerator, covered, for up to 1 week.

SMALL BITES, LOW RISK

Travel, trade and immigration have produced an interesting side effect: culinary exchange. Very likely, you can have your pick of ethnic cuisines from all over the world within an hour's drive of your home. But the less adventurous eaters among us can be slow to try new flavors. And that's one reason I love to serve appetizers. I get to introduce my guests to unfamiliar tastes in nonintimidating quantities. Even the most dedicated meat-and-potatoes type will usually try the Wasabi–Sour Cream Sauce if it's only a few bites. Chances are, he or she will love it, and next time, you can incorporate it into your main course.

VEGETABLE TERRINE PROVENÇALE

MAKES 10 SERVINGS

We eat first with our eyes. Our initial impression of the food presented to us is a visual one, so it's important to make everything we eat look as delicious as it tastes. This terrine is a perfect example. Using a spray bottle to mist olive oil onto the vegetables really helps to bind the layers together while keeping the amount of oil you use to a minimum. This terrine is best made a day or two ahead to allow the flavors to marry fully.

2 medium eggplants, peeled and sliced lengthwise into ½-inch strips

3 large zucchini, cut lengthwise into ½-inch strips

Olive oil and canola oil in a spray bottle, or 2 tablespoons plus 2 teaspoons olive oil

¼ cup balsamic vinegar

½ teaspoon kosher salt, optional

1 teaspoon freshly ground black pepper, optional

3 medium red bell peppers

2 ounces thinly sliced smoked salmon

¾ cup part-skim ricotta cheese

20 fresh basil leaves, cut into very thin strips

Mixed greens for serving, washed and patted dry

Rosemary sprigs for garnish

Kalamata or Niçoise olives for garnish

Lightly spray the eggplant and zucchini with 1 teaspoon olive oil and transfer to a large mixing bowl. Stir in the balsamic vinegar, salt and black pepper, if using; marinate for 30 minutes.

Preheat a grill, stovetop grill or broiler. Lightly spray or brush the red bell peppers with 1 teaspoon olive oil; grill or broil for 5 minutes, turning so that all sides are charred. Transfer to a plastic bag and seal; set aside for about 10 minutes, or until the peppers are cool enough to handle. Remove the skin and seeds and cut each into 10 equal-size pieces. Set aside.

Remove the eggplant from the marinade and spray or brush with 1 teaspoon olive oil, if necessary. Grill or broil for 3 to 4 minutes per side, or until the eggplant just begins to soften. Remove from the grill and set aside. Remove the zucchini from the marinade; grill or broil for 3 to 4 minutes per side, or until it begins to soften.

Line a 9 $\frac{1}{2}$ x 2 $\frac{1}{2}$-inch terrine pan with plastic wrap and spray or brush with 1 teaspoon olive oil. Place the smoked salmon into the pan, arranging it so that the bottom of the pan is covered. Place four slices of grilled eggplant on top of the salmon. Mist the eggplant with 1 teaspoon olive oil. Using a spatula, spread on a layer of ricotta cheese. Scatter some of the basil strips on top of the cheese. Press on 5 to 6 grilled zucchini slices, mist with 1 teaspoon olive oil and spread with another layer of ricotta and basil. Add a layer of roasted red pepper and mist again with 1 teaspoon olive oil. Top with another layer of ricotta and basil. Repeat the process until all the grilled vegetables have been used, finishing with a layer of zucchini and eggplant and a final misting of olive oil. Gently press down and cover the terrine with plastic. Press the terrine with another empty terrine pan or loaf pan of the same size; refrigerate overnight.

Carefully remove the vegetable terrine from the pan by pulling up on the plastic wrap. Place on a cutting board. Using a sharp knife, carefully cut it into 1-inch slices. Place the terrine slices on a bed of mixed greens and garnish with rosemary sprigs and olives; serve. The Vegetable Terrine Provençale can be kept in the refrigerator, covered, for 3 to 4 days.

A TASTE OF THE MEDITERRANEAN

I spent some time working in the renowned chef Roger Vergé's Moulin de Mougins in the south of France; while there I prepared several vegetable terrines and really came to appreciate what a wonderfully elegant first course they can make, especially with a glass of chilled rosé. Every time I prepare the Vegetable Terrine Provençale, with its fragrant layers of eggplant, zucchini and roasted pepper, I'm transported back to the south of France.

VEGETABLE CRUDITÉ WITH ROASTED RED PEPPER AND BASIL MAYONNAISE

MAKES 6 SERVINGS

Every day at 10:45 A.M. and 3:45 P.M. guests take a break and gather near the pool to get recharged and to practice one of the cornerstones of the Golden Door eating philosophies: eat often, eat less. I prepare a vegetable tray using whatever is fresh and abundant in the garden. Carrots and celery do not a crudité make; let your senses determine what vegetables and fruits should appear on your crudité tray.

1 head butter lettuce or red leaf let-
    tuce, washed and patted dry
1 bunch asparagus (about 10 ounces)
1 cup broccoli florets (about 8 ounces)
14 to 18 cherry tomatoes
2 fennel bulbs, cored and cut in
    $\frac{1}{2}$-inch slices

12 baby carrots, peeled
1 bunch radishes, trimmed
Roasted Red Pepper and Basil
    Mayonnaise (page 206)

Line a large basket with lettuce. Set aside.

Bring a large pot of water to a boil. Prepare a bowl of ice water. Immerse the asparagus in the boiling water for 1 or 2 minutes, or until tender-crisp. Remove from the pot with tongs or a slotted spoon and plunge into the ice water for 30 seconds to stop the cooking process. Drain, pat dry and set aside. Repeat the process with the broccoli.

Arrange the asparagus, broccoli, tomatoes, fennel, carrots and radishes in the basket on top of the lettuce and serve with Roasted Red Pepper and Basil Mayonnaise.

THE HERB GARDEN

Herbs are an indispensable addition to the spa kitchen—and any other kitchen, for that matter. Herbs (not to be confused with spices, which are typically made from seeds and barks, not leaves) add flavor and complexity to foods. Put them in salads, pastas, stews, dressings, mayonnaise and dips, or sprinkle them on most any dish just before you are ready to serve. Heat can retard the flavor of herbs, so adding them at the last minute guarantees that they will retain their full flavor. Look for herbs in bloom: flowering herbs make a colorful, flavorful, beautiful garnish. Wash herbs gently and pat them dry to preserve their essential oils. To store your herbs, wrap them in damp paper towels and keep them in the refrigerator. I like to use fresh herbs, but if they are not available, dried herbs are a fine substitute. Use a smaller amount, as the flavor of dried herbs is more concentrated. Here's a quick guide to some herbal favorites:

Basil: Best known in this country for its fresh taste in pesto and tomato-based Italian sauces, basil is also used in Southeast Asian cookery. It makes a welcome addition to soups, salads, pastas, stir-fries and mayonnaise.

Chervil: A delicate leafy herb whose flavor combines elements of both fennel and parsley, chervil should be used as whole leaves rather than chopped. It's lovely floating on the surface of a soup, sprinkled over salads or mixed into sauces.

Chive: It looks like a grass, but once you smell and taste its mild oniony aroma and flavor, you won't mistake it for anything else. Snip it with scissors to top soups, salads, baked potatoes or any savory dish. Flowering Chinese chive with its garlicky flavor is one variety that I particularly like, especially for Asian-style soups.

Cilantro: Some call this herb *coriander;* others use the term *coriander* to refer to the seeds (ground as a spice) and *cilantro* to refer exclusively to the leaves. Most of us in North America know it as a hallmark of Mexican cooking, but it actually originated in Asia. It has a wonderful cooling effect and is delightful in curries, soups, salads and salsas.

Dill: Feathery leaves make this herb not just a flavorful addition to seafood, cucumbers and dairy-based sauces (which it is), but a beautiful garnish as well.

Fennel: Many people discard the feathery top of the fennel bulb, quite unaware that it can serve as an herb. Its anise-like flavor helps counter the oiliness of some foods, and it pairs well with fatty fish such as salmon.

Marjoram: Similar to oregano, marjoram has a light fragrance. It is used in sauces and dressings.

Mint: One of the most widely used herbs, mint can be added to teas, incorporated into desserts, mixed into some Middle Eastern–style dishes and pressed into service as a pretty, aromatic garnish.

Oregano: Although it can be found fresh, oregano is often used in its more potent dried form. It's great in sauces, pasta, pizzas and dressings. The fresh leaves are mild enough to chop and add to dressings, much like parsley. Just be sure you know which variety you are chopping. The Greek and Spanish varieties of oregano have a stronger flavor.

Parsley: This ever-present herb has been so overused as a garnish that it is sometimes taken for granted. But whether in flat-leaf or curly form, parsley adds a mild, slightly tangy and sweet flavor to soups, salads, mushroom dishes and many other savory foods. One thing I'm adamant about: never use dried parsley—it has no flavor.

Rosemary: Pleasantly pungent with pine and camphor aromas, this herb is used to flavor meats, potatoes, breads and, in smaller quantities, dressings and cooked vegetables. It can also be crushed or minced and mixed with olive oil and minced garlic to make a rub for meat and fish. Rosemary makes a beautiful garnish; I particularly like the flowering variety for this purpose. (It's not one to sprinkle raw on the top of a finished dish, however; it's best when it has a chance to cook a bit.)

Sage: With its strong aroma and flavor, sage is a popular seasoning for sausage, poultry, omelets, cooked vegetables and stuffings. The oblong leaves make a pretty garnish, especially the variety called gold sage. (Like rosemary, it's not an herb to use raw, except as a garnish.)

Summer Savory and Winter Savory: With their peppery notes, winter and summer savory are ideal for spicing up vegetables and grains.

Tarragon: With its strong floral aroma and vaguely anise flavor, tarragon is an herb that should be used in moderation in vinaigrettes, sauces, marinades and salads. It's wonderful when chopped with parsley.

Thyme: Excellent for long cooking times, thyme makes a wonderful addition to stocks, soups, sauces and dressings. I like the variety called lemon thyme, which has undertones of lemon and is great for lightening up poultry dishes and winter soups.

ARTICHOKE AND BASIL DIP

MAKES 2 CUPS

It's traditionally laden with mayonnaise, but this slimmed-down version of artichoke dip gets its rich texture from cottage cheese. (You can also use low-fat cream cheese.) Artichokes tend to oxidize and turn brown when trimmed; to avoid this, rub them with lemon juice. Serve with Golden Door Chips, our easy, light chips that you make from tortillas or pita bread.

4 artichokes

1 tablespoon fresh lemon juice

1 tablespoon olive oil

1 tablespoon minced shallots

2 teaspoons minced garlic

1 bay leaf

4 sprigs fresh thyme

1 cup water

1 cup low-fat cottage cheese

$\frac{1}{4}$ cup very thinly sliced fresh basil

Salt and freshly ground black pepper
   to taste

Golden Door Chips (page 220)

Remove the tough outer leaves of the artichoke to reveal the tender inner leaves. Trim the stem and cut off the top third of the artichoke. Trim around the base and remove any remaining tough, dark green spots. Quarter the artichoke and remove the fuzzy choke with a melon ball scoop. Slice thinly. Rub with lemon juice to prevent browning. Repeat with remaining artichokes.

Pour the olive oil into a nonstick pan set over medium heat. Add the shallots and garlic; sauté, stirring, for 3 minutes. Add the artichokes, bay leaf, thyme and water; simmer for 15 minutes, or until the artichokes are tender.

Remove the bay leaf and thyme sprigs from the water. Drain the artichokes and transfer with the shallots and garlic to a blender or food processor fitted with a metal blade. Add the cottage cheese; process until smooth. Transfer to a mixing bowl, stir in the basil and season with salt and black pepper. Serve with Golden Door Chips. Artichoke and Basil Dip can be kept in the refrigerator, covered, for 1 day.

ASPARAGUS GUACAMOLE

MAKES 2 ½ CUPS

Despite their high fat content, avocados can still be part of a healthy eating plan. Avocados contain the "good" fat—the monounsaturated kind. Still, it's best to lower overall fat consumption, so I've reduced the amount of avocado in this guacamole by blending it with fresh asparagus and yogurt—with no sacrifice of flavor. If you want a hotter version, use serrano chilies instead of the Anaheim. Serve with Golden Door Chips.

1 medium Anaheim or serrano chili

Olive oil and canola oil in a spray bottle, or 1 teaspoon olive oil

5 or 6 fresh asparagus spears, ends trimmed

½ cup nonfat plain yogurt

½ small avocado

1 plum tomato, seeded and diced

1 tablespoon chopped scallions

¼ cup chopped fresh cilantro

½ teaspoon salt, optional

½ teaspoon freshly ground black pepper, optional

Golden Door Chips (page 220)

Preheat a grill, stovetop grill or broiler. Lightly spray the chili peppers with olive oil; grill or broil for 5 minutes, turning so that all sides are charred. Transfer to a plastic bag and seal; set aside for about 10 minutes, or until the peppers are cool enough to handle. Remove the stem, skin and seeds from the peppers; cut into small dice. Set aside.

Bring a pot of water to a boil. Prepare a bowl of ice water. Immerse the asparagus in the boiling water for 3 to 4 minutes and drain. Plunge the asparagus into the ice water to stop the cooking process. Remove from the ice water and drain. Chop the cooled asparagus into 1-inch pieces. Transfer to a blender or food processor fitted with a metal blade. Add the yogurt and avocado; process until smooth. Transfer to a mixing bowl and stir in the chili, tomatoes, scallions, cilantro, and salt and black pepper, if using. Cover and refrigerate until ready to use. Serve with Golden Door Chips. Asparagus Guacamole can be kept in the refrigerator, covered, for 1 to 2 days.

CANNELLINI BEAN AND ROASTED GARLIC DIP

MAKES 2 CUPS

Roasted garlic should be part of every spa cook's repertoire. It can be spread like butter on bread, swirled into soups, blended into dips and mashed potatoes, and served by the head with a roasted chicken. Here it is blended with puréed cannellini beans for a garlic lover's dream dip. Serve with Golden Door Chips.

1 head garlic

2 tablespoons olive oil

3/4 cup cannellini beans, soaked for 2 hours or overnight and rinsed

3 cups Chicken Stock (page 200) or Vegetable Broth (page 201) or water

1 bay leaf

2 tablespoons fresh lemon juice

1 teaspoon finely chopped fresh thyme

1 teaspoon finely chopped fresh rosemary

Golden Door Chips (page 220)

Preheat the oven to 350 degrees F.

Cut and discard the top third of the head of garlic; drizzle 2 tablespoons of olive oil on top of the remaining garlic. Loosely wrap in aluminum foil; place on a baking sheet and bake for 35 to 45 minutes, or until the garlic is golden brown and caramelized. Remove from the oven and set aside until cool enough to handle. Then, grasp the root end of the garlic and gently squeeze to remove the soft, caramelized cloves from the papery skin. Discard the skin and reserve the caramelized garlic.

Meanwhile, combine the beans, stock, broth or water, and bay leaf in a small pot set over medium-high heat. Cover and simmer for 45 minutes, or until the beans are tender.

Remove the bay leaf from the pot. Drain the beans, reserving the liquid, and transfer the beans and 1/2 of the cooking liquid to a blender or food processor fitted with a metal blade. Add the roasted garlic and lemon juice; process until smooth. Add the thyme and rosemary; pulse until the herbs are incorporated. Serve with Golden Door Chips. Cannellini Bean and Roasted Garlic Dip can be kept in the refrigerator, covered, for 2 to 3 days.

It comes as a surprise to some Golden Door guests that their love for soup has been re-kindled during their stay. Activity-filled days would seem to call for big refueling meals at lunch and dinner, but just the opposite turns out to be true as the rhythm of a seven-day stay unfolds. Instead of heavy dishes at midday or in the evening, many of us crave plenty of liquids. Soups, steaming hot or chilled, filled with tender vegetables, seem to satisfy an elemental need. Simple to eat and easy to digest, they are the very soul of "comfort."

Soups make us feel that someone is taking care of us, thinking of our best interests, warming us. When a fragrant broth waits for our spoon to reveal the mysteries beneath that steaming sea, we are transported back to our mothers' tables. Some of the most vivid and fragrant memories of my Belgian childhood are set in my mother's kitchen, where I learned to make delicious soups at a very young age. Her gentle ways with me as a child were not unlike her respect for the ingredients in her soups. She treated them with great care, knowing that the best soups are not an afterthought made from leftovers, but a culinary art form worthy of careful shopping at the farmers market.

In this chapter you will find that the Golden Door's Bourride with Fennel and Monkfish, and our Root Vegetable Soup with Dilled Sour Cream, are slim versions of the sort of hearty main-course soups my mother made. Corn Tortilla Soup and Summer Corn Chowder with Crabmeat have been inspired by the ingredients available to us here on the West Coast, just

SOUPS

an hour from the Mexican border. Thanks also to the climate and plentiful produce of southern California, my passion for soup making has evolved beyond the stovetop to include wonderful chilled vegetable and fruit soups; they're perfect for lunch when accompanied by a salad, or as a first course at dinner.

Several recipes in this chapter are inherently low-fat, but others rely on some of my essential techniques for "de-calorizing" soups that are traditionally high in fat. For example, something as smooth and creamy as my Chilled Chayote and Avocado Soup may look and taste sinful, but the chayote fills in and cuts the fat content of a purely avocado-based soup. In the Root Vegetable Soup with Dilled Sour Cream, you'll discover how nonfat sour cream can replace the full-fat version without loss of flavor or silken feel. In so many soups, sprightly fresh herbs are a key: they help many base ingredients spring to life.

Most of the soups here are very simple to make, especially if you've taken a little extra time to prepare homemade stock and freeze it. But even if you don't prepare in advance, soups can easily become a frequent part of your repertoire. Just remember to follow this basic rule: soups will only taste as fresh as the ingredients that go into the pot, and should not be used as a way to clean out a refrigerator's produce drawer. And, as we used to say when I was a boy in Belgium, soup is always better the next day. Just give it some fresh peas or diced celery, shredded spinach or chopped fresh herbs—something fresh.

BOURRIDE WITH FENNEL AND MONKFISH

MAKES 6 SERVINGS

Bourride is a classic Mediterranean fish soup, typically thickened with egg yolks and served with garlic mayonnaise. Creamy simmered leeks, potatoes and fennel give the Golden Door version its rich texture without all the fat. Flavor the soup with a dash of Pernod just before serving for an enhanced anise flavor. Be sure to wash the leeks thoroughly, as sand often collects inside them as they grow.

1 teaspoon olive oil

2 small leeks, washed well, trimmed and sliced

1 bay leaf

4 sprigs fresh thyme

4 fingerling potatoes, sliced

1 pound monkfish fillet, trimmed and cut into 2-inch pieces

1 teaspoon kosher salt, or to taste

$\frac{1}{2}$ teaspoon freshly ground black pepper

4 cups Fish Stock (page 202)

1 bulb fennel, halved, core removed, and thinly sliced

1 teaspoon Pernod or anise-flavored liqueur, optional

$\frac{1}{4}$ cup chopped fresh chervil

Heat the olive oil in a heavy skillet set over medium heat. Add the leeks, bay leaf and thyme; sauté for 5 minutes, stirring periodically. Add the potatoes; sauté, stirring, for another 2 minutes.

Season the monkfish with 1 teaspoon salt and $\frac{1}{2}$ teaspoon black pepper; place it on top of the leek-potato mixture. Pour in the stock and bring to a simmer. Reduce the heat to medium-low and add the sliced fennel; simmer for 10 to 15 minutes, or until the potatoes are just cooked. If you wish, season the soup with a little more salt and a dash of Pernod. Remove the bay leaf and discard.

Ladle into soup bowls, garnish with chervil and serve.

CHILLED HONEYDEW MELON SOUP WITH MINT

MAKES 4 SERVINGS

Chilled soup can be a light, refreshing staple in your home spa kitchen. Trim and chop the melon, and the rest is effortless. If honeydew melons are not available, try using casaba or crenshaw melons. Edible rose petals, available at specialty markets, make a colorful garnish.

1 large honeydew melon (about 2 $\frac{1}{2}$
   pounds), seeded, rind removed, and
   diced
2 tablespoons fresh lemon juice
1 $\frac{1}{2}$ cups low-fat buttermilk

$\frac{2}{3}$ cup apple juice
1 tablespoon honey, optional
1 tablespoon finely chopped fresh mint
4 sprigs fresh mint for garnish
Edible rose petals for garnish, optional

Process the melon in a blender or food processor fitted with a metal blade until smooth.

Transfer to a medium-size mixing bowl; stir in the lemon juice, buttermilk, apple juice, honey, if using, and chopped mint. Cover and refrigerate until well chilled.

Serve cold in chilled bowls. Garnish with fresh mint sprigs or rose petals, if desired.

SOME LIKE IT COLD

In summertime, I prefer cold soup. It's refreshing and not too heavy. When fresh corn is at its sweetest, there's nothing better than Golden Gazpacho (see page 40). You might have to coax the folks at your table to try a cold fruit soup—but only the first time. Peaches and ripe melons make excellent soups that can serve as starters or light desserts.

CHILLED CHAYOTE AND AVOCADO SOUP

MAKES 6 SERVINGS

The hiking trails and walking paths at the Golden Door are blessed with lush avocado trees, their fruit strewn on the ground, much to the delight of guests who make the trek up the mountain each morning at dawn. It's not unusual for some to come into the kitchen with a few cradled in their T-shirts, asking me to share a recipe. This one is among my favorites. To cut down the fat content, I've supplemented the avocado with chayote, a white-fleshed, pear-shaped fruit with mild flavor, to make a delicious chilled soup. If the chayote skin is thick, remove it so it doesn't make the soup stringy or gritty.

1 teaspoon olive oil

$\frac{1}{2}$ medium onion, diced

2 celery ribs, diced

3 chayote (about $1\frac{1}{2}$ pounds), peeled and diced

3 sprigs fresh parsley

1 bay leaf

3 cups Chicken Stock (page 200) or Vegetable Broth (page 201)

1 teaspoon salt

1 small avocado, peeled and pitted

$\frac{1}{3}$ cup nonfat sour cream

3 tablespoons fresh lime juice

$\frac{1}{4}$ teaspoon cayenne pepper, optional

Heat the olive oil in a large pot set over medium-high heat. Add the onion and celery; sauté, stirring, for 2 to 3 minutes, or until translucent and soft. Add the chayote, parsley and bay leaf; sauté, stirring, for another 2 to 3 minutes. Stir in the stock or broth and salt; simmer for 20 minutes. Prepare a cold water bath by filling a bowl large enough to hold the soup pot with ice water. When the soup is done, remove it from the heat, place the pot into the water bath and let cool.

Remove the bay leaf from the soup and discard. In batches, transfer the cooled chayote mixture to a blender or food processor fitted with a metal blade; process until smooth. Strain the soup through a fine-mesh sieve and return it to the food processor or blender. Add the avocado and sour cream; process until smooth and creamy. Transfer to a large bowl or storage container and stir in the lime juice and cayenne pepper, if using. Cover and refrigerate for 1 hour, or until chilled.

Serve cold in chilled soup bowls.

COLD CARROT AND ORANGE SOUP WITH CUMIN

MAKES 4 SERVINGS

The sweetness of carrots and the warm, mellow heat of cumin are made for each other. Use fresh orange juice if possible. If not, squeeze in a little fresh lime juice to lift the flavor.

1 teaspoon canola oil

1/3 small onion, cut into 1/4-inch slices

2 teaspoons ground cumin

5 medium carrots, diced

6 cups Chicken Stock (page 200) or
  Vegetable Broth (page 201)

1 teaspoon kosher salt, optional

1 cup fresh orange juice

2 teaspoons fresh lime juice, optional

1 tablespoon grated orange zest
  for garnish

6 sprigs fresh dill for garnish, optional

Heat the canola oil in a medium-size pot set over medium-high heat. Add the onion; sauté, stirring, for 2 to 3 minutes, or until soft and translucent. Stir in the cumin; cook for about 2 minutes to bring out the pungent aroma of the spice. Stir in the carrots, stock or broth and salt, if using; simmer, partially covered, for 30 to 40 minutes, or until the carrots are tender. Remove from the heat and let cool.

Transfer the soup to a blender or food processor fitted with a metal blade and process until smooth. Blend in the orange juice and lime juice, if using. Transfer to a bowl or storage container, cover and refrigerate until well chilled.

Serve cold in chilled soup bowls. Garnish with orange zest and dill, if desired.

GOLDEN GAZPACHO

Yellow tomatoes and corn kernels shaved from the cob give this soup its golden hue. If you prefer a quicker method, use canned vegetable broth and let your food processor chop the vegetables. Pulse the tomatoes and peppers guardedly so as not to overblend them.

2 ears fresh corn, shucked and rinsed

4 yellow tomatoes, seeded and cut into small dice

1 small red onion, minced

1 large yellow bell pepper, stem removed, seeded and finely diced

1 large cucumber, peeled, seeded and finely diced

$^{1}/_{4}$ cup Chicken Stock (page 200) or Vegetable Broth (page 201)

2 tablespoons chopped fresh parsley

2 tablespoons olive oil

1 teaspoon kosher salt

$^{1}/_{2}$ teaspoon freshly ground black pepper

Fresh parsley sprigs for garnish

$^{1}/_{4}$ cup sliced almonds, lightly toasted, for garnish

Cut the kernels off the corncob by holding it vertically on a cutting board and cutting downward with a sharp knife, until all the kernels are removed.

In a large bowl, combine the corn kernels, tomato, red onion, yellow bell pepper, cucumber, stock or broth, chopped parsley, olive oil, salt and pepper. Cover and refrigerate for 1 to 2 hours.

Serve cold in chilled soup bowls. Garnish with parsley sprigs and toasted almonds.

CORN TORTILLA SOUP

MAKES 6 SERVINGS

A Mexican staple, authentic tortilla soup generally calls for sautéing the onions and garlic in lard, an ingredient that we replace with olive oil. Use tortillas that are slightly stale, if possible, and bake well—if they are not crisp, the soup will turn to glue. In Mexico, this soup is enriched with whatever ingredients are available—cheese, chicken, avocado. For a lighter version, you can add a tablespoon of brown rice or a few slices of poached chicken to make it a meal.

4 corn tortillas, cut into small pieces

1 corn tortilla, halved and cut into thin strips

Olive oil and canola oil in a spray bottle, or 1 teaspoon olive oil

2 teaspoons olive oil

1 small white onion, diced

3 cloves garlic, minced

2 tablespoons chili powder

1 tablespoon ground cumin

1 teaspoon dried thyme

2 teaspoons salt

3 tomatoes, seeded and diced

$\frac{1}{2}$ cup canned tomato purée

8 cups Chicken Stock (page 200) or Vegetable Broth (page 201)

$\frac{1}{4}$ cup chopped fresh cilantro

Preheat the oven to 350 degrees F. Spread the small pieces of the 4 tortillas on a baking sheet and bake for 10 minutes, or until lightly browned.

Place the strips of the remaining tortilla into a separate baking pan and spray or brush with 1 teaspoon olive oil; bake for 15 to 20 minutes, or until crisp, tossing once during the baking time.

Meanwhile, heat the 2 teaspoons olive oil in a large pot set over medium-high heat. Add the onion, garlic and lightly browned tortilla pieces; sauté, stirring, for 3 to 4 minutes, or until the onion is translucent and soft. Stir in the chili powder, cumin, thyme, salt and tomatoes; cook for 1 to 2 minutes. Add the tomato purée and stock or broth; simmer, uncovered, for 25 minutes, stirring occasionally until the soup thickens and the flavors blend. Remove from the heat and let cool for 15 minutes.

Transfer the soup to a blender or food processor fitted with a metal blade; process until smooth. Return the soup to the pot, stir in the cilantro, and heat through.

Ladle the soup into warm soup bowls and garnish with the crispy tortilla strips.

LEMON CHICKEN SOUP

MAKES 6 SERVINGS

This is the spa version of *avgolemono*, the Greek lemon-chicken soup, which is always finished with egg yolks. Here, egg whites are used instead, poured into the soup in a thin stream, cooking as they hit the hot broth. Serve this with the Arugula, Grapefruit and Shaved Parmesan Salad (page 55) for the perfect winter lunch.

1 tablespoon olive oil

2 (4-ounce) skinless, boneless chicken breast halves

1 tablespoon minced garlic

2 leeks, washed well, trimmed and finely diced

1 medium onion, finely diced

2 medium carrots, finely diced

7 cups Chicken Stock (page 200)

1 $^1/_2$ cups Steamed Fluffy Brown Rice (page 223)

5 egg whites

$^1/_4$ cup fresh lemon juice

$^1/_4$ cup finely chopped fresh parsley

$^1/_4$ cup finely chopped fresh basil

2 tablespoons grated Asiago cheese

Heat the olive oil in a nonstick skillet set over medium-high heat. Place the chicken breast halves into the skillet in a single layer. Sauté for 2 to 3 minutes, being careful not to brown the chicken. Stir in the garlic, leeks, onion and carrots; sauté, stirring, for another 3 to 5 minutes, or until the vegetables are soft. Add the stock and cooked brown rice; simmer for 10 to 15 minutes. The chicken should be cooked through and no longer pink.

Remove the cooked chicken breast from the skillet and transfer to a plate to cool. Using your fingers, shred the chicken into small pieces; return it to the soup.

Whisk together the egg whites, lemon juice, parsley and basil in a mixing bowl. In a thin stream, slowly pour the egg white mixture into the hot soup, whisking constantly, so that the egg cooks and forms thin tissue-like strands.

Ladle into warm soup bowls and garnish with the Asiago cheese; serve.

Vegetable, Chicken and Barley Soup

MAKES 6 SERVINGS

Pearl barley is packed with B vitamins, minerals, iron and calcium. Combined with chicken and vegetables, it makes a very filling, nutritious soup. Add more stock to the soup if you are reheating it, since the barley will absorb the liquid over time.

$3/4$ cup pearl barley, rinsed

3 cups water

1 bay leaf, optional

3 teaspoons kosher salt

3 (4-ounce) skinless, boneless chicken breast halves

6 cups Chicken Stock (page 200), plus more if needed

1 teaspoon olive oil

$1/2$ small onion, finely diced

1 leek, washed well, trimmed and finely diced

1 celery rib, finely diced

1 small carrot, finely diced

1 small yellow squash, trimmed and finely diced

3 scallions, thinly sliced (about $1/4$ cup)

1 lime, cut into 6 wedges

Combine the barley, water, bay leaf and 2 teaspoons salt in a small pot set over medium-high heat. Cover and bring to a simmer. Simmer for 40 minutes, or until the barley is plump and the water has been absorbed. Add more water if necessary.

Place the chicken breast halves into a medium-size pot and pour in the stock; set over medium-high heat and bring to a simmer. Simmer for 15 minutes, or until the chicken is cooked through and no longer pink. Remove the chicken breasts from the stock and set aside until cool enough to handle. Reserve the stock. Dice the chicken into $1/4$-inch cubes. Strain the stock through a fine-mesh sieve and set aside.

In the same pot, heat the olive oil over medium-high heat. Add the onion, leek, celery, carrot and squash; sauté, stirring, for 3 to 5 minutes, or until the vegetables are just beginning to soften. Stir in the diced chicken and stock; simmer for 10 to 15 minutes. Remove the bay leaf from the barley and discard. Add the cooked barley and remaining salt to the soup; simmer for another 5 minutes. Add additional stock if the soup is too thick. Ladle equal portions of the soup into warm soup bowls; garnish with the scallions and a squeeze of lime.

MULLIGATAWNY SOUP

My years in England in the early 1960s were pretty dark, foodwise, until I discovered curries. Mulligatawny, meaning "pepper water," sustained me through that time. In this version, thin slices of sweet apples temper the intense heat of the curry.

2 teaspoons canola oil

2 Anaheim chilies, stemmed, seeded and finely diced

1 small onion, finely diced

2 celery ribs, finely diced

1 large carrot, finely diced

2 tablespoons Madras curry powder

$^1/_2$ cup canned tomato purée

6 cups Chicken Stock (page 200)

1 teaspoon kosher salt

$^3/_4$ cup Steamed Fluffy Brown Rice (page 223)

1 green apple, peeled, cored and thinly sliced

1 tablespoon fresh lime juice

3 scallions, thinly sliced (about $^1/_4$ cup)

Heat the canola oil in a medium-size pot set over medium-high heat. Add the Anaheim chilies, onion, celery and carrot; sauté, stirring, for 3 to 4 minutes, or until the vegetables just begin to soften. Stir in the curry powder and tomato purée; cook, stirring, for another 2 minutes. Pour the stock into the pot and add the salt; simmer for 10 to 15 minutes.

Spoon equal portions of cooked rice and apple slices into warm soup bowls. Ladle the hot soup over the apples and stir a splash of lime juice into each bowl. Garnish with scallions and serve.

A COMPLETE MEAL

I make it a point to leave the kitchen and go out and chat with our Golden Door guests every day. It's a good way to find out what they're interested in. One day, we had Mulligatawny Soup on the menu, and one of the guests stopped me to ask if she could add cooked shrimp to the soup if she made it at home. "Of course," I said. "That way, it's a complete meal." You can do the same thing with most of the soups in this book. Cooked shrimp, roasted turkey breast and cooked chicken can all be added to make heartier soups—one-pot meals.

RED BELL PEPPER SOUP WITH FRESH BASIL

MAKES 6 SERVINGS

Roma tomatoes and red peppers give this soup a wonderful color. Be careful not to over-process or it will lose its vibrant red hue. The rustic flavor of the peppers melds perfectly with fresh basil. As an alternative, serve chilled with chunks of crabmeat, lobster, or avocado. Hot or cold, this soup makes a great start to any meal.

2 teaspoons olive oil

½ medium onion, minced

2 cloves garlic, minced

4 large red bell peppers,
    seeded and diced

5 plum tomatoes, quartered, seeded
    and diced

1 pinch saffron

3 cups Chicken Stock (page 200) or
    Vegetable Broth (page 201)

1 bay leaf

1 teaspoon salt, optional

2 tablespoons very thinly sliced
    fresh basil leaves

Heat the olive oil in a small pot set over medium heat. Add the onion, garlic and red bell pepper; sauté, stirring, for 4 to 5 minutes, or until the vegetables begin to soften. Add the tomatoes; cover and simmer for about 2 to 3 minutes, or until they are soft. Stir in the saffron, stock or broth, bay leaf and salt, if using; simmer, partially covered, for 30 minutes. Remove from the heat and let cool. Remove the bay leaf and discard.

Transfer the soup to a blender or food processor fitted with a metal blade; process until just smooth. Be careful not to overprocess, or the soup will discolor and turn orange. Strain the soup through a fine-mesh sieve back into the soup pot; heat through.

Ladle into warm soup bowls and garnish with basil; serve.

ROOT VEGETABLE SOUP WITH DILLED SOUR CREAM

MAKES 6 SERVINGS

When I make this soup, I purée the beets separately from the other root vegetables, and then swirl the purée into each bowl before serving. Or you can toss them into the blender with the other ingredients, and garnish with the dilled sour cream only. Vegetarians will enjoy this hearty soup using Vegetable Broth instead of Chicken Stock.

2 small beets

1 tablespoon olive oil

1 leek, washed well, trimmed and finely diced

1 large celery rib, finely diced

1 large carrot, finely diced

12 ounces celery root, peeled and diced

1 bay leaf

1 teaspoon dried thyme

1 teaspoon kosher salt

1 teaspoon freshly ground black pepper

6 cups Chicken Stock (page 200) or Vegetable Broth (page 201)

$^1/_4$ cup nonfat sour cream

2 tablespoons finely minced fresh dill

In a small pot set over medium-high heat, boil the beets in enough water to cover, for 40 minutes, or until tender. Remove the beets from the pot, reserving $^1/_4$ cup of the cooking liquid; let cool slightly. Remove the outer skin from the beets and cut into quarters. Transfer to a blender or food processor fitted with a metal blade; process until smooth, adding the reserved cooking liquid as needed. Set aside.

Heat the olive oil in a medium-size pot set over medium-high heat. Add the diced leek, celery, carrot and celery root; sauté, stirring, for 5 minutes. Add the bay leaf, thyme, salt and black pepper; cook for another 3 to 5 minutes. Pour in the stock or broth; bring to a simmer. Simmer for 20 minutes, or until the vegetables are soft. Let cool. Remove the bay leaf and discard.

Transfer to a blender or food processor fitted with a metal blade; process until smooth. (You might need to do this in two batches, depending on the size of the food processor or blender.) Return the puréed soup to the pot and keep warm.

Pour the nonfat sour cream into a small mixing bowl and add the dill; mix well.

Ladle the hot soup into warm soup bowls and swirl in the beet purée. Garnish each bowl with a dollop of dilled sour cream; serve.

SHIPWRECK SOUP

MAKES 6 SERVINGS

If I were stranded on an exotic island, I'd try to make this soup. Succulent shrimp and aromatic seasonings are simmered together for an invigorating soup. It works as an opening course or as a main dish.

2 teaspoons canola oil or peanut oil	2 cups Swiss chard leaves
2 cloves garlic, sliced	8 cups Fish Stock (page 202) or Vegetable Broth (page 201)
1 stalk lemongrass, trimmed and smashed with the side of a knife	1 pound large shrimp, shelled and deveined
1 (1-inch) piece fresh gingerroot, smashed with the side of a knife	$\frac{1}{2}$ cup low-fat coconut milk
1 serrano chili pepper, seeded and diced	2 tablespoons low-sodium soy sauce
	$\frac{1}{4}$ cup fresh lime juice

Heat the oil in a large pot set over medium-high heat. Add the garlic, lemongrass, gingerroot and chili pepper; sauté, stirring, for 3 minutes. Add the Swiss chard, stock or broth and shrimp; bring to a low simmer. Simmer for 10 to 15 minutes, or until the shrimp are pink and cooked through. Using tongs or a slotted spoon, remove the lemongrass and gingerroot. Stir in the coconut milk, soy sauce and lime juice.

Ladle into warm bowls and serve.

A PAINTING IN A BOWL

We eat with our eyes first. For that reason, I think about color and texture with every dish—and soups are no exception. They should look as good as they taste. And sometimes, as with many other dishes, a bit of color contrast is all it takes: a sprinkling of chopped chives, a feathery sprig of dill, a small handful of bright red diced tomato or a dollop of fat-free sour cream. These simple additions can transform a nice-looking soup into a beautiful still life.

SPICED PEACH AND GINGER SOUP

MAKES 4 SERVINGS

A perfectly ripe peach, eaten out of hand, is nearly impossible to top; there is little a cook can do to compete with Mother Nature. This gently spiced cold soup makes a wonderful dessert when fresh whole peaches are too casual an offering. To make fast work of peeling peaches, immerse them in a pot of boiling water for 1 minute, drain, then drop them into a bowl of ice water for 30 seconds and drain again. Peel them when they are cool enough to handle.

8 medium peaches (about 2 pounds), peeled and pitted

2 tablespoons fresh lemon juice

1 cup low-fat buttermilk

$3/4$ cup apple juice

$1/2$ teaspoon grated gingerroot

$1/4$ teaspoon ground cinnamon

$1/8$ teaspoon grated nutmeg

Cut all of the peaches into quarters and toss with the lemon juice. Cut 8 of the quarters into slices and set aside.

In a blender or food processor fitted with a metal blade, process the quartered peaches until smooth. Transfer to a mixing bowl and stir in the buttermilk, apple juice, gingerroot, cinnamon and nutmeg. Cover and refrigerate until well chilled. Ladle into chilled bowls and garnish with reserved fresh peach slices.

SPLIT PEA AND FRESH PEA SOUP WITH BASIL

MAKES 6 SERVINGS

Famed chef Jean-Georges Vongerichten made an unforgettable split pea and fresh pea soup at his restaurant, Jo Jo, in New York City. It inspired my home-style version, which is slightly chunky. Heat the fresh pea mixture until just warm, or the peas will lose their fresh-from-the-garden flavor. I love to garnish this soup with colorful flowering herbs such as thyme, rosemary or garlic. If they aren't available, use parsley or chervil.

1 tablespoon olive oil

1 medium leek, washed well, trimmed, and cut into $\frac{1}{2}$-inch slices

1 medium carrot, cut into $\frac{1}{2}$-inch rounds

$\frac{1}{3}$ small onion, diced

1 cup green split peas, rinsed

1 teaspoon dried thyme

1 bay leaf

1 teaspoon kosher salt

$\frac{1}{2}$ teaspoon freshly ground black pepper

8 cups Chicken Stock (page 200) or Vegetable Broth (page 201)

$1\frac{1}{2}$ cups fresh peas, or sugar snap peas or frozen petite peas

$\frac{1}{4}$ cup fresh basil leaves

Heat the olive oil in a medium-size pot set over medium heat. Add the leek, carrot and onion; sauté, stirring, for 4 to 6 minutes, or until the onion is soft and translucent. Stir in the split peas, thyme, bay leaf, salt and black pepper; cook, stirring, for 2 to 3 minutes. Pour in the stock or broth; simmer, partially covered, for about 1 hour and 15 minutes, or until the split peas are soft. Remove from the heat and let cool slightly. Remove the bay leaf and discard.

Just before serving, pour about $\frac{1}{3}$ of the soup and all of the fresh peas into a food processor or blender; process until smooth. Add the basil; pulse until it is just incorporated. Return the fresh pea mixture to the soup pot, stir and cook until heated through. Ladle into warm soup bowls and serve.

LAST-MINUTE ADDITIONS

Adding fresh herbs to your soups just before serving elevates them to a higher level. The herbs add color, complementing or contrasting with the soup's hue. And, too, herbs add their own lovely fragrances, which mingle with those of the soup. Very thinly sliced basil, chopped chives, Italian parsley, oregano, cilantro — each contributes its own special character, which makes for a more complex, delicious soup.

SUMMER CORN CHOWDER WITH CRABMEAT

MAKES 6 SERVINGS

Don't be tempted to use canned or frozen corn in this recipe. Make it when fresh corn is in season. Make sure the broth simmers rather than boils; boiled broth makes the chowder cloudy.

4 ears corn, shucked and rinsed

2 teaspoons olive oil

2 leeks, washed well, trimmed and diced

3 celery ribs, diced

2 medium carrots, diced

8 cups Chicken Stock (page 200)

3 red potatoes, diced

10 ounces cooked crabmeat, diced

1/2 cup thinly sliced fresh basil leaves

3 scallions, including tops, thinly sliced (about 1/4 cup)

Cut the kernels off the corncob by holding it vertically on a cutting board and cutting downward with a sharp knife until all the kernels are removed.

Heat the olive oil in a large pot set over medium-high heat. Add the leeks, celery and carrots; sauté, stirring, for 3 to 5 minutes, or until the vegetables begin to soften. Add the corn kernels; cook, stirring, for another 2 to 3 minutes. Pour in the stock and bring to a simmer. Simmer for 10 to 15 minutes.

Meanwhile, to keep the chowder clear, cook the potatoes in a separate pot before adding them to the soup. Place the diced potatoes into a small pot with enough lightly salted water to cover. Set over medium-high heat; bring to a simmer. Simmer, uncovered, for 6 to 8 minutes. The potatoes should be firm. Drain the potatoes, add them to the chowder and let simmer for 5 minutes.

Place the diced crabmeat, basil and scallions into warm soup bowls. Ladle the chowder into the bowls; serve.

Miso Soup with Tofu, Scallions and Enoki Mushrooms

MAKES 6 SERVINGS

A staple in the Japanese pantry, miso is a paste of fermented soybeans combined with either a barley, rice or soybean base. We use it in all manner of Japanese-style dishes, the lighter miso in delicate soups and salad dressings, the darker in heartier dishes. I use light *shiromiso* in this soup, but you can experiment with the different varieties to find the one you like best. There are those who believe that miso has healing properties; to preserve these properties, don't let the soup boil.

6 ounces firm tofu, drained

2 tablespoons low-sodium soy sauce

1 (1 1/4-inch) piece fresh gingerroot, skin on

6 cups Chicken Stock (page 200) or Vegetable Broth (page 201)

3 teaspoons shiromiso (white miso)

3 ounces enoki mushrooms

2 tablespoons diagonally sliced scallions, including tops

Press the tofu by patting it dry and wrapping it in a kitchen towel. Place a heavy plate on top and let stand for 20 to 30 minutes to extract any extra liquid. Cut the pressed tofu into 1/4-inch cubes.

Place the tofu into a glass or ceramic dish, pour in the soy sauce and marinate for 30 minutes. Using a cheese grater, coarsely grate the gingerroot. Then, working over a small bowl, squeeze the grated gingerroot with your hands to extract the juices until you have 2 teaspoons. Reserve the juices and discard the ginger pulp.

Bring the stock or broth to a simmer in a medium-size soup pot set over medium-high heat. Whisk in the miso and gingerroot juice; continue to simmer, being careful not to let it boil.

Place equal portions of marinated tofu into soup bowls and ladle the miso broth over it. Garnish the soup with enoki mushrooms and scallions.

Mixed greens. What a world of possibilities that little culinary term opens up! The complexity of curly endive, the shocking variegated colors of radicchio, the fragile undulation of butter lettuce, and the strongly-ribbed crispness of romaine. Flavors ranging from bitter to sweet, hot to buttery, pungent to understated. The dressings—a shelf full of vinegars, artisan-pressed olive and nut oils, plump fresh garlic cloves, acidic citrus juices, tangy yogurt and sprinklings of shaved dry cheeses. And all this variety comes without turning on a burner or oven. In fact, the elemental raw nature of salads may lie at the heart of their attraction.

Tour a farmers market, health food or gourmet grocer, or your own backyard garden, and you're just as apt to be fingering the leaves of a cress, exotic Asian green, or purslane as you are the big-leafed watery lettuces that dominated the supermarkets and garden seed packets just a few decades ago.

Times change, tastes change, but salad principles remain simple: the ingredients must be impeccably fresh and seasonal and the salad itself must be lovely to look at. I don't plan my salads ahead; I visit the garden each morning and look around, just as you can do in your favorite market. Because I combine four or fewer ingredients in many of my salads, each ingredient must be flavorful enough to stand on its own. For example, Arugula, Grapefruit and Shaved Parmesan Salad must be peppery sharp and tart, with each ingredient con-

SALADS

tributing fully to its refreshing flavor. The same is true for Frisée with Garden-Fresh Strawberries, where the just-bitter-enough greens balance the juicy sweetness of berries.

Sometimes a salad can consist of simply the very best greens tossed in a piquant dressing, as in Spinach and Buckwheat Sprout Salad. Or it can be heartier and more elaborate, ample enough to eat as a main course. I love to combine seafood and fruit in a Curried Papaya and Crabmeat Salad for a delicious luncheon, and I will often add more protein to salads to make them complete meals, such as Mexican-Style Chicken Taco Salad and Thai-Style Chicken Salad.

Most salads rely on dressings to bind them together, and many are overly dressed with flavor-masking fatty ingredients. In this chapter, you will find some salads tossed in vinaigrettes flavored with fresh herbs and spices, and others in dressings made creamy with silken tofu, mustard and miso paste. I've also included salads based on cabbage or fruits or beans, with no "mixed greens" to be seen. Heartier, they make wonderful main or side dishes.

Salads are on the Door's lunch and dinner menus every day. I enjoy the wonderful challenge of creating different combinations of ingredients and dressings while visualizing them on the plate. Take the time to choose your ingredients well, and arrange them in a way that gives you pleasure. As we do at the spa, consider sprinkles of edible flowers as a final flourish. They always draw the oohs and aahs.

SPRING WILD RICE SALAD

Freshly squeezed lemon juice and lemon thyme give this rice salad a bright tangy taste. Serve it at room temperature for the best flavor. If you can't find lemon thyme, use the more common variety. This salad makes a wonderful complement to the Five-Spice Duck Breast Salad with Garden Arugula and Watercress (page 68).

$1/2$ cup wild rice, rinsed

$2\,1/4$ cups water

1 bay leaf

$1/4$ cup fresh lemon juice

1 tablespoon olive oil

1 cup corn kernels

$1/2$ cup chopped scallions

2 large plum tomatoes, seeded and diced

$1/2$ cup finely chopped parsley

2 teaspoons finely chopped fresh lemon thyme or common thyme

1 teaspoon kosher salt, optional

Freshly ground black pepper to taste, optional

Combine the rice, water and bay leaf in a small pot set over medium-high heat; cover and bring to a simmer. Simmer for 35 minutes, or until the rice is tender. Transfer to a mixing bowl and let cool. Remove the bay leaf. Stir in the lemon juice, olive oil, corn, scallions, tomatoes, parsley, lemon thyme and salt, if using. Mix well and refrigerate for 30 minutes. Season with black pepper, if desired.

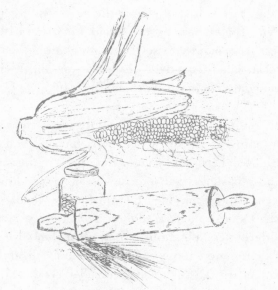

ARUGULA, GRAPEFRUIT AND SHAVED PARMESAN SALAD WITH PEPPERCORN-CHIVE VINAIGRETTE

MAKES 4 SERVINGS

It only takes three ingredients to make this Golden Door favorite, but the freshness of each ingredient is key. Arugula is fragile and can spoil quickly if not properly stored. Put the stems in water and cover the leaves loosely with paper towels, or wrap loosely in a plastic bag and store in the refrigerator. Use a cheese slicer to shave the Parmesan paper-thin. The pink or red peppercorns in the dressing are in fact dried berries that release an enticing citrus fragrance when crushed. The flavor is sweet and slightly piquant, with hints of citrus. Garnish the salad with a sprinkle of arugula flowers, if available.

For the vinaigrette:

2 tablespoons Champagne vinegar or sherry vinegar

1 tablespoon Dijon mustard

$\frac{1}{4}$ cup water

2 tablespoons chardonnay

2 tablespoons fresh lemon juice

1 tablespoon pure maple syrup

2 tablespoons olive oil

1 tablespoon crushed pink peppercorns

2 tablespoons finely chopped fresh chives

For the salad:

2 white grapefruit, peeled, pith removed and separated into segments

6 cups arugula, washed and patted dry

$\frac{1}{4}$ cup thinly shaved Parmesan cheese

Arugula flowers for garnish, optional

To make the vinaigrette, combine the vinegar, mustard, water, chardonnay, lemon juice and maple syrup in a blender; process at low speed. With the motor running, slowly pour in the olive oil. Or put all of these ingredients except the oil into a mixing bowl and beat with a fork. Pour in the oil in a steady stream with one hand and continue beating with the other hand. (If you need a "third" hand to keep the bowl from moving, set it on a wet dish towel.) Transfer the dressing to a mixing bowl and stir in the peppercorns and chives. *Makes 1 cup.*

To prepare the salad, cut the outer membrane from the grapefruit segments. Tear the arugula into bite-sized pieces and distribute equal portions onto chilled salad plates. Top each with $\frac{1}{4}$ of the grapefruit segments, sprinkle with the shaved Parmesan cheese, garnish with arugula flowers, if using, and drizzle each salad with 2 tablespoons Peppercorn-Chive Vinaigrette; serve. Peppercorn-Chive Vinaigrette can be kept in the refrigerator, covered, for up to 5 days.

FRISÉE WITH GARDEN-FRESH STRAWBERRIES AND MANGO-TAHINI DRESSING

MAKES 4 SERVINGS

Fresh fruit and greens are a popular combination at the Golden Door; our gardens overflow with them practically year-round. I make this in early summer, when the strawberries are plump to bursting. If you can find edible geranium leaves and flowers, toss them into the salad as you would any other green. They add a subtle pepper flavor to the dish.

4 cups frisée lettuce, washed and patted dry

2 cups fresh strawberries, stems removed and quartered

$^1/_2$ cup Mango-Tahini Dressing (page 209)

$^1/_4$ cup scented geranium leaves and flowers, optional

Combine the frisée lettuce, strawberries and Mango-Tahini Dressing in a mixing bowl; toss to coat. Place equal portions onto chilled plates and sprinkle with scented geranium flowers and leaves, if using; serve.

SIMPLIFY, SIMPLIFY

A salad need not be complicated. Four ingredients or fewer often make the best salads. And the dressing can be as simple as a good-quality olive oil and a dash of aged balsamic vinegar. (Forget the lumpy, gloppy, gluey bottled dressings.) The key is to get the best and freshest produce possible—and often that means shopping at a farmers market, where the goods have come right from the farm (not from farm to warehouse to supermarket). The fresher the produce, the more flavorful and visually appealing and the less you need to rely on complicated additions. Nature does it all for you.

Papaya, Orange and Bermuda Onion Salad

MAKES 4 SERVINGS

I love this combination, and so do my guests. The vinaigrette is very acidic and tangy, perfectly suited to the supersweet combination of papaya, orange and red onion.

$^{1}/_{2}$ small Bermuda onion, thinly sliced

1 tablespoon sherry vinegar

$^{1}/_{4}$ cup fresh orange juice

1 tablespoon fresh lime juice

1 tablespoon olive oil

2 oranges, peeled, pith removed and
    separated into segments

4 cups mixed greens, washed and
    patted dry

1 large papaya, peeled, seeded and
    sliced lengthwise into 12 strips

4 nasturtium flowers, optional

In a small mixing bowl, combine the Bermuda onion and sherry vinegar; marinate for 15 minutes.

Prepare the dressing by whisking together the orange juice, lime juice and olive oil in a small bowl.

Using a sharp knife, cut the outer membrane from the orange segments.

Place equal portions of the mixed greens onto chilled salad plates. Arrange the sliced papaya around the greens and top with the orange segments and marinated onions. Drizzle the dressing over the top and garnish with the nasturtiums, if using; serve.

THE MARKET OPTION

When you shop for salad, keep an open mind. Then, when you see something wonderful, grab it. Say you intended to make the Papaya, Orange and Bermuda Onion Salad above, but when you get to the market, you find beautiful yellow bell peppers and so-so papaya. By all means, substitute the peppers! Some of the greatest salads are born of serendipity. And somehow, they always work.

SPINACH AND BUCKWHEAT SPROUT SALAD WITH SWEET AND SOUR DRESSING

MAKES 4 SERVINGS

A salad of spinach and sprouts? On the days when your body is telling you (and, amazingly, it does) to eat your greens, this is the salad to make. Buckwheat sprouts are the most mild-mannered member of the sprout family, but you can use whatever sprouts you like best. Sunflower sprouts, mung bean sprouts and pea shoots also work well. The dressing was created by my sous-chef, Dean Rucker, and it became an instant hit with our guests.

For the dressing:
$1/_3$ cup fresh lime juice
$1/_3$ cup low-sodium soy sauce
$1/_4$ cup brown sugar
1 serrano chili, stemmed, seeded and minced
2 cloves garlic, minced
2 tablespoons canola oil

For the salad:
6 cups baby spinach leaves, washed and patted dry
1 cup buckwheat or other sprouts

To make the dressing, combine the lime juice, soy sauce, brown sugar, serrano chili, garlic and canola oil in a blender or food processor fitted with a metal blade; process briefly so that the ingredients are combined but the solids stay slightly chunky. *Makes 1 cup.*

To prepare the salad, place equal portions of spinach and sprouts onto chilled salad plates; drizzle about $1^1/_2$ tablespoons of the dressing on each. Sweet and Sour Dressing can be kept in the refrigerator, covered, for up to 5 days.

ASPARAGUS, BEAN SPROUT AND SCALLION SALAD

MAKES 4 SERVINGS

This combination makes an excellent salad course on its own, or it can become a main course with the addition of crabmeat or grilled chicken. Buy asparagus from stores that sell it out of a water-filled bucket. Use medium-thick stalks that are bright green and have tight tips with a purple blush. When trimming the asparagus, snap the stalks with your fingers, allowing them to break naturally; then trim the ends with a knife.

8 stalks asparagus, trimmed

1 cup bean sprouts or sunflower sprouts

$1^1/_2$ scallions including tops, diagonally sliced (about 2 tablespoons)

$^1/_2$ cup Lime-Miso Dipping Sauce and Dressing (page 211)

4 cups mixed greens, washed and patted dry

2 teaspoons sesame seeds, optional

Bring a pot of water to a boil over high heat. Prepare a bowl of ice water. Slice the asparagus diagonally into 1-inch pieces. Immerse the asparagus in the boiling water for 1 to 2 minutes, drain and plunge into the ice water for 30 seconds to stop the cooking process. Drain and pat dry.

Combine the cooled asparagus, bean sprouts and scallions in a mixing bowl. Pour the Lime-Miso Dipping Sauce and Dressing over the vegetables; toss gently to coat.

Place equal portions of the mixed greens onto chilled salad plates, and top each with $^1/_4$ of the asparagus mixture. Sprinkle with sesame seeds, if desired; serve.

ABOUT SPROUTS

I love sprouts of all kinds—pea, sunflower, radish and, yes, plain old mung bean sprouts. They add flavor and crunch to all kinds of foods. If your local market sells them, by all means buy sprouts that still have their seeds attached—sprouted already, of course. Don't buy sprouts that smell bad or whose stems are brown and spoiled. Sprouts tend to be fragile. Don't expect to keep sprouts too long; instead plan to use them right away. Alfalfa sprouts have been associated with *E. coli* bacteria; avoid them altogether. If you can't find the more exotic sprouts, fresh crisp mung bean sprouts are a lovely choice. And if you can't find them, scallion tops will work, too.

GRILLED ASPARAGUS WITH RADICCHIO AND ROASTED ANAHEIM CHILI VINAIGRETTE

MAKES 4 SERVINGS

A fiery vinaigrette dresses this salad, which offers a combination of smoky, tart and bitter flavors. I love the mix of warm and cold ingredients; it makes every bite interesting. You can use the dressing with chicken salad or as a dip for vegetables. The combination of smoky Anaheim chilies and tangy apple cider vinegar makes this dressing irresistible.

For the vinaigrette:

2 large Anaheim chilies

Olive oil and canola oil in a spray bottle, or 1 teaspoon olive oil

1 small shallot, minced

2 tablespoons apple cider vinegar

½ cup water

1 tablespoon Dijon mustard

1 tablespoon honey

½ teaspoon freshly ground black pepper

1 tablespoon fresh cilantro leaves

For the salad:

16 stalks asparagus

2 heads radicchio, washed and patted dry

1 large grapefruit, peeled, pith removed and separated into segments

Olive and canola oil in a spray bottle, or 1 teaspoon olive oil

1 ½ cups trimmed, chopped romaine lettuce

4 fresh cilantro sprigs, optional

To make the dressing, preheat a charcoal, gas or stovetop grill. Spray or brush the Anaheim chilies with olive oil; grill or broil them for 5 minutes, turning so that all sides are charred. Transfer to a plastic bag, seal and set aside to cool. When cool enough to handle, remove the skin, seeds and stems; chop coarsely.

Combine the roasted chilies, shallot, cider vinegar, water, mustard, honey and black pepper in a blender or food processor fitted with a metal blade; process until smooth. Add the cilantro; pulse to incorporate. *Makes 1 cup.*

To prepare the salad, preheat a charcoal, gas or stovetop grill. Bring a pot of water to a boil over high heat; prepare a bowl of ice water.

Trim the asparagus by snapping the stalks with your fingers, allowing them to break naturally; then trim the ends with a knife. Using a vegetable peeler, trim the lower half of the asparagus so that the tough outer skin is removed. Immerse the trimmed asparagus in the boiling water for 1 to 2 minutes. Remove with tongs or a slotted spoon, then plunge into the ice water for 30 seconds to stop the cooking process. Drain and set aside.

Remove 4 whole radicchio leaves from their heads and set aside for garnish. Finely chop the remaining radicchio. Using a sharp knife, cut the outer membrane from the grapefruit segments.

Spray or brush the blanched asparagus with olive oil; grill for 3 to 4 minutes, or until lightly charred. Transfer to a work surface and slice diagonally into 1-inch pieces. Place the asparagus pieces into a large salad bowl and stir in the shredded radicchio, chopped romaine lettuce, grapefruit segments and ½ cup Roasted Anaheim Chili Vinaigrette; toss well.

Place 1 radicchio leaf on each chilled plate and top with equal portions of the salad. Garnish with fresh cilantro sprigs, if desired. Roasted Anaheim Chili Vinaigrette can be kept in the refrigerator, covered, for up to 5 days.

VINAIGRETTE GOES ON A DIET

The classic vinaigrette recipes call for three parts oil to one part vinegar, plus salt, black pepper and, if you wish, other flavorings. You can get just as much flavor and enjoyment with a lightened-up version. My rule of thumb is one part oil, one part vinegar and one part water. For a really light touch, pour your olive oil into a spray bottle and mist your salad lightly. Then sprinkle a tiny amount of vinegar on. Remember that a vinaigrette—especially a lighter one—is a simple affair, so it's important to choose the best ingredients you can find: good-quality olive oil, an aged balsamic vinegar or herbed vinegar or some fresh lemon juice.

CELERY ROOT AND ORANGE SALAD WITH GINGER, PEANUT AND CILANTRO DRESSING

MAKES 4 SERVINGS

This salad exemplifies the fusion of Eastern (lime, scallions, ginger) and Western (celery root, oranges) ingredients, and the result is a beautifully balanced dish. Celeriac, or celery root, the root of a variety of cultivated celery, tastes somewhat like common celery, but with a hint of sharpness reminiscent of parsley. Choose celery root that is small, about the size of an apple (anything over 2 pounds is flavorless), with bright green leaves and no knobs.

9 ounces celery root, peeled, rinsed and cut into thin strips

1 tablespoon fresh lime juice

2 tablespoons fresh orange juice

2 oranges

$^1/_2$ cup diagonally sliced scallions

$^1/_4$ cup Ginger, Peanut and Cilantro Sauce and Dressing (page 210)

Fresh cilantro sprigs for garnish

Combine the celery root, lime juice and orange juice in a mixing bowl; toss to coat.

Bring a small pot of water to a boil over high heat. Prepare a small bowl of ice water. Using a vegetable peeler, trim the zest from one of the oranges and cut into matchstick-sized strips, making sure to remove any pith. Immerse the orange zest in the boiling water for 1 minute, drain, then plunge into the ice water for 30 seconds to stop the cooking process. Drain again and stir the zest into the celery root.

Peel the oranges and remove any white pith. Using a sharp knife, cut the outer membrane from the orange segments. Stir into the celery root; then mix in the scallions.

Pour $^1/_4$ cup of the Ginger, Peanut and Cilantro Sauce and Dressing over the celery root salad; mix well. Place equal portions of celery root salad onto chilled plates. Garnish with fresh cilantro sprigs.

RUBY RED GRAPEFRUIT COLESLAW

MAKES 6 SERVINGS

This winter slaw is simple enough to make for dinner on a busy weeknight yet pretty enough to serve on the holiday table—and both the napa cabbage and red grapefruit are excellent sources of vitamin A. Other seasonal ingredients, such as tangerines, pomegranates and blood oranges, can be combined with, or substituted entirely, for the red grapefruit. Segment the grapefruit over a bowl so that every bit of juice can be used for the dressing.

1 ruby red grapefruit, peeled, pith removed and separated into segments

10 cups trimmed, shredded napa cabbage

1 medium red onion, thinly sliced

1 carrot, shredded

$1/4$ cup fresh cilantro leaves

$1/3$ cup fresh grapefruit juice

1 tablespoon mirin (sweet rice wine)

1 tablespoon dark sesame oil

1 teaspoon low-sodium soy sauce

1 teaspoon Vietnamese chili sauce

2 tablespoons sesame seeds

Using a sharp knife, cut the outer membrane from the grapefruit segments. Combine the shredded cabbage, red onion, carrot, cilantro and grapefruit segments in a large bowl.

Whisk together the grapefruit juice, mirin, sesame oil, soy sauce and chili sauce in a small mixing bowl. At least 10 minutes before serving, toss the slaw with the dressing and allow to marinate. Sprinkle with sesame seeds; serve.

Mexican-Style Chicken Taco Salad with Cumin Salad Dressing

MAKES 4 SERVINGS

Much of the fat in restaurant-style taco salads comes from the fried corn tortillas and the sour cream that are typically served with them. Here, the corn chips are baked and the salad is dressed with flavorful low-fat Cumin Salad Dressing. Toasting the cumin in a hot, dry skillet helps release its aroma and aids in mellowing its slightly bitter characteristic.

For the dressing:

$1/_2$ cup silken tofu

$1/_2$ cup nonfat plain yogurt

2 teaspoons ground cumin, toasted for 2 to 3 minutes in a hot, dry skillet

1 teaspoon cayenne pepper

2 tablespoons fresh lime juice

For the salad:

4 (4-ounce) skinless, boneless chicken breast halves

$1/_2$ red onion, coarsely chopped

1 celery rib

1 bay leaf

$1 ^3/_4$ cups Chicken Stock (page 200)

2 tablespoons fresh lime juice

$1/_2$ red onion, thinly sliced

2 tablespoons red wine vinegar

1 teaspoon fructose or sugar

1 small avocado

4 cups baby romaine lettuce, cut into 1-inch strips

16 Golden Door Chips (page 220)

2 plum tomatoes, finely diced

To make the dressing, combine the silken tofu, yogurt, cumin, cayenne pepper and lime juice in a blender or food processor fitted with a metal blade; process until smooth, then refrigerate until ready to serve. *Makes 1 cup.*

To prepare the salad, place the chicken, onion, celery and bay leaf into a nonstick pan, pour in the stock, set the pan over medium heat and bring it to a simmer. Poach the chicken for 15 to 20 minutes, or until it is thoroughly cooked and no longer pink. Remove the poached chicken from the liquid and set aside to cool. When cool enough to handle, shred the chicken, transfer the pieces to a bowl and toss with lime juice.

Combine the red onion, red wine vinegar and fructose or sugar in a small bowl; marinate for 30 minutes.

When you are ready to serve, slice the avocado into thin strips. Arrange equal portions of the lettuce on chilled salad plates; top with the shredded chicken, Golden Door Chips, marinated red onion, and diced tomato. Drizzle 2 tablespoons of Cumin Salad Dressing over each salad and top with slices of avocado. Cumin Salad Dressing can be kept in the refrigerator, covered, for up to 5 days.

THAI-STYLE CHICKEN SALAD

MAKES 4 SERVINGS

A lean, clean version of a favorite takeout Thai specialty. Look for lemongrass in Asian markets and specialty stores.

2 tablespoons low-sodium soy sauce

2 tablespoons fresh lime juice

1 teaspoon minced gingerroot

1 teaspoon minced garlic

$\frac{1}{2}$ teaspoon trimmed, minced lemongrass

4 (4-ounce) skinless, boneless chicken breast halves

Canola oil in a spray bottle, or 1 teaspoon canola oil

2 ounces cellophane or bean-thread noodles

$\frac{1}{4}$ cup seasoned rice vinegar

$\frac{1}{4}$ cup minced fresh chives

2 cups mixed salad greens, washed and patted dry

2 cups shredded napa cabbage

$\frac{1}{2}$ cup Lime-Miso Sauce and Dressing (page 211)

Fresh chives, for garnish, optional

Combine the soy sauce, lime juice, gingerroot, garlic and lemongrass in a glass or ceramic bowl; mix well. Add the chicken breast halves and turn a few times to coat all sides. Cover and refrigerate for 30 to 40 minutes, turning the chicken once.

Preheat the oven to 350 degrees F. Spray or grease a nonstick ovenproof pan with canola oil and heat over medium-high heat. Remove the chicken from the marinade; discard the marinade. Place the chicken into the pan and sear for 2 minutes on each side. Transfer the chicken to the oven and bake for 12 to 15 minutes, or until the meat is cooked through and no longer pink, and its juices run clear. Remove from the oven; set aside to cool.

Bring a pot of water to a boil. Place the noodles into a bowl and pour the boiling water over them. Cover and let stand for 10 to 15 minutes, or until the noodles are soft and glassy. Drain the noodles well and toss with rice vinegar and chives. Set aside.

Place equal portions of the mixed greens and shredded cabbage onto large, chilled salad plates; top with equal portions of the seasoned noodles. Cut each chicken breast half on the bias and fan it over the noodles. Drizzle 2 tablespoons Lime-Miso Sauce and Dressing over each chicken breast and garnish each plate with chives, if desired.

CURRIED PAPAYA AND CRABMEAT SALAD WITH CURRIED MANGO DRESSING

MAKES 4 SERVINGS

Curry is a combination of spices ranging from as few as five ingredients to as many as thirty. Some of the spices found in curry powder most often are turmeric, chili powder, allspice, ginger, cinnamon, clove and cardamom. The pungency of the curry depends on the amount of chili powder in it, and can range from mild to intense. Try to avoid generic curry powders in the supermarket but explore local Asian and Middle Eastern markets for high-quality curry. When scooping the flesh from the papaya, hold it over a bowl to catch the juices. The juices help bind the salad together without adding any fat.

For the dressing:
$^3/_4$ cup Silken Tofu Mayonnaise
    (page 206)
$^1/_4$ cup apple juice or mango nectar
$^1/_2$ ripe mango, peeled, pitted and diced
1 tablespoon Madras curry powder
2 tablespoons finely chopped parsley

For the salad:
2 papayas
12 ounces cooked crabmeat, with
    4 large pieces reserved for garnish
$^1/_3$ cup diced jicama
1 celery rib, finely diced
2 teaspoons Madras curry powder
2 tablespoons finely chopped parsley
4 cups mixed greens, washed and
    patted dry

To make the dressing, combine the Silken Tofu Mayonnaise, apple juice or mango nectar, mango and curry powder in a blender or food processor fitted with a metal blade; process until smooth. Transfer to a bowl or storage container and stir in the parsley. Refrigerate until ready to serve. *Makes 1 $^1/_4$ cups.*

To prepare the salad, cut the papaya in half and remove the seeds. Gently scoop out the papaya flesh and transfer to a mixing bowl. Stir in the crabmeat (except for the 4 pieces reserved for garnish), jicama, celery, curry powder and parsley; mix well. Fill the papaya halves with the salad mixture.

Arrange equal portions of the mixed greens on chilled salad plates and place a stuffed papaya in the center of each. Garnish each papaya with a large piece of crabmeat and drizzle each salad with 2 tablespoons Curried Mango Dressing. Curried Mango Dressing can be kept in the refrigerator, covered, for up to 5 days.

TENDER SPRING GREENS AND SHRIMP SALAD

MAKES 4 SERVINGS

A simple seasoning of parsley and lemon coats the succulent shrimp in this easy-to-make salad. The warm shrimp wilt the baby lettuces slightly, making the tender greens perfect to the bite.

Canola oil in a spray bottle, or
   1 teaspoon canola oil

12 medium shrimp (about 1 pound),
   shelled and deveined

1 tablespoon finely chopped fresh
   parsley

$\frac{1}{2}$ teaspoon kosher salt

$\frac{1}{2}$ teaspoon freshly ground
   black pepper

2 tablespoons fresh lemon juice

6 cups mixed baby lettuce leaves,
   washed and patted dry

$\frac{1}{2}$ cup Mango-Tahini Dressing
   (page 209)

1 lemon, cut into wedges

$\frac{1}{4}$ cup calendula petals, optional

Spray or grease a nonstick pan with canola oil and set over medium-high heat. Add the shrimp; sauté, stirring, for 2 to 3 minutes on each side, or until pink. Reduce the heat to medium-low and sprinkle the shrimp with parsley, salt and black pepper, and drizzle with lemon juice. Cover and cook for another 2 minutes. Remove from the heat and let cool.

Place equal portions of the greens onto chilled plates and top with the shrimp. Drizzle 2 tablespoons of Mango-Tahini Dressing over each; garnish with lemon wedges and calendula petals, if desired.

FIVE-SPICE DUCK BREAST SALAD WITH GARDEN ARUGULA AND WATERCRESS

MAKES 4 SERVINGS

Duck breast meat is rich enough to handle assertively flavored marinades like this mixture of soy sauce, balsamic vinegar and mirin. Remove the fatty skin from the duck breast before marinating to reduce the fat content of the dish.

For the marinade:

1 teaspoon grated fresh gingerroot

1 teaspoon minced garlic

2 tablespoons low-sodium soy sauce

1 (1-inch) piece lemongrass, trimmed and smashed with the side of a knife

1 tablespoon chopped fresh mint

1 tablespoon mirin (sweet rice wine)

1 tablespoon rice wine vinegar

For the salad:

1 (12 to 14-ounce) duck breast, trimmed

Canola oil in a spray bottle, or 1 teaspoon canola oil

3 corn tortillas, cut into $1/4$-inch strips

2 cups arugula, washed and patted dry

2 cups watercress, washed and patted dry

3 cups finely shredded napa cabbage

$1/2$ cup radish or mung bean sprouts

3 medium carrots, cut into thin strips (about 1 cup)

$1/2$ cup Lime-Miso Dipping Sauce and Dressing (page 211)

4 sprigs fresh cilantro, optional

To prepare the marinade, combine the gingerroot, garlic, soy sauce, lemongrass, mint, mirin and rice wine vinegar in a shallow dish.

Place the duck breast into the marinade, turn a few times to coat, cover and refrigerate for 2 hours. When you are ready to cook, remove the duck from the marinade; discard the marinade.

Preheat the oven to 375 degrees F. Spray or grease a baking sheet with canola oil and set aside.

Spray a nonstick ovenproof pan with canola oil and set over medium-high heat. Place the marinated duck breast into the pan and sear each side for 2 to 3 minutes, or until lightly browned. Transfer the duck to the oven and cook for 10 to 15 minutes for medium-rare or longer to taste. Remove from the oven and set aside to cool.

Place the corn tortilla strips onto the prepared baking sheet; bake for 10 minutes, tossing once or twice, or until the strips are golden brown and crisp. Remove from the oven and let cool.

When you are ready to serve, slice the duck breast thinly on the bias. Combine the arugula, watercress, napa cabbage, sprouts and carrots in a large mixing bowl; toss well. Place equal portions of the salad into chilled salad bowls. Top each with 4 to 5 slices of the duck breast and baked corn strips. Drizzle each salad with 2 tablespoons Lime-Miso Dipping Sauce and Dressing and garnish each plate with a sprig of cilantro.

A GUIDE TO GREENS

The selection of greens available has increased exponentially in the last few years. Of course we still enjoy old favorites like romaine, Boston or Bibb lettuce (even iceberg lettuce is enjoying a comeback); but now we have so many more choices, ranging from mild to bitter, tender to crisp. Buy the freshest greens you can—and buy what you'll need over the next day or so. Don't try to stockpile, as many greens wilt and spoil easily. Wash greens well and spin them dry if you think they can withstand it without bruising; but if they are delicate, pat them dry thoroughly with a paper towel and store in your refrigerator's vegetable bin. Here's a quick guide to some favorites:

Arugula: Also known as *roquette* in France and *rucola* in Italy, its tender leaf belies its peppery flavor.

Belgian Endive: Its oblong leaves can be sliced into salads or kept whole to serve as edible containers for dips and such. Light, almost white, it has a mild bitter flavor.

Curly Endive: Also known as *frisée*, curly endive is a kind of chicory. The leaves are coarse, prickly and slightly bitter. Look for curly endive that is pale green to white; it will be milder and more tender than the deep green leaves.

Dandelion Greens: Tart and tangy, they can be eaten raw or cooked.

Mâche: A fragile leaf with a sweet nutty flavor, mâche is also called lamb's lettuce.

Mizuna: A member of the mustard family, mizuna has feathery leaves and a delicate flavor.

Pea Shoots: Everything on the first five inches of a snow pea vine—tendrils, leaves, pods and the actual vine—comprise the pea shoot, a crisp delicious component of salads and Asian-inspired dishes.

Radicchio: Deep purple streaked with white, radicchio grows as round heads or long leaves and has a bitter flavor.

Spinach: Popeye's favorite, spinach was one of the first "alternative" greens to be used in salads, and it's still a delicious choice.

Tofu Niçoise Salad with
Crispy Potato Scallops and Mustard Vinaigrette

MAKES 4 SERVINGS

I often turn to this classic dish as a basis for my recipes. Here, a Niçoise salad is reinterpreted with seared garlic, tarragon-infused tofu, and potatoes, accented with a tangy Mustard Vinaigrette.

For the vinaigrette:

$^1\!/_2$ cup water

3 tablespoons apple cider vinegar

1 shallot, sliced

1 tablespoon olive oil

3 tablespoons Dijon mustard

1 tablespoon honey, optional

$^1\!/_2$ teaspoon freshly ground
   black pepper

$^1\!/_2$ teaspoon dried tarragon or thyme

2 tablespoons chopped fresh parsley

For the salad:

6 ounces firm tofu, drained

3 purple potatoes

1 cup green beans (about 4 ounces)

1 teaspoon minced garlic

1 tablespoon chopped tarragon

2 tablespoons apple cider vinegar

2 tablespoons apple juice

1 teaspoon canola oil

$^1\!/_2$ teaspoon kosher salt

$^1\!/_2$ teaspoon freshly ground
   black pepper

Olive oil and canola oil in a spray
   bottle, or 1 teaspoon olive oil

4 cups mixed greens, washed and
   patted dry

2 large ripe tomatoes, cut in
   $^1\!/_4$-inch slices

$^1\!/_4$ cup pitted Kalamata or
   Niçoise olives

2 tablespoons capers, drained

$^1\!/_4$ teaspoon fresh thyme leaves

$^1\!/_4$ teaspoon fresh rosemary leaves

$^1\!/_4$ cup chopped fresh parsley

To prepare the vinaigrette, combine the water, vinegar, shallot, olive oil, mustard, honey, if using, and black pepper in a blender; process until smooth. Pulse in the tarragon and parsley. *Makes 1 cup.*

To prepare the salad, wrap the tofu in a clean kitchen towel and cover with a heavy plate for 30 minutes.

Place the potatoes into a medium-size pot with enough water to cover and bring to a boil. Boil for about 15 minutes, or until fork-tender but still firm. Remove from the heat, drain and let cool. Peel and slice the cooled potatoes into $\frac{1}{4}$-inch rounds.

Bring another pot of water to a boil and prepare a bowl of ice water. Immerse the green beans in the boiling water for 4 to 5 minutes, or until they are tender-crisp. Drain and plunge the beans into the ice water for 30 seconds to stop the cooking process. Drain.

Slice the tofu into thin pieces. Combine the tofu slices, garlic, tarragon, apple cider vinegar and apple juice in a glass or ceramic dish. Cover and marinate for 30 minutes.

Spray or grease a nonstick pan with canola oil and set over medium-high heat. Add the marinated tofu and sear for 3 to 5 minutes on each side, or until it is medium-crisp. Set aside and let cool.

Season the cooked, sliced potatoes with the salt and black pepper. Spray or grease a separate nonstick pan with olive oil and set over medium-high heat. Add the potato slices and sear on both sides for 3 to 4 minutes, or until the potatoes are crisp. Remove the potato slices from the pan and let cool.

Place equal portions of mixed greens onto chilled plates. Top with the crispy tofu and potatoes, arrange the sliced tomatoes, green beans and olives next to the tofu and potatoes, and scatter the capers around each plate. Sprinkle with thyme, rosemary and parsley. Drizzle 2 tablespoons Mustard Vinaigrette over each salad and serve. Mustard Vinaigrette can be kept in the refrigerator, covered, for up to 1 week.

GOLDEN DOOR SALAD WITH TONNATA DRESSING

MAKES 4 SERVINGS

I love this salad, with its classic French ingredients dressed in a classic Italian tuna dressing. *Tonnata* is an Italian dressing made with tuna and mayonnaise, which traditionally accompanies cold sliced veal, but it works beautifully with a salad of tuna, hard-cooked egg whites and veggies.

For the dressing:

Olive oil and canola oil in a spray bottle, or 1 teaspoon olive oil

1/2 medium onion, finely diced

1 tablespoon minced garlic

3 anchovy fillets, rinsed and patted dry

1/2 cup silken tofu (about 5 ounces)

1/2 cup Chicken Stock (page 200) or Vegetable Broth (page 201) or water

2 tablespoons fresh lemon juice

1 teaspoon fresh thyme leaves, or 1/2 teaspoon dried thyme

3 ounces canned light tuna packed in water, drained

1/2 teaspoon freshly ground black pepper

1/3 cup chopped parsley

2 tablespoons capers, drained

For the salad:

1 cup French-style green beans

4 small red potatoes

Olive oil and canola oil in a spray bottle, or 1 teaspoon olive oil

2 eggs, hard-cooked and cooled

4 cups baby romaine lettuce, washed and patted dry

2 yellow tomatoes, cut into wedges

2 red tomatoes, cut into wedges

8 ounces canned light tuna packed in water, drained

To prepare the dressing, spray or grease a nonstick pan with olive oil and set over medium heat. Add the onion and garlic; sauté, stirring, for 3 to 5 minutes, or until the onion is translucent and soft. Transfer the mixture to a blender or food processor fitted with a metal blade. Add the anchovies; silken tofu; stock, broth or water; lemon juice; thyme and tuna; process until smooth. Add the black pepper, parsley and capers; pulse to incorporate. Refrigerate until ready to serve. *Makes 1 cup.*

To prepare the salad, bring a large pot of water to a boil and prepare a bowl of ice water. Immerse the green beans in the boiling water for 4 to 5 minutes, or until the beans are tender. Drain the beans and plunge them into the ice water for 30 seconds to stop the cooking process. Drain.

Place the potatoes into a small pot, add enough water to cover, set the pot over medium-high heat, and bring to a simmer. Simmer for 20 minutes, or until the potatoes are just tender. (Be careful not to overcook them or they will fall apart when you try to slice them.) When the potatoes are done, drain them in a colander and run under cold water to stop the cooking process. Drain. Slice the cooled potatoes and spray or brush with olive oil. Set aside.

Peel the hard-cooked eggs, remove and discard the yolks, and chop the egg whites finely.

Place equal portions of the romaine leaves on chilled salad plates. Arrange the potato slices, red and yellow tomato wedges, and blanched green beans around the lettuce. Place equal portions of tuna on each plate and sprinkle each with chopped egg whites. Drizzle each salad with 2 tablespoons Tonnata Dressing; serve. Tonnata Dressing can be kept in the refrigerator, covered, for up to 5 days.

MESCLUN

Mesclun is a French term that means a combination of baby lettuces (such as curly endive, romaine, oak leaf, butter lettuce, radicchio and arugula). It is also called gourmet lettuce. I like to add nasturtium flowers to the mix, both for their brilliant colors and distinctive peppery flavor.

Herbed Bean Salad

MAKES 8 SERVINGS

Here is a contemporary twist on the traditional three-bean salad; it calls for fava, flageolet and Anasazi beans. Fava beans, also known as broad beans, are rich in nutrients. Look for favas in pods that are not full to bursting, an indication that the beans are old. If fava beans are unavailable, use blanched haricot verts or edamame (fresh soybeans). Flageolet beans are tiny, tender French kidney beans, while Anasazi beans are speckled red-and-white beans; you can use navy or white kidney beans in their place if necessary. Add brown rice, barley or quinoa to this salad and you have a complete vegetarian meal. It's an excellent accompaniment to grilled chicken or poached salmon.

1 cup shelled fava beans

$^3/_4$ cup flageolet beans, soaked for 2 hours or overnight and rinsed

$^3/_4$ cup Anasazi beans, soaked for 2 hours or overnight and rinsed

$^1/_2$ cup minced red onion

1 cup seeded diced tomato

$^1/_4$ cup finely chopped fresh basil

$^1/_4$ cup finely chopped fresh parsley

4 tablespoons olive oil

1 teaspoon freshly ground black pepper

1 teaspoon kosher salt, optional

$^1/_4$ cup calendula petals, optional

Bring a small pot of water to a boil and prepare a bowl of ice water. Immerse the fava beans in the boiling water for 1 to 2 minutes, drain and plunge into ice water for 30 seconds to stop the cooking process. To remove the fibrous outer shell, make a small incision with your fingernail on one end of the shell, pop the bean out and discard the shell. Transfer the beans to a bowl and set aside.

Drain the soaked flageolet and Anasazi beans. Place each variety into separate pots and pour $3^1/_2$ cups of water into each; bring to a simmer and simmer for 40 minutes, or until the beans are just tender to the bite. Drain the beans, reserving any excess cooking liquid; set aside to cool.

Combine the fava beans, flageolet beans, Anasazi beans, red onion, tomato, basil, parsley and olive oil in a mixing bowl; mix well. Stir in $^1/_2$ cup of the reserved cooking liquid and season the salad with salt and black pepper. Cover and refrigerate for 30 minutes. Garnish the salad with calendula petals, if desired.

SOUTHWEST CAESAR SALAD

MAKES 4 SERVINGS

Corn and jicama are tossed with green romaine lettuce, for a twist on a classic Caesar salad. For more southwestern flavor, the salad is served with lime rather than the traditional lemon. The Southwest Caesar Dressing contains the salad's traditional anchovies, but the addition of toasted cumin gives it a southwestern flair.

For the dressing:

3 anchovy fillets, rinsed and patted dry

1/2 cup low-fat buttermilk

2 tablespoons 1 percent low-fat cottage cheese

1 shallot, minced

1 clove garlic, coarsely chopped

1 tablespoon fresh lime juice

1/2 teaspoon white Worcestershire sauce or white balsamic vinegar

1/2 teaspoon freshly ground black pepper

1 teaspoon ground cumin, toasted for 2 to 3 minutes in a hot, dry skillet

1/4 cup flat-leaf parsley leaves

1/2 teaspoon chili-pepper flakes

For the salad:

Canola oil in a spray bottle, or 1 teaspoon canola oil

2 (6-inch) corn tortillas, cut into 2-inch strips

2 heads romaine lettuce, trimmed, washed, patted dry and cut into 2-inch strips

2 heads Belgian endive, trimmed, washed, patted dry and cut into 2-inch strips

1 cup peeled, diced jicama

1/2 cup corn kernels

1/4 cup crumbled feta cheese

1 lime, cut into wedges

To make the dressing, combine the anchovies, buttermilk, cottage cheese, shallot, garlic, lime juice, Worcestershire sauce or balsamic vinegar, black pepper and cumin in a blender or food processor fitted with a metal blade; process until smooth and creamy. Add the parsley leaves and chili-pepper flakes; pulse to combine. Be careful not to overprocess or the dressing will turn a uniform green. Refrigerate until ready to serve. *Makes 1 cup.*

To prepare the salad, preheat the oven to 375 degrees F. Spray or grease a baking sheet with canola oil. Place the tortilla strips on the prepared baking sheet; bake for 8 to 10 minutes, tossing once or twice, until the strips are crisp and golden brown. Remove from the oven and let cool.

Place equal portions of the lettuce and endive leaves onto chilled plates. Scatter equal portions of the baked corn tortilla strips, jicama, corn and feta cheese on each. Drizzle 2 tablespoons of the dressing over each salad and garnish with lime wedges. Southwest Caesar Dressing can be kept in the refrigerator, covered, for 1 week.

We emphasize fruits and vegetables at the Golden Door in our breakfasts, lunches and snacks, but meat has its place at our dinners. Meat portions at the spa are small but big on flavor and very satisfying when complemented by hearty side dishes. In the early days, founder Deborah Szekely would sometimes remind guests that a good rule of thumb for any meat portion was to make it about the size of a deck of cards (before cooking). Now, especially with the Asian influences that I incorporate into my cooking, it's easier than ever to let meat act as a flavoring rather than as a source of bulky satisfaction.

Chicken is a frequent meat choice in our low-fat mantra. We use simple techniques for sealing in the juicy flavor of lean breast meat without adding fat. For example, many of the chicken dishes in this chapter call for first sautéing the chicken breast, then simmering it in chicken broth to preserve tenderness. Another excellent technique for sealing in moisture and flavor is to sauté the breast briefly before broiling or baking.

Chicken is so plentiful at the home cook's nearest supermarket that it has become a generic staple—one that doesn't seem to require a lot of fuss. But we contend that poultry is worthy of careful selection for taste, flavor and provenance. We use chicken breasts from free-range birds raised on organic feeds. The birds are hormone- and antibiotic-free.

Why the particular fuss over organic? First, we support and practice sustainable agriculture as much as possible at the Golden Door. Using chickens raised in vast factory farms brings

POULTRY, MEAT AND GAME

up all kinds of environmental and ethical questions that may concern you. They concern us. And simply put, free-range, organic grain–fed chickens taste better. Their texture is meaty and fork-tender when properly prepared, never artificially plumped and tenderized with the watery additives common in frozen breasts these days. Their taste is rich, obviously tied to the wholesomeness of their whole-grain diet supplemented by their foraging during the day.

We also enjoy ways of serving turkey that are inspired by recipes typically featuring beef, such as our Turkey Meatballs, Turkey Sausage, and a phyllo dough pouch filled with seasoned turkey. All of them are prepared using techniques that seal in their delicious juices. I begin with a mixture of white and dark turkey meat, as the dark meat is essential for moist fillings.

If you are looking for healthy recipes for entertaining, consider quail, a naturally low-in-fat bird. Boned quail needs little more than freshly ground pepper and salt and a sprinkle of thyme before grilling to make it delicious and elegant. Seared Duck Breast is also one of my favorite dishes, perhaps because it harkens back to my training as a chef in France. At the Golden Door, I remove the skin from the duck breast—the source of much of its fat—and cook it to only medium-rare for best flavor. I've also included two of my favorite lamb recipes: small chops dashed with the piquancy of mustard, and a curried leg of lamb in which the pungent spices are gorgeously offset by the sweetness of currants and mangoes. Whether you are cooking for yourself each night or sharing dinnertime with a gathering of friends, you will find recipes in this chapter that surprise you again and again.

Chicken Duxelle with Steamed Baby Carrots

MAKES 4 SERVINGS

My version of this quintessential French mushroom dish is fragrant with freshly ground nutmeg, an essential ingredient in the spa kitchen. Always buy whole nutmeg and grate it yourself for the freshest flavor. Here, we have added spinach to the duxelle for additional nutritional value and fresh flavor.

1 pound crimini or button mushrooms

1 medium shallot, minced

Olive oil and canola oil in a spray bottle, or 1 tablespoon olive oil

2 tablespoons uncooked whole-wheat couscous

$\frac{1}{8}$ teaspoon grated nutmeg

4 cups spinach, trimmed, washed and patted dry but still damp

$\frac{1}{4}$ cup crumbled feta cheese

4 baby carrots, peeled with tops trimmed

4 (4-ounce) skinless, boneless chicken breast halves

$\frac{1}{2}$ teaspoon kosher salt

$\frac{1}{2}$ teaspoon freshly ground black pepper

$\frac{1}{2}$ teaspoon fresh thyme leaves or dried thyme

$\frac{1}{2}$ cup Chicken Stock (page 200)

1 lemon, cut into 8 wedges

Fresh parsley sprigs for garnish

Place the mushrooms and shallot into a blender or food processor fitted with a metal blade; process until finely chopped. Spray or grease a medium-size pan with 1 teaspoon olive oil and set over medium heat; add the mushroom mixture and stir in the couscous. Sauté, stirring, for 10 minutes, or until the mushrooms have released their liquid and it is absorbed by the couscous. Stir in the nutmeg.

Spray or grease a sauté pan with 1 teaspoon olive oil and set over medium-high heat. Add the spinach; sauté, stirring, for 2 to 3 minutes, or until it wilts. Wipe out the blender or food processor, and transfer the spinach into it; process until finely chopped. Set aside.

Stir the spinach and feta cheese into the mushroom mixture; sauté, stirring, for 3 to 5 minutes, until thoroughly combined. Remove from the heat and set aside.

Bring a pot of water to a boil. Prepare a bowl of ice water. Immerse the carrots in the boiling water and cook for 3 to 5 minutes, or until they are fork-tender. Drain and plunge them into the ice water for 30 seconds to stop the cooking process. Drain and keep warm.

Season the chicken with salt, black pepper and thyme. Spray or grease a saucepan with 1 teaspoon olive oil and set over medium-high heat. Place the chicken breast halves into the pan in a single layer; cook for 3 to 5 minutes on each side, or until the chicken is lightly browned. Pour in the stock and simmer for 10 to 15 minutes, or until the chicken is cooked through and no longer pink, and its juices run clear.

Place equal portions of the mushroom-spinach duxelle onto warm serving plates. Cut the chicken breasts on the bias and fan 1 sliced breast half over each mound of the duxelle. Garnish each plate with 1 baby carrot and 2 lemon wedges and fresh parsley sprigs. Serve immediately.

BABY VEGGIES ON THE SIDE

At dinnertime at the Golden Door, every main course automatically comes with several kinds of simply steamed baby vegetables that are lightly misted with olive oil from a spray bottle when they come out of the steamer. Baby carrots, haricots verts, baby zucchini, eggplant, leeks, broccoli or cauliflower—the combination is determined by what's fresh from the garden that day. This side dish, which can be had in unlimited quantities, rounds out the meal and is especially important for those on limited calorie diets. The veggies provide a satisfying crunch, a generous dose of nutrition and a welcome dash of color.

CURRIED PINEAPPLE CHICKEN BREAST WITH CARDAMOM-SPICED BASMATI RICE

MAKES 4 SERVINGS

Curries talk back, so if you're craving something exciting and spicy, this is the dish to make. Turmeric gives the curry powder its yellow color, while chili pepper gives it pungency. I prefer Madras curry powder; it's intense but not overpowering. If you wish, you can adjust the amount of curry powder to control the piquancy of the curry.

For the chicken:

1 teaspoon dark sesame oil

1 tablespoon Madras curry powder

$\frac{1}{2}$ cup pineapple juice

Canola oil in a spray bottle, or
    1 teaspoon canola oil

4 (4-ounce) skinless, boneless chicken
    breast halves

1 cup finely diced pineapple

$\frac{1}{2}$ cup finely diced celery

$\frac{1}{2}$ cup finely diced red bell pepper

$\frac{1}{2}$ cup Chicken Stock (page 200)

2 teaspoons arrowroot powder
    dissolved in 2 tablespoons water

$\frac{1}{2}$ cup diagonally sliced scallions for
    garnish

For the rice:

$\frac{3}{4}$ cup basmati rice, rinsed and drained

1 $\frac{1}{2}$ cups Chicken Stock (page 200)

2 pods cardamom, smashed

1 teaspoon ground cinnamon

1 stalk lemongrass, trimmed and
    smashed with the side of a knife

1 teaspoon kosher salt, optional

$\frac{1}{2}$ teaspoon freshly ground
    black pepper, optional

To prepare the chicken, combine the sesame oil, curry powder and pineapple juice in a shallow glass or ceramic dish; add the chicken, and turn to coat. Cover and refrigerate for 1 hour.

Meanwhile, combine the rice, 1 $\frac{1}{2}$ cups stock, cardamom, cinnamon and lemongrass in a medium-size pot set over medium-high heat; bring to a simmer. Cover and cook for 25 minutes, or until the liquid has been absorbed. Remove the cardamom pods and lemongrass and fluff with a fork. Season the rice with salt and black pepper, if desired. Keep warm until ready to serve.

When you are ready to cook the chicken, preheat the oven to 350 degrees F. Spray or grease a large, ovenproof nonstick skillet with canola oil and set over medium-high heat. Place the chicken breast halves into it in a single layer, reserving the marinade. Sear the chicken breasts for 2 to 3 minutes on each side, or until golden. Transfer the skillet to the oven and bake for 10 to 12 minutes, or until the chicken is cooked through and no longer pink, and its juices run clear. Remove the chicken breasts from the skillet, cut them in half and keep warm, taking care to reserve all the chicken juices in the skillet.

Add the reserved marinade, pineapple, celery and red bell pepper to the skillet, and set it over medium heat; sauté, stirring, for 5 minutes, or until the vegetables soften. Add the stock and stir well; cook for 5 minutes, or until the liquid reduces in volume by half. To thicken the curry, add the dissolved arrowroot and simmer for 1 minute, or until thickened. Return the chicken to the curry and mix well.

To serve, spoon equal portions of Cardamom-Spiced Basmati Rice on warm plates, place a chicken breast half on each and scatter the scallions on top. Serve immediately.

THE SECRET TO MOIST, LUSCIOUS CHICKEN

We trim the skin and fat off chicken breasts and pieces at the Golden Door. That makes it light and healthful, but it also leaves it open to becoming too dry during cooking—the worst sin in the spa kitchen. You can avoid this by paying strict attention to timing—and don't start cooking too far in advance or you will increase the chances that your food will dry out. Always keep some chicken stock on hand; if your poultry looks like it's getting dry, spoon a little stock over it. Also, use a pan that is just big enough to contain the chicken—too much room is yet another reason foods dry out. If you sear your poultry before proceeding with the recipe, cover the pot when you are finished searing.

GINGER-MARINATED CHICKEN WITH SOBA NOODLES AND GINGER, PEANUT AND CILANTRO SAUCE

MAKES 4 SERVINGS

The juice from the fibrous gingerroot is the key to the flavorful marinade in this dish. Grate the ginger, skin-on, gather the shavings in your hands, and squeeze the juice into the marinade mixture. Traditionally, buckwheat soba noodles are served with *dashi*, a Japanese broth made from seaweed, but they are also an ideal counterpoint to this tangy dish.

For the chicken:

2 tablespoons low-sodium soy sauce

1 tablespoon mirin (sweet rice wine)

1 teaspoon dark sesame oil

$^{1}/_{2}$ teaspoon minced garlic

2 tablespoons grated gingerroot

4 (4-ounce) skinless, boneless chicken breast halves

Ginger, Peanut and Cilantro Sauce and Dressing (page 210)

$^{1}/_{2}$ cup garlic flowers, optional

For the noodles:

4 ounces soba noodles

$^{1}/_{4}$ cup diagonally sliced scallions

2 tablespoons fresh cilantro leaves

1 tablespoon mirin (sweet rice wine)

2 tablespoons low-sodium soy sauce

1 teaspoon dark sesame oil

$^{1}/_{2}$ cup Chicken Stock (page 200)

To prepare the chicken, combine the soy sauce, mirin, sesame oil and garlic in a glass or ceramic dish. Squeeze the grated ginger into the dish to extract its juices; discard the pulp. Mix well, place the chicken into the dish, and turn to coat. Cover and refrigerate for 30 minutes.

To prepare the noodles, bring a medium-size pot of lightly salted water to a boil. Add the noodles and reduce the heat to medium; simmer for 5 minutes, or until tender. Drain in a colander and run under cold water to stop the cooking process. Transfer to a mixing bowl and stir in the scallions, cilantro, mirin, soy sauce and sesame oil. Mix well, cover and set aside.

When you are ready to cook the chicken, remove it from the marinade, reserving the liquid. Place the chicken breast halves into a nonstick skillet in a single layer and set over medium-high heat; sauté, stirring, for 3 to 5 minutes on each side, or until lightly browned. Add the reserved marinade and reduce the heat to medium; cook, covered, for another 5 to 8 minutes, or until the chicken is cooked through and no longer pink, and its juices run clear. Remove the chicken from the skillet. Set aside until it is cool enough to handle.

Return the noodles to the pan and add the stock; cook until heated through. Shred the chicken into long strips. Place equal portions of noodles onto 4 warm plates. Top with chicken and drizzle with Ginger, Peanut and Cilantro Sauce and Dressing. Toss in the garlic flowers, if using, and serve.

Glazed Orange-Basil Chicken with Baked Yams and Wilted Spinach

MAKES 4 SERVINGS

The secret to keeping this dish moist is to cook it in a pan just large enough to accommodate the chicken breast halves. You can marinate the chicken a day in advance, tightly wrapped and refrigerated. The marinade will work with all kinds of poultry as well as shrimp.

For the chicken:

$^1/_4$ cup chopped fresh basil

1 tablespoon grated orange zest

$^1/_2$ cup fresh orange juice

1 teaspoon Dijon mustard

$^1/_2$ teaspoon kosher salt, optional

$^1/_2$ teaspoon freshly ground black pepper, optional

4 (4-ounce) skinless, boneless chicken breast halves

Canola oil in a spray bottle, or 1 teaspoon canola oil

For the yams:

3 medium-to-large yams (about 12 ounces each)

1 teaspoon olive oil

For the spinach:

Olive oil and canola oil in a spray bottle, or 1 teaspoon olive oil

6 cups spinach, stems removed, washed and patted dry but slightly damp

Kosher salt, optional

To prepare the chicken, mix the basil, orange zest, orange juice, mustard, salt and black pepper, if using, in a shallow glass or ceramic dish. Place the chicken into the marinade and turn to coat; cover and refrigerate for 1 hour, turning once or twice.

Meanwhile, to prepare the yams, preheat the oven to 350 degrees F. Scrub the yams, oil them and bake for 50 minutes, or until fork-tender.

When you are ready to cook the chicken, preheat the broiler. Spray or grease a baking sheet with canola oil and set aside. Remove the chicken from the marinade, reserving the liquid. Place the chicken onto the prepared baking sheet and spoon the reserved marinade on top. Broil for 15 to 20 minutes, turning the chicken breast once, until the top of the chicken is golden brown and glazed.

Meanwhile, spray or grease a nonstick pan with olive oil and set it over medium-high heat. Add the spinach, stirring constantly with a wooden spoon for 2 to 3 minutes, or until wilted. Season with salt if desired.

To serve, slice each yam into 4 ($^1/_2$-inch) rounds and place 3 rounds each on warm plates. Place a chicken breast half on each plate, spoon equal portions of spinach beside it and serve.

Grilled Chicken on Petite Ratatouille Provençale with Balsamic Sauce

MAKES 6 SERVINGS

This garlicky ratatouille is inspired by the lush flavors of southern France. Make this dish a day in advance to bring out the best flavor.

For the ratatouille:

2 teaspoons olive oil

1 1/2 tablespoons minced garlic

1/2 red onion, minced

1 1/2 medium red bell peppers, seeded and finely diced

1 small zucchini, seeded and finely diced

1 small yellow squash, seeded and finely diced

1 small eggplant, peeled and finely diced

4 plum tomatoes, seeded and finely diced

1/2 cup canned tomato purée or sauce

3/4 cup finely sliced fresh basil

1 tablespoon fresh thyme leaves

1 teaspoon kosher salt

2 teaspoons freshly ground black pepper

For the chicken:

6 (4-ounce) skinless, boneless chicken breast halves

Olive oil and canola oil in a spray bottle, or 1 teaspoon olive oil

Salt and freshly ground black pepper to taste

1/2 cup Balsamic Sauce (page 204)

Fresh basil sprigs for garnish

To make the ratatouille, heat the oil in a large, nonstick pan set over medium heat. Add the garlic and onion; sauté, stirring, for 1 to 2 minutes, or until softened. Add the red bell pepper, zucchini, yellow squash and eggplant; sauté, still stirring, for 5 to 10 minutes, or until the vegetables have just begun to soften. Mix in the tomatoes, tomato purée or sauce, basil, thyme, salt and black pepper; stir well. Cover and cook for another 5 minutes, or until the vegetables are tender but not mushy. Keep warm until ready to serve.

To prepare the chicken, preheat a grill, stovetop grill or broiler. Spray or brush the chicken with olive oil and season lightly with salt and black pepper.

If you are using a grill: grill the chicken breast halves for 5 to 6 minutes on each side, turning to make diamond-shaped grill marks. Move the chicken breast halves to the sides of the grill away from the direct heat and cover; continue to cook for another 5 to 10 minutes, or until the chicken is cooked through and no longer pink, and its juices run clear.

If you are using a broiler: place the chicken into a pan that is just large enough to contain the 4 breast halves—no larger. Place it 4 to 6 inches away from the heating element; broil for 5 to 6 minutes on one side, turn, and broil for 5 to 6 minutes on the other side. Turn again and broil for 3 to 4 minutes, or until the chicken is cooked through and no longer pink, and its juices run clear. Remove from the grill and keep warm.

Spoon equal portions of the ratatouille onto warmed plates and top each with a grilled chicken breast half. Drizzle with Balsamic Sauce and garnish with sprigs of fresh basil.

POACHED CHICKEN BREAST WITH SPRING FAVA BEANS

MAKES 4 SERVINGS

I make this hearty soup for dinner in early spring, when the nights are still a bit chilly and the season's warmer days bring fresh favas and leeks from the Golden Door's organic garden. Look for young favas, which are bright green and flatter than more mature beans. Older favas lose their tender texture and sweetness as they age. Fresh favas are truly a treat, but if you can't find them, substitute fresh whole sugar snap peas or edamame beans.

1 cup fava beans, shelled, or sugar-snap peas or edamame beans

4 (4-ounce) skinless, boneless chicken breast halves

2 medium leeks, washed well, trimmed and cut into long strips

4 fingerling potatoes, cut in half lengthwise

4 cups Chicken Stock (page 200)

$\frac{1}{2}$ cup finely chopped fresh parsley

1 tablespoon finely chopped fresh tarragon

4 teaspoons fresh lemon juice

4 sprigs fresh tarragon for garnish

Bring a pot of water to a boil. Prepare a bowl of ice water. Immerse the fava beans in the boiling water for 1 to 2 minutes. Drain and plunge the beans into the ice water for 30 seconds to stop the cooking process. Drain. To remove the fibrous shells from the blanched fava beans, make an incision on one end of the shell with your fingernail, pop the bean out, and discard the shells. Set aside.

Place the chicken breasts, leeks and potatoes into a medium-size pot; add the stock, set over medium heat and bring to a simmer; cook, covered, for 15 to 20 minutes. Stir in the fava beans, parsley and tarragon; continue to simmer for 2 to 3 minutes.

Remove the chicken from the broth and cut into thin slices. Place equal portions of chicken into warmed soup bowls. Divide the hot broth and beans, leeks and potatoes between the bowls, and drizzle 1 teaspoon lemon juice into each bowl. Garnish with tarragon sprigs. Serve immediately.

TAMARIND CHICKEN STIR-FRY

MAKES 4 SERVINGS

I love wok cooking—it's one-pot cooking at its most dynamic. This wok-based dish features tamarind, a tart, highly acidic fruit available in paste or pulp form from Asian markets. The pulp form should be soaked in warm water before using. If you can't find it, substitute hoisin sauce. Plain rice—white or brown—is all you need for this flavorful stir-fry, as it makes its own sauce. I like fragrant jasmine rice, another staple of Southeast Asian cooking.

2 teaspoons minced fresh garlic

2 teaspoons minced fresh gingerroot

2 tablespoons low-sodium soy sauce

$\frac{1}{2}$ cup Chicken Stock (page 200)

1 tablespoon light brown sugar

$1\frac{1}{2}$ tablespoons tamarind paste

4 (4-ounce) skinless, boneless chicken breast halves, diagonally sliced into 4 or 5 ($\frac{3}{4}$-inch) strips

Steamed Fluffy Jasmine Rice (page 223)

2 teaspoons canola oil

1 cup snow peas, trimmed

1 cup thinly sliced carrots

2 cups Swiss chard leaves, washed, patted dry and cut into 1-inch pieces

Combine the garlic, gingerroot, soy sauce, $\frac{1}{4}$ cup stock, brown sugar and tamarind paste in a shallow glass or ceramic dish; mix well. Add the chicken pieces and toss to coat. Cover and refrigerate for at least 1 hour.

Prepare the rice as directed on page 223, and keep warm.

In a large nonstick wok or pan, heat the canola oil over medium-high heat. Drain the chicken, reserving the marinade. Carefully place the chicken into the wok and stir-fry for 10 minutes, or until the chicken is seared and golden. Add the remaining marinade to the pan and continue to cook until the meat is browned and thoroughly cooked. Remove the chicken from the wok and keep warm.

While the wok is still hot, add the remaining stock, snow peas, carrots and Swiss chard; stir-fry for 5 minutes, or until the vegetables soften. Return the cooked chicken to the wok; heat thoroughly. To serve, mound equal portions of rice on warm plates. Top with chicken, vegetables and sauce.

SEARED FIVE-SPICE CHICKEN WITH SHIITAKE MUSHROOM SAUCE

MAKES 4 SERVINGS

Chinese five-spice powder is a combination of star anise, Szechwan peppercorns, cloves, fennel and cinnamon. In Chinese tradition, the number five is thought to be a sign of good health, so many Chinese dishes incorporate this exotic spice blend. For the sauce, you can use fresh or dried shiitake mushrooms. To reconstitute the dried form, soak them in warm water for about 30 minutes. Remove the tough stems; then rinse well to remove any grit or dirt. Shiitakes have an earthy flavor that stands up to assertively seasoned food, as does the brown rice that accompanies the dish.

For the chicken:

1 teaspoon five-spice powder

1 teaspoon dark sesame oil

1 tablespoon low-sodium soy sauce

$\frac{1}{2}$ cup Chicken Stock (page 200)

4 (4-ounce) skinless, boneless chicken breast halves

Canola oil in a spray bottle, or 1 teaspoon canola oil

$\frac{1}{4}$ cup diagonally sliced scallions for garnish

Steamed Fluffy Brown Rice (page 223)

For the sauce:

12 ounces fresh shiitake mushrooms, or 8 ounces dried shiitake mushrooms, soaked in water and drained

Canola oil in a spray bottle, or 1 teaspoon canola oil

1 teaspoon minced garlic

2 tablespoons low-sodium soy sauce

$\frac{3}{4}$ cup Chicken Stock (page 200)

2 teaspoons arrowroot powder dissolved in 2 tablespoons of water

To prepare the chicken, combine the five-spice powder, sesame oil, soy sauce and stock in a shallow glass or ceramic dish; mix well. Place the chicken breasts into this marinade and turn to coat. Cover and refrigerate for at least 1 hour.

Prepare the rice as directed on page 223; keep warm.

Meanwhile, to make the sauce, remove the stems from the shiitake mushrooms and quarter them. Spray or grease a nonstick pan with canola oil and set over medium-high heat. Add the shiitake mushrooms and garlic; sauté, stirring, for 3 to 5 minutes, or until the mushrooms are soft. Add the soy sauce and chicken stock; simmer for 5 to 10 minutes. Stir in the dissolved arrowroot; simmer until the sauce thickens. Keep warm until ready to serve.

When you are ready to cook the chicken, preheat the oven to 350 degrees F. Remove the chicken from the marinade, reserving the liquid. Spray or grease a nonstick ovenproof skillet with canola oil and set over medium-high heat. Add the chicken breast halves in a single layer; sear for 3 to 4 minutes on each side, or until lightly browned. Pour the remaining marinade over the chicken and transfer to the oven; bake for 10 minutes, or until the chicken is thoroughly cooked and no longer pink, and its juices run clear.

To serve, mound equal portions of rice on warmed plates. Top with the chicken breast halves and drizzle with the sauce. Scatter scallions over each plate and serve immediately.

TASTY MARINADES FOR POULTRY

Marinades tenderize and add flavor to poultry and meat. It's best to marinate in a glass or ceramic pan, so that the acids in the marinade don't mix with the container and impart a metallic taste to the food. Always marinate animal protein in the refrigerator. And remember to discard the marinade or cook it along with the meat; never ever spoon raw marinade back onto cooked meat or you run the risk of bacterial contamination. (If you are grilling and want the marinade to drizzle over the meat at the table, first bring it to a boil.)

Here are a few of the marinades that I like to use for poultry. They can also be used for fish; just remember that the proteins in fish are far more delicate than in meat and poultry, so you don't need to marinate fish as long—30 minutes to an hour should do it as opposed to 2 hours to overnight for meat and poultry.

For 4 (4-ounce) servings of poultry:

Asian: 2 teaspoons grated fresh ginger, 2 teaspoons minced garlic, 2 tablespoons light soy sauce, 2 tablespoons mirin (sweet rice wine), 1 teaspoon dark sesame oil, 1 teaspoon chopped lemongrass.

Citrus: 2 tablespoons olive oil, 2 tablespoons lemon zest, 1 tablespoon fresh lemon juice, 2 tablespoons chopped fresh basil, $\frac{1}{4}$ teaspoon freshly ground black pepper, or to taste.

Herb: 2 tablespoons olive oil, 1 teaspoon chopped fresh tarragon, 2 tablespoons chopped fresh parsley, 1 teaspoon chopped fresh sage, 1 teaspoon chopped fresh oregano, $\frac{1}{4}$ teaspoon freshly ground black pepper, or to taste.

Hot and Spicy: 2 teaspoons grated ginger, 1 to $1\frac{1}{2}$ teaspoons chili-pepper flakes or (for more heat) chopped Thai chili, 1 teaspoon dark sesame oil, 2 tablespoons low-sodium soy sauce, 1 tablespoon lime juice.

CHICKEN ROULADE AND RED POTATOES WITH CHERVIL

MAKES 4 SERVINGS

If your recipe repertoire consists of only a few dishes, this colorful, elegant chicken should be among them. I prepare this for my weekly cooking class at the Golden Door because it is perfectly suited to home cooking—and it makes an excellent dish for entertaining, as it can be made in advance. You'll need cheesecloth to wrap the chicken for baking. I like to serve the dish with Red Potatoes with Chervil, but you can use parsley, scallions, chives or any soft herbs or seasonings you like.

For the potatoes:

1 pound red potatoes, quartered

1 teaspoon olive oil

1 teaspoon kosher salt, optional

$\frac{1}{2}$ teaspoon freshly ground black pepper

2 tablespoons chopped fresh chervil

For the chicken:

1 small red bell pepper

4 (4-ounce) skinless, boneless chicken breast halves

Olive oil and canola oil in a spray bottle, or 1 teaspoon olive oil

2 cups spinach, stems removed, washed and patted dry but slightly damp

$\frac{1}{2}$ teaspoon minced garlic

1 teaspoon grated lemon zest

1 teaspoon kosher salt

1 teaspoon freshly ground black pepper

2 tablespoons crumbled feta cheese

2 tablespoons finely chopped fresh basil

4 cups Chicken Stock (page 200)

$\frac{1}{4}$ cup chopped scallions or chives

4 teaspoons fresh lemon juice, optional

To prepare the potatoes, place them into a small pot and add enough lightly salted water to cover. Set over medium heat and bring to a simmer. Cook for 15 to 20 minutes, or until the potatoes are just fork-tender. Drain well and transfer to a bowl. Toss with the olive oil, salt, black pepper and chervil. Keep warm until ready to serve.

Preheat a grill, stovetop grill or broiler. Spray or brush the red bell peppers with olive oil; grill or broil them for 5 minutes, turning so that all sides are charred. Transfer to a plastic bag, seal and set aside to cool. When cool enough to handle, remove the skin, seeds and stems and cut into $\frac{1}{4}$-inch strips. Set aside.

Wrap 1 chicken breast half loosely in plastic wrap and place it on a work surface. Using the smooth side of a mallet, the side of a large chef's knife or the bottom of a sauté pan, gently pound the chicken breast half until it is about $\frac{1}{4}$ inch thick. Repeat the process with the remaining chicken breast halves, place them into a covered container and refrigerate until ready to use.

Spray or grease a sauté pan with olive oil and set over medium-high heat. Add the spinach, garlic and lemon zest; sauté, stirring, for 3 to 4 minutes, or until the spinach has wilted. Transfer to a work surface and chop the spinach coarsely. Set aside.

When you are ready to cook the chicken, prepare 4 (7 x 5-inch) pieces of cheesecloth. Remove the pounded chicken breast halves from the refrigerator and place them on a work surface. Season with salt and black pepper. Spread 2 tablespoons of the chopped spinach over each chicken breast. Top with $\frac{1}{4}$ of the roasted red pepper strips and sprinkle with $\frac{1}{4}$ of the feta cheese and basil. Carefully roll up the chicken to form small roulades, or rolls, and place each on a piece of cheesecloth. Wrap the roulades tightly in the cheesecloth and tie the ends with cooking twine.

Transfer the roulades to a pot and add the stock. Set over medium heat and bring to a simmer; cook, covered, for 35 to 40 minutes, adding more stock if necessary. Using tongs or a slotted spoon, carefully remove the roulades from the pot, reserving the stock. Unwrap the roulades and slice each diagonally into 4 pieces.

To serve, place the sliced roulades into warm bowls, and spoon the potatoes next to them. Ladle the hot stock over the chicken and potatoes. Sprinkle each bowl with 1 tablespoon scallions or chives, and drizzle with lemon juice if desired. Serve immediately.

Butternut Squash and Smoked Chicken Ravioli with Vine-Ripened Tomato Coulis

MAKES 6 SERVINGS

Years ago, we used to offer pasta-making classes at the Golden Door. Our guests loved them; they especially enjoyed making ravioli, perhaps because they never had or never would make it in their own kitchens. Wonton wrappers are an excellent substitute for the homemade version. And it's even easier when you make this dish assembly-line style with a helper. It's best to let the ravioli dry, uncovered, for 1 to 2 hours before cooking. If you wish, you can make them a day ahead. If smoked chicken is not available, use smoked turkey breast.

Olive oil and canola oil in a spray
    bottle, or 2 teaspoons olive oil

1 small butternut squash
    (about 10 ounces)

Vine-Ripened Tomato Coulis
    (page 205)

$\frac{1}{4}$ cup low-fat ricotta cheese

$\frac{1}{3}$ cup finely diced smoked skinless,
    boneless chicken breast

2 tablespoons minced fresh basil

2 tablespoons minced fresh parsley

1 teaspoon minced fresh thyme

$\frac{1}{2}$ teaspoon kosher salt, optional

$\frac{1}{2}$ teaspoon freshly ground
    black pepper

Semolina flour for dusting

48 wonton wrappers

1 egg white, lightly beaten

6 tablespoons grated Asiago or
    Parmesan cheese

Preheat the oven to 375 degrees F. Spray or brush the squash with 1 teaspoon olive oil and place it on a baking sheet; bake for 1 hour, or until fork-tender.

Prepare the Vine-Ripened Tomato Coulis as directed on page 205 and set aside.

Remove the squash from the oven and set aside until cool enough to handle. When cool, cut into the neck of the squash and scoop out 1 cup of the cooked flesh. (Reserve the remainder for another use.) Chop coarsely and transfer to a mixing bowl. Stir in the ricotta cheese, smoked chicken, basil, parsley, thyme, salt and black pepper; mix well.

Dust a baking sheet with semolina flour and set aside. Place 2 wonton wrappers on a work surface and brush with beaten egg white. Place 1 tablespoon of the squash-chicken filling in the center of one of the wrappers and place the second wrapper on top, with the egg-brushed side facing down. Using your fingers, gently press the edges of the wrappers together, releasing any air pockets. Repeat the process with the remaining filling and wonton wrappers to make 24 ravioli. Transfer the ravioli to the prepared baking sheet and set aside to dry, uncovered, for 1 to 2 hours or up to one day, refrigerated.

Bring a large pot of lightly salted water to a boil. Immerse the ravioli in the water and simmer for 3 to 4 minutes, or until they are cooked al dente. To serve, spoon a little tomato coulis into warm bowls; using a slotted spoon, remove the ravioli from the pot, drain and place 4 into each bowl. If you wish, you can spray or brush with a little olive oil to keep them from sticking. Ladle the Vine-Ripened Tomato Coulis over them immediately, sprinkle with grated cheese and serve.

CHICKEN, MANGO AND ANAHEIM CHILI QUESADILLAS

MAKES 4 SERVINGS

A true quesadilla is made with some of the mild white cheeses of Mexico, which, while delicious, might be difficult to find in the U.S. I use feta cheese here, but any good-quality, firm cheese, used sparingly, will serve the purpose. The tortillas must be warmed briefly on the griddle to soften them before you can assemble the quesadillas. They're excellent for brunch or lunch and can also be cut into bite-size wedges for a filling appetizer. They're ideal for entertaining, as you can assemble them up to 4 hours ahead of time and cook them just before serving. Serve with Salsa Mexicana.

2 Anaheim chilies

Olive oil and canola oil in a spray bottle, or 2 teaspoons olive oil

2 (4-ounce) skinless, boneless chicken breast halves

$\frac{1}{4}$ teaspoon kosher salt, optional

$\frac{1}{8}$ teaspoon freshly ground black pepper, optional

1 medium red onion, halved and thinly sliced

4 fat-free whole-wheat flour tortillas

1 mango, peeled and thinly sliced, or more to taste

$\frac{1}{2}$ cup crumbled feta cheese or goat cheese

$\frac{1}{4}$ cup fresh cilantro leaves

Fresh cilantro sprigs for garnish

Salsa Mexicana (page 212)

Preheat a grill, stovetop grill or broiler. Spray or brush the Anaheim chilies with 1 teaspoon olive oil; grill or broil them for 5 minutes, turning so that all sides are charred. Transfer to a plastic bag, seal and set aside to cool, leaving the grill or broiler on. When the chilies are cool enough to handle, remove the skin, seeds and stems; dice.

Meanwhile, season the chicken with the salt and black pepper.

If you are using a grill: grill the chicken breast halves for 5 to 6 minutes per side. Move the chicken breast to the side of the grill, away from the direct heat, and cover; continue to cook for another 5 to 8 minutes, or until the chicken is cooked through and no longer pink, and its juices run clear.

If you are using a broiler: place the chicken into a pan that is just large enough to contain the breast halves—no larger. Place it 4 to 6 inches away from the heating element; broil for 5 to 6 minutes on one side, turn and broil for 5 to 6 minutes on the other side. Turn again and broil for 3 to 4 minutes, or until the chicken is cooked through and no longer pink, and its juices run clear.

Transfer the chicken to a work surface and chop coarsely. Cover and keep warm.

Spray or grease a nonstick pan with 1 teaspoon olive oil and set over medium-high heat. Add the onion; sauté, stirring, for 5 minutes, or until golden brown and soft. Stir in the roasted chilies and continue to cook, stirring, for another 2 minutes. Transfer to a bowl and let cool.

Place the tortillas on a griddle or nonstick pan set over medium-high heat; heat briefly on both sides, flipping with a spatula.

Place 2 of the warm tortillas on a work surface and spoon equal portions of the onion-chili mixture and chopped chicken over each. Top with mango slices and sprinkle with the feta cheese and cilantro. Place the 2 remaining tortillas on top, and gently press together. (At this point, the quesadillas can be refrigerated for up to 4 hours before cooking. Place waxed paper between them if stacked.)

Using a large spatula, carefully place the quesadillas back onto the griddle; cook for 1 to 2 minutes on each side, or until crisp. Remove from the heat and cut in half. Slice each half into three equal-size pieces, place 3 pieces on each warm plate, and serve immediately. If desired, garnish with additional mango slices, cilantro sprigs and Salsa Mexicana.

Turkey Basil Mozzarella Pizza

MAKES 1 LARGE OR 8 SMALL PIZZAS

This leaner pizza lacks nothing in the flavor department. It's a delicious, nutritious family dinner and wonderful as casual party fare. You can even let your guests make their own. The game plan is simple: Mix up the Semolina Dough and while it is rising the first time, see to the toppings that need prepping. After the dough has risen once, form the pizza crust, and let rise again. Bake just until firm, then top and bake again.

For the crust:

Vegetable oil in a spray bottle, or
  2 teaspoons vegetable oil

Semolina flour for dusting

Semolina Dough (page 215), mixed
  and allowed to rise once

For the toppings:

8 ounces ground turkey or turkey-
  fennel sausage, casing removed

2 red onions, thinly sliced

3 cups crimini mushrooms, sliced

2 teaspoons minced garlic

2 teaspoons dried oregano

$1/2$ cup canned tomato purée or sauce

$2 1/2$ cups seeded, diced plum
  tomatoes

2 cups baby spinach, washed and
  patted dry

1 cup torn fresh basil leaves

1 cup grated mozzarella cheese
  (about 6 ounces)

$1/4$ teaspoon freshly ground
  black pepper

Olive and canola oil in a spray bottle,
  or 1 teaspoon olive oil

Preheat the oven to 375 degrees F. For one large pizza, spray or grease a 19-inch pizza pan with vegetable oil and dust lightly with semolina flour. For 8 small pizzas, spray or grease 2 baking sheets and dust lightly with semolina flour.

Prepare the Semolina Dough as directed on page 215, and while it is rising, prepare the toppings.

Spray or grease a nonstick ovenproof pan with 1 teaspoon vegetable oil and place the turkey into it, spreading it in a fairly even layer. Bake for 15 to 20 minutes, or until lightly browned but still moist. Remove from the oven and transfer the turkey to a work surface. Chop into bite-size pieces.

Spray or grease another nonstick pan with 1 teaspoon vegetable oil, set it over medium heat, add the onion, mushrooms, garlic and oregano; sauté, stirring, for 4 to 5 minutes, or until softened. Transfer to a plate and let cool.

Place the once-risen dough on a lightly floured work surface and knead well for 1 or 2 minutes: Alternate pressing with the heel of your hand and folding the dough over. If you are making 1 large pizza, use a rolling pin to roll the dough to fit the pan. If you are making 8 small pizzas, divide the dough into 8 equal portions and shape into small balls. With your fingertips, spread each ball into an 8-inch circle. Let the dough rise for 10 minutes.

Use your fingers to poke holes into the risen dough; bake for 15 minutes, or until the crust is firm and begins to brown on the bottom. Remove from the oven.

Using a spoon or pastry brush, spread the tomato purée or sauce on the baked pizza crust. Top with the onion-mushroom mixture and spread to form an even layer. Top with the spinach and basil; scatter the chopped turkey and tomato over them. Sprinkle with mozzarella cheese and season with black pepper. Spray lightly with olive oil and return to the oven; bake for 15 to 20 minutes, or until the cheese is lightly browned. Serve immediately.

Roasted Yam, Fennel and Turkey Sausage Turnover

MAKES 4 SERVINGS

Aromatic Moroccan spices mingle with flavorful yams, fennel, leeks and mushrooms in these turnovers. The filling can be prepared in advance and the turnovers assembled just before baking. I love to use turkey sausage infused with fennel, but any low-fat sausage or an equal amount of seared tempeh or tofu will work just as well. Frozen phyllo dough makes a fast, easy turnover pastry; this recipe calls for 4 sheets, but you can freeze any left-over dough for another use. Or, you can transform the turnovers into calzones by substituting Semolina Dough (page 215) for the phyllo. I like to serve these turnovers with a salad of Frisée with Garden-Fresh Strawberries (page 56).

Vegetable oil in a spray bottle, or
   1 tablespoon plus 1 teaspoon
   vegetable oil

1 tablespoon olive oil

1 medium leek, washed well,
   trimmed and diced

1 small yam, peeled and diced

1 large fennel bulb, trimmed, cored
   and diced

6 whole crimini mushrooms, stems
   removed, quartered

1 clove

1/4 teaspoon ground cinnamon

1 tablespoon pitted, chopped
   Kalamata olives

4 tablespoons crumbled feta cheese

6 leaves fresh basil

1 tablespoon chopped fresh oregano

1/4 teaspoon minced orange zest

1/2 teaspoon kosher salt

1/2 teaspoon freshly ground
   black pepper

4 ounces turkey sausage, casing
   removed, crumbled

4 sheets frozen phyllo dough, thawed

Preheat the oven to 375 degrees F. Spray or brush a baking sheet with 1 teaspoon vegetable oil and set aside.

Heat the olive oil in a nonstick pan set over medium heat. Add the leek, yam and fennel; sauté for 5 to 7 minutes, or until the root vegetables begin to soften. Stir in the mushrooms, clove and cinnamon; sauté for another 3 to 4 minutes. Add the olives, feta cheese, basil, oregano, orange zest, salt and black pepper; mix well. Remove from the heat, transfer to a bowl and let the mixture cool slightly. Remove the clove.

Wipe the same pan clean with a towel and place the crumbled turkey sausage into it. Cook, stirring, for 5 minutes, or until the crumbled sausage is cooked thoroughly and browned. Transfer the sausage to the vegetable mixture and mix well.

To assemble the turnovers, spray or brush 2 sheets of phyllo dough with ¹/₂ teaspoon vegetable oil each, carefully stack them on top of each other and cut them in half lengthwise to make 2 strips. Place 3 tablespoons of the roasted root vegetable mixture on the end of one strip. Carefully fold the dough over the mixture to form a triangle (as though you were folding a flag) and fold again to make a smaller triangle, using the entire strip of phyllo. Repeat with the remaining strip. Then repeat the entire process with 2 more sheets of phyllo dough and the remaining filling.

Place the turnovers onto the prepared baking sheet and spray or brush with 1 teaspoon vegetable oil; bake for 10 to 15 minutes, or until golden brown and flaky. Serve hot with Frisée with Garden-Fresh Strawberries or the salad of your choice.

BEGGAR'S PURSE WITH GROUND TURKEY

MAKES 4 SERVINGS

The beggar's purse is a traditional Chinese dish that is typically filled with pork. In my updated version, I like to use a mixture of white- and dark-meat turkey. The white breast meat is lower in fat, but the dark meat provides essential moisture and richer flavor. Ask your butcher to grind three parts of white meat to two parts dark. I also use easy-to-work-with phyllo dough for the "purses." Slice scallions lengthwise to create "purse-strings" to tie the purses closed.

Vegetable oil in a spray bottle, or
    2 teaspoons vegetable oil

3 plum tomatoes

2 teaspoons olive oil

10 ounces ground turkey

2 tablespoons uncooked cracked wheat

2 tablespoons minced shallots

1 teaspoon finely chopped fresh thyme

2 cups packed spinach, washed, patted
    dry and chopped

1 cup sliced mushrooms

$\frac{1}{2}$ teaspoon kosher salt

$\frac{1}{2}$ teaspoon freshly ground
    black pepper

2 tablespoons Chicken Stock
    (page 200) or water, if needed

6 sheets frozen phyllo dough, thawed

1 scallion, sliced lengthwise into
    thin strips

Balsamic Sauce (page 204)

$\frac{1}{4}$ cup chopped fresh chives or fresh
    parsley for garnish

Preheat the oven to 375 degrees F. Spray or grease a baking sheet with 1 teaspoon vegetable oil and set aside.

Bring a pot of water to a boil. Prepare a bowl of ice water. Using a sharp knife, carve an "X" on the bottom of each tomato and immerse in the boiling water for 1 minute. Remove with a slotted spoon and plunge into the ice water for 30 seconds to stop the cooking process. Drain. Peel the tomatoes (the skin should now come off easily) and cut them into quarters. Scoop out the seeds; then dice into small cubes. Set aside.

Heat the olive oil in a large saucepan set over medium-high heat, and add the ground turkey; sauté for 5 to 6 minutes, breaking up the meat into small pieces with a spatula. Add the cracked wheat; sauté, stirring, for another 2 minutes. Stir in the shallots, thyme, tomatoes, spinach, mushrooms, salt and black pepper; cook for 10 minutes, or until the vegetables are soft. Stir in the stock or water if the mixture is too dry.

To make the individual purses, spray each piece of phyllo dough with vegetable oil and stack three sheets together. This will make two stacks of phyllo dough. Cut out 4 (10 x 10-inch) squares, discarding any phyllo scraps; place 5 tablespoons of the filling into the center of each square. Lift the corners of the phyllo dough into the center of the purse and pinch gently. Spray or brush with vegetable oil, tie a thin strip of scallion to secure the purse, and transfer to the prepared baking sheet; bake for 30 to 35 minutes, or until golden.

To serve, place the beggar's purses on warmed plates, drizzle each with 1 tablespoon Balsamic Sauce and sprinkle with 1 tablespoon chives or parsley.

TURKEY RICE MEATBALLS IN TOMATO BROTH

MAKES 4 SERVINGS

My dear wife, Irma, makes these delicious turkey meatballs at home. This quick combination of ground turkey, herbs and spices results in meatballs that have wonderful texture and flavor as well as a low fat content. If you can, use ground turkey that is 70 percent white meat and 30 percent dark. You can vary the vegetables in the broth depending on what's in your refrigerator. These meatballs can be made a day ahead and are perfect for a family meal. Make 2 cups of Steamed Fluffy Brown Rice. Use $\frac{1}{3}$ cup in the meatballs and serve the rest as a side dish.

For the meatballs:

2 cups Steamed Fluffy Brown Rice (page 223)

1 egg white, lightly beaten

12 ounces ground turkey

1 small carrot, finely diced

1 celery rib, finely diced

$\frac{1}{4}$ cup finely sliced scallions

1 tablespoon coarsely chopped fresh cilantro

$\frac{1}{2}$ teaspoon dried oregano

$\frac{1}{8}$ teaspoon freshly ground black pepper

$\frac{1}{8}$ teaspoon ground cumin

For the broth:

Olive oil and canola oil in a spray bottle, or 1 teaspoon olive oil

1 medium onion, diced

1 medium carrot, diced

$3\frac{1}{2}$ cups Chicken Stock (page 200)

$\frac{1}{2}$ cup canned tomato purée

1 cup corn kernels

2 medium zucchini, diced

2 tablespoons chopped fresh cilantro or parsley for garnish

Lemon and lime wedges for garnish

A few drops of commercial chili sauce, optional, for serving

Prepare the rice as directed on page 223 and keep warm.

Combine the egg white, turkey, carrot, celery, scallions, cilantro, oregano, black pepper, cumin and $\frac{1}{3}$ cup cooked rice in a mixing bowl; mix well. Form 16 meatballs and place into a shallow nonstick baking pan. Set aside.

Spray or grease a large, heavy pan with olive oil and set over medium heat. Add the onion and carrot; sauté for 3 to 4 minutes, or until the vegetables begin to soften. Place the meatballs into the pan, then add the stock and tomato purée; bring to a simmer. Add the corn and zucchini; simmer for 20 to 25 minutes.

To serve, spoon equal portions of the remaining cooked rice into warm bowls. Top with 4 meatballs in each bowl and ladle hot tomato broth and vegetables into each. Garnish with cilantro and lemon or lime wedges. If you like it spicy, stir in chili sauce to taste.

GRILLED QUAIL WITH SPRING VEGETABLE ORZO

MAKES 4 SERVINGS

When it is properly grilled, good quality quail—or any other poultry—needs only a simple seasoning of salt, pepper and fresh herbs. Ask your butcher to butterfly the quail so that they will lie flat on the grill rack for even cooking. Or try butterflying them yourself: simply cut the backbone-side of the quail with a sharp knife and open the bird so that it is one flat piece of meat. To keep the small birds succulent, cook them to medium doneness.

For the orzo:

Vegetable oil in a spray bottle,
    or 1 teaspoon vegetable oil

1 small carrot, minced

1 medium yellow squash, minced

4 ounces green peas (about $\frac{1}{2}$ cup),
    cooked

1 cup orzo (Greek "long grain" pasta)

3 tablespoons finely chopped parsley

2 teaspoons olive oil

1 teaspoon lemon juice

1 teaspoon kosher salt

$\frac{1}{2}$ cup Chicken Stock (page 200)

For the quail:

4 quail, boned and butterflied

1 teaspoon kosher salt, optional

1 teaspoon freshly ground
    black pepper

1 teaspoon finely chopped fresh thyme

1 bunch watercress, washed well and
    patted dry, for garnish

To make the orzo, spray or grease a nonstick pan with vegetable oil, set it over medium-high heat, and add the carrots and squash; sauté, stirring, for 2 to 3 minutes, or until the vegetables begin to soften. Add the peas and cook for 1 to 2 minutes, or until heated through. Remove from the heat and keep warm.

Bring a small pot of lightly salted water to a boil, and add the orzo; simmer for 8 minutes, or until the orzo is al dente. Drain through a fine-mesh sieve and transfer to a bowl. Stir in the cooked vegetables, parsley, olive oil, lemon juice and salt; mix well. Add the stock to prevent the orzo from sticking and keep warm until ready to serve.

When you are ready to cook the quail, preheat a grill, stovetop grill or broiler. Spray or brush the quail with olive oil and season with salt, black pepper and thyme. Place the quail on the grill or broiler rack, skin-side down, and grill or broil for 3 to 4 minutes on each side for medium doneness. Turn to make diamond-shaped grill marks.

To serve, mound equal portions of orzo on warm plates. Rest the quails on the orzo. Garnish with watercress.

SEARED DUCK BREAST WITH CHERRY SAUCE AND BUTTERNUT SQUASH–ORANGE RISOTTO

MAKES 4 SERVINGS

Rich duck breast cries out for slightly acidic fruit accents; cherry sauce and orange-laced risotto answer the call here. The risotto is not made according to the classic recipe; this updated version is quicker, lighter and very tasty. Ask the butcher to trim the duck breast of excess fat for you. Cook the breasts to medium-rare or medium for the most succulent flavor.

For the risotto:

$^3/_4$ cup brown basmati rice

1 tablespoon ground fennel seed

1 bay leaf

$1^1/_2$ cups Chicken Stock (page 200)

1 tablespoon olive oil

$1^1/_4$ cups butternut squash, trimmed, peeled and finely diced

$^1/_2$ cup fresh orange juice

1 teaspoon minced orange zest

$^1/_4$ cup finely chopped fresh parsley

$^1/_4$ cup Asiago cheese

For the duck:

2 (8-ounce) duck breast halves, excess fat removed

$^1/_2$ teaspoon freshly ground black pepper

1 tablespoon grated lemon zest

2 teaspoons dried basil

1 teaspoon canola oil

Fresh mint sprigs for garnish

For the sauce:

3 tablespoons dried sour cherries

$^1/_2$ cup cherry juice or cranberry juice cocktail

$^1/_2$ cup Chicken Stock (page 200)

2 tablespoons sherry vinegar

2 tablespoons honey

2 teaspoons arrowroot powder dissolved in 2 tablespoons water

To prepare the risotto, combine the rice, fennel seed, bay leaf and stock in a small pot set over medium heat and bring to a simmer; cook for 30 minutes, or until all of the liquid is absorbed. Remove the bay leaf and fluff with a fork. Cover and keep warm.

Meanwhile, heat the olive oil in a small sauté pan set over medium-high heat and add the squash; sauté, stirring, for 1 to 2 minutes, or until the squash just begins to soften. Add the orange juice and zest; sauté, stirring, for another 3 to 4 minutes. Spoon the squash into the warm rice and stir in the parsley and Asiago cheese; keep warm.

To prepare the duck, preheat the oven to 375 degrees F. Rub the duck breast with the black pepper, lemon zest and basil; cover and refrigerate until ready to cook.

Start the sauce by combining the dried cherries and cherry or cranberry juice in a small pot set over medium heat; bring to a simmer and cook for 1 to 2 minutes. Remove from the heat and let stand for 15 minutes. Drain the cherries, reserving the juice, and set aside until ready to use.

Heat the canola oil in a nonstick ovenproof skillet set over medium-high heat and add the duck breasts; sear for 2 to 3 minutes on each side, or until lightly browned. Transfer the skillet to the oven and bake for 10 to 15 minutes for medium-rare, or 20 minutes for medium. Remove the duck breast from the skillet, transfer to a warm platter, cover and keep warm. Reserve the skillet with its juices intact.

Deglaze the skillet by pouring in the stock, sherry vinegar, honey and reserved cherry juice. Stir well, scraping the pan with a wooden spoon to loosen any flavorful browned bits, and pour the blended liquids into a saucepan. Set it over medium-high heat and bring to a simmer; cook until the liquid reduces in volume by half. To thicken the sauce, stir in the dissolved arrowroot; simmer for 1 to 2 minutes. Strain the sauce through a fine-mesh sieve. Add the plumped cherries and heat through before serving.

To serve, mound equal portions of the risotto on warmed plates. Slice the seared duck breast on the bias and place equal portions next to the risotto mounds. Drizzle with the cherry sauce and garnish with mint sprigs.

CORNISH GAME HEN GREMOLATA
WITH LEMON-PARSLEY MASHED POTATOES

MAKES 4 SERVINGS

This recipe features a dry rub, an intensely fragrant combination of lemon zest, oregano and crushed fennel seeds—a wonderful combination for rubbing on any poultry. A squeeze of lemon juice when the hens come out of the oven adds extra zing and complements the accompanying Lemon-Parsley Mashed Potatoes well.

For the game hens:

2 (1-pound) Cornish game hens

For the gremolata:

1 tablespoon grated lemon zest

2 tablespoons chopped fresh
     flat-leaf parsley

1 tablespoon chopped fresh oregano
     or 1 teaspoon dried oregano

2 teaspoons crushed fennel seed

$\frac{1}{2}$ teaspoon kosher salt, optional

$\frac{1}{2}$ teaspoon freshly ground
     black pepper

1 tablespoon olive oil

Olive oil and canola oil in a spray
     bottle, or 1 teaspoon olive oil

1 lemon, cut into 4 wedges

$\frac{1}{4}$ cup dry white wine

4 sprigs fresh oregano

For the potatoes:

1 pound white potatoes, scrubbed
     and quartered

$1\frac{1}{2}$ tablespoons grated lemon zest

$\frac{1}{4}$ cup nonfat sour cream

2 tablespoons finely chopped
     fresh parsley

1 teaspoon kosher salt

$\frac{1}{2}$ teaspoon freshly ground
     white pepper

To prepare the hens, split them in half lengthwise with a sharp knife. Remove and discard the wings and backbones; then trim away all excess fat and skin.

Make the gremolata by combining the lemon zest, parsley, oregano, fennel seed, salt and black pepper in a small bowl; pour in 1 tablespoon olive oil and mix well. Rub the gremolata mixture on all sides of the birds; cover and refrigerate for 30 minutes to 1 hour.

Preheat the oven to 375 degrees F. Spray or grease a nonstick ovenproof pan with 1 teaspoon olive oil and set it on the stove over medium-high heat. Place the hens into the pan and sear on each side for 1 minute. Pour in the wine, cover the pan and transfer to the oven.

Bake for 40 to 45 minutes, or until the hens are cooked through and are no longer pink and their juices run clear.

Meanwhile, place the potatoes into a pot and add enough lightly salted water to cover. Set over medium-high heat and simmer. Cook for 30 to 35 minutes, or until tender.

Bring a small pot of water to a boil. Prepare a bowl of ice water. Immerse the lemon zest in the boiling water for 1 minute, drain and plunge into the ice water for 30 seconds to stop the cooking process. Pat dry and set aside.

Drain the potatoes well and mash by hand or with an electric mixer. Do not overmix or they will become gluey. Stir in the lemon zest, sour cream and parsley; fluff with a fork until light and fluffy. Season with salt and white pepper. Keep warm until ready to serve.

To serve, remove the split hens from the pan and place on warm serving plates. Squeeze the juice of $1/4$ lemon over each and mound $1/4$ of the Lemon-Parsley Potatoes next to them. Garnish with oregano sprigs.

MASHED POTATOES FOR ALL SEASONS

If there's anything better than mashed potatoes, it's seasoned mashed potatoes. Garlic mashed potatoes have become a staple of restaurant menus, but you can season your potatoes with all kinds of flavors. I like to vary my seasonings with the seasons.

For 3 to 4 potatoes ($1 1/2$ to 2 pounds)

Spring: Add 1 tablespoon fresh thyme leaves, 2 tablespoons chopped fresh parsley, 2 tablespoons blanched orange zest and a dash of freshly ground pink peppercorn.

Summer: Add 4 to 5 peeled, seeded and diced tomatoes, sautéed for 2 to 3 minutes with $1/2$ cup chopped fresh basil.

Fall: Add $1 1/2$ cups steamed, chopped (in the food processor) broccoli florets.

Winter: Add $1/4$ cup caramelized shallots and 2 tablespoons chopped chives to taste.

Any Season: Wilt 3 cups spinach in a little oil, season with a dash of grated nutmeg and mash with potatoes.

Classic Roasted-Garlic Mashed Potatoes: Cut off the top of a head of garlic, mist the head lightly with oil, wrap it in foil and bake for 45 minutes at 350 degrees F, or until tender. Squeeze the roasted garlic into the potatoes, then mash.

APPLE-STUFFED QUAIL WITH POTATO-ONION GALETTE

MAKES 4 SERVINGS ·

These are especially nice to make if you are having a holiday meal for a small crowd. The fragrance of apple and sage wafting through the air whets the appetite and puts you in the mood for a festive meal. Have your butcher bone the quail for you.

For the potatoes:

3 fingerling potatoes (about 2 ounces each), skin on

1 ½ teaspoons olive oil

¾ red onion, halved and thinly sliced (about 1 cup)

½ teaspoon dried thyme

1 bay leaf

For the quail:

1 ½ teaspoons olive oil

1 Fuji apple, peeled, cored and cut into 12 wedges

4 quail, boned

4 leaves finely chopped fresh sage

¾ cup Chicken Stock (page 200)

½ teaspoon kosher salt

1 teaspoon freshly ground black pepper

1 small orange, quartered

2 tablespoons minced fresh parsley

For the Potato-Onion Galette, place the fingerling potatoes into a small pot, add enough lightly salted water to cover, set over medium-high heat and bring to a simmer. Cook for 10 minutes, or until fork-tender but still firm. Let cool slightly, then slice on the bias.

Heat 1 ½ teaspoons olive oil in a nonstick sauté pan set over medium-high heat. Add the onions; sauté, stirring, for 4 to 5 minutes, until lightly browned. Add the thyme and bay leaf; sauté, stirring, for another 2 to 3 minutes. Transfer the onions to a nonstick baking dish. Remove the bay leaf. Top with the sliced fingerling potatoes and set aside.

Preheat the oven to 375 degrees F. Using the same nonstick sauté pan, heat the olive oil over medium-high heat and add the apple wedges; sauté for 3 to 5 minutes, or until they are lightly browned. Remove from the heat and let cool slightly. Fill the cavities of the quails with the caramelized apple wedges and fresh sage. Return the sauté pan to medium-high heat, place the quail into it in a single layer, working in batches if necessary. Sear the quail for 2 to 3 minutes on each side, or until they are lightly browned. Place the seared quail on top of the onion-potato mixture.

Deglaze the pan by adding the stock, scraping the pan with a wooden spoon to loosen any flavorful browned bits. The stock should take on an amber color. Season the stock with salt and black pepper and pour over the potatoes, onions, and quail; bake for 30 to 35 minutes, or until the quail are thoroughly cooked but still pink. Remove from the oven. Place a stuffed quail on each warm plate and mound ¼ of the Potato-Onion Galette next to each. Drizzle the juice of ¼ orange over each quail, sprinkle each with parsley and serve.

BROILED LAMB CHOPS WITH WHOLE-GRAIN MUSTARD AND BELGIAN ROOT VEGETABLE MASH

MAKES 4 SERVINGS

If you're in the mood for a meal that seems fancier than your average weeknight fare yet is fairly quick and easy to prepare, you'll love these lamb chops, slathered with mustard, and the accompanying Belgian Root Vegetable Mash. When I was growing up in Belgium, we always stored root vegetables in our cellar, and I grew up eating dishes like this—full of sweet flavor and packed with nutrients. If you like, a glass of Pinot Noir will complement the meal beautifully.

For the vegetables:

2 pounds potatoes, peeled and cut into 1-inch pieces

1 large leek, washed well, trimmed and diced

2 medium carrots, diced

2 celery ribs, diced

1 parsnip, diced

2 bay leaves

2 sprigs fresh thyme

$1/4$ cup light sour cream

2 teaspoons kosher salt

1 teaspoon freshly ground black pepper

For the lamb chops:

4 lamb chops, double ribbed, trimmed and fat removed

2 tablespoons whole-grain mustard

2 teaspoons chopped fresh rosemary

To prepare the Belgian Root Vegetable Mash, preheat a grill, stovetop grill or broiler. Place the potatoes, leek, carrots, celery and parsnip into a pot. Add enough water to barely cover the vegetables; then add the bay leaves and thyme, cover, and bring to a boil. Remove the lid and cook, uncovered, over medium-high heat for 10 to 15 minutes, or until almost all the water has been absorbed. Using a wire whisk or potato masher, mash the vegetables with the sour cream until the mixture takes on the consistency of a coarse purée. Season with salt and black pepper and keep warm.

Coat each lamb chop with mustard and sprinkle with rosemary. Heat a broiler. Set the chops on a broiler pan and place it about 4 inches below the heating element. Broil for 3 to 4 minutes on each side, until browned. The lamb should be pink in the center. Remove from oven and keep warm.

To serve, mound equal portions of root vegetable mash on warm plates and place a chop next to each.

CURRIED LEG OF LAMB WITH CURRANTS, MANGO AND DEBORAH'S BASMATI RICE

MAKES 6 SERVINGS

Lamb's strong, almost gamy, flavor marries well with piquant curry spices and tart, sweet fruits. If you can't find mangoes, you can substitute sweet ripe pineapple or apple wedges. I developed the basmati rice with sweet corn for Deborah Szekely, the founder of the Golden Door, who absolutely loves fresh sweet corn, especially when we come up with new ways to use it. The nutty rice and sweet corn balance the spicy curry nicely.

For the rice:

$3/4$ cup long-grain brown basmati rice, rinsed and drained

$1/2$ teaspoon fennel seeds

2 cups Vegetable Broth (page 201) or water

2 medium ears corn, shucked and rinsed

1 small red bell pepper, seeded and diced

$1/3$ cup thinly sliced scallions, including tops

For the lamb:

2 teaspoons canola oil

1 pound lamb leg, boned, trimmed and diced

1 tablespoon plus 1 teaspoon Madras curry powder

$1/4$ teaspoon freshly ground black pepper

2 teaspoons minced garlic

$1/2$ onion, diced

1 medium carrot, diced

2 Anaheim chilies, seeded, trimmed and diced

$3/4$ cup Chicken Stock (page 200) or Vegetable Broth (page 201) or water

2 tablespoons canned tomato purée

2 medium red potatoes, scrubbed and diced

2 tablespoons currants

Salt to taste

$1/2$ mango, peeled and diced

To prepare the rice, place it in a medium-size saucepan, add the fennel seeds and $1 1/2$ cups broth, and set over medium-high heat. Bring to a simmer, then reduce the heat to medium; simmer, covered, for about 35 minutes. Remove from the heat and let stand for 5 minutes. Then, remove the cover and fluff with a fork. Cover again and keep warm.

Meanwhile, cut the kernels off the corncob by holding it vertically on a cutting board and cutting downward with a sharp knife until all the kernels are removed. Place the kernels into a small sauté pan, add the red bell peppers and remaining broth, set over medium-high heat and bring to a simmer. Simmer for 2 to 3 minutes. Mix the vegetables into the rice. Remove from the heat and stir in the scallions.

To prepare the curry, heat the canola oil in a heavy skillet set over medium-high heat and add the diced lamb; cook, stirring occasionally, for 4 to 5 minutes, or until the meat is lightly browned. Add the curry powder and black pepper; stir to coat. Add the garlic, onion, carrot and Anaheim chilies; stir well and cook for about 4 to 5 minutes, until the vegetables begin to soften. Add the stock, broth or water, tomato purée and diced red potatoes. Cover and simmer for about 35 minutes, or until the meat is fork-tender and thoroughly cooked. Add the currants and salt. Mound equal portions of the rice on warmed plates. Spoon the curry on top, and garnish with diced mango. Serve immediately.

WHERE'S THE BEEF?

At the Golden Door, we don't pass on red meat altogether. Instead, we choose the leaner red meats—bison and lamb, for example—and serve them sparingly, most often once during the standard weeklong guest stay. Bison is low in fat and cholesterol, but very tender and flavorful. Turkey is also a good choice when you are craving something meaty. It works beautifully in many dishes that are traditionally made with beef, such as meatballs and chili.

As a child, my eyes grew wide with displays of fresh seafood in front of Belgium's better restaurants. In the still-life tradition of great Flemish painters of the sixteenth and seventeenth centuries, these lavish displays could magically draw a diner inside as if by an invisible leash, there to feast in a brasserie setting on such Belgian favorites as mussels or *waterzooi*, a kind of national fish soup. Fresh fish and shellfish from the North Sea have always been especially important to residents of Brussels, and atmospheric neighborhoods such as Ste-Catherine have been devoted to seafood dining for many generations.

But this is not a Belgian cookbook, and the past serves only to illustrate my ongoing obsession with fresh fish. Now that I have lived in California for more than three decades, I have embraced a new ocean, and its somewhat different array of fish than the one that I gazed on as a child. I've also shifted many of my preparation techniques toward the Pacific Rim, with influences ranging from Mexico to Japan and Southeast Asia. I especially enjoy grilling fish. I live in a land that loves to barbecue, and I do it year-round, for the Golden Door and the San Diego region have near-perfect climates. Why not be outdoors whenever you can, tending a fragrantly smoking bed of charcoal and sizzling salmon steaks? Chargrilling works best for steaklike fish such as salmon, yellowtail, mahi mahi and tuna.

Not to be confused with steaming, poaching involves cooking the fish in a very gently simmering broth. A delicious exchange of flavors takes place; the fish infuses the broth, and

SEAFOOD

the broth moistens and flavors the fish. I think you'll enjoy my version of classic poached salmon, especially when this assertively flavored fish marries with the tang of Sweet and Sour Red Cabbage and the hearty, deeply satisfying heft of Parsnip Mashed Potatoes. I'd say that this is as worthy of being called "comfort food" as any stew or meat loaf.

I wouldn't be true to my Belgian roots if I didn't include shellfish in this collection. Shrimp excites the eye as much as the palate. Unlike many fillets of fish whose pallid color must be carefully accompanied by some eye appeal (such as my jewel-toned salsas or vegetable side dishes), shrimp hold their own with their brilliant color and the way the delicate shells crack open to reveal a few wonderful bites, each plump, savory and steaming. I think you'll love the spiciness of my Firecracker Shrimp. I include recipes for two popular Golden Door scallop and lobster dishes as well, wonderful for special-occasion dinners.

Any chef will admonish you to use only the freshest fish you can find. I am no different. I use sight, smell and touch without shame when purchasing fish, and you should too. Do you fear you will insult your fishmonger if you ask to raise an unwrapped fillet to your nose before deciding? Then perhaps you need another fishmonger. Discuss your purchase with the persons across the counter, taking note of their knowledge as well as their pride. When you find those who consistently give you the freshness you deserve, keep them as friends. Or marry them. But do whatever you can to show your gratitude, for good fish is certainly a key to enjoying a lifetime of creative cooking.

POACHED SALMON WITH SWEET AND SOUR
RED CABBAGE AND PARSNIP MASHED POTATOES

MAKES 4 SERVINGS

Make this in the cold months, when cabbage and apples are piled high at the market. This dish is wonderful served with Parsnip Mashed Potatoes. The sweet and sour flavors of the cabbage make a tart counterpoint to the rich, creamy salmon.

For the potatoes:

3 medium russet potatoes, scrubbed and quartered

3 small parsnips, peeled and diced

$1/3$ cup nonfat sour cream

1 tablespoon creamed horseradish

2 tablespoons chopped fresh parsley

For the cabbage:

Vegetable oil in a spray bottle, or 1 teaspoon vegetable oil

$1/2$ cup finely diced onion

$1/2$ cup red wine vinegar

$1/3$ cup cabernet sauvignon

$1/2$ cup brown sugar

1 bay leaf

2 cloves

$1/2$ medium head red cabbage (about 1 pound), cored and shredded

$1/2$ cup water

2 Granny Smith apples, peeled, cored and thinly sliced

$1/2$ teaspoon kosher salt

$1/2$ teaspoon freshly ground black pepper

For the salmon:

6 cups Court Bouillon (page 203)

4 (4-ounce) salmon fillets

To prepare the potatoes, place them and the parsnips into a medium-size pot, add enough lightly salted water to cover, set over medium-high heat and bring to a simmer. Cook for 25 to 30 minutes, or until the potatoes are fork-tender. Drain and mash by hand or with an electric mixer until light and fluffy. Do not overmix or they will become gluey. Stir in the sour cream, horseradish and parsley. Keep warm.

To prepare the cabbage, spray or grease a ceramic pot with vegetable oil; set over medium-high heat and add the onion; sauté, stirring, for 2 to 3 minutes, or until the onion is translucent and soft. Stir in the vinegar, wine, brown sugar, bay leaf and cloves; bring to a simmer. Add the cabbage, water, apples, salt and pepper. Simmer, partially covered, for 35 to 40 minutes, stirring once or twice, or until the cabbage is tender. Remove from the heat, remove the bay leaf and cloves and keep warm.

Meanwhile, bring the bouillon to a simmer in a separate pot set over medium heat; simmer for 5 to 10 minutes. Immerse the salmon fillets in the bouillon and simmer for 5 to 7 minutes. Turn off the heat and let the salmon stand in the liquid for 5 minutes. Then, using a slotted spoon, gently remove the salmon from the bouillon and blot dry with a kitchen towel.

To serve, place equal portions of the cabbage and potatoes onto warm plates and top each with a poached salmon fillet.

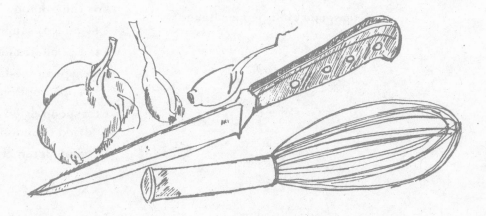

GRILLED SALMON WITH THREE SALSAS

MAKES 4 SERVINGS

Grilled salmon is a blank canvas for all kinds of accompaniments. Here, three colorful, flavorful salsas—Gingered Cranberry-Cherry Salsa, Papaya-Kiwi Salsa and Corn, Jicama and Pineapple Salsa—render it bold and bright. When pomegranates are in season, I substitute their bright, colorful, slightly tart seeds for the cranberries or cherries.

For the Gingered Cranberry-Cherry Salsa:

$\frac{1}{2}$ cup dried cranberries

$\frac{1}{2}$ cup pitted cherries

2 tablespoons sugar

2 tablespoons apple juice

2 tablespoons minced candied ginger

1 teaspoon grated orange zest

For the Papaya-Kiwi Salsa:

1 papaya, peeled, seeded and diced

1 kiwifruit, peeled and diced

2 tablespoons fresh lime juice

2 tablespoons fresh cilantro leaves

1 tablespoon minced scallions

$\frac{1}{8}$ teaspoon chili-pepper flakes

For the Corn, Jicama and Pineapple Salsa:

$\frac{1}{2}$ medium jicama, peeled and diced (about 1 cup)

$\frac{1}{2}$ cup diced fresh pineapple

$\frac{1}{2}$ cup corn kernels

1 serrano chili or habanero chili, seeded and minced

2 tablespoons chopped fresh cilantro

2 tablespoons fresh lime juice

1 clove garlic, minced

Salt to taste, optional

Freshly ground black pepper to taste, optional

For the salmon:

4 (4-ounce) salmon fillets

1 teaspoon kosher salt, optional

$\frac{1}{2}$ teaspoon freshly ground black pepper, optional

1 teaspoon dried lemon thyme or dried common thyme

12 whole fresh chives

To prepare the Gingered Cranberry-Cherry Salsa, combine the cranberries, cherries, sugar, apple juice, candied ginger and orange zest in a medium-size saucepan set over medium heat and bring to a simmer; cook for 5 minutes, or until the cranberries are plump and soft. Remove the salsa from the heat and let cool. *Makes 2 cups.*

To make the Papaya-Kiwi Salsa, combine the papaya, kiwifruit, lime juice, cilantro, scallions and chili-pepper flakes in a mixing bowl. Cover and set aside. *Makes 1 1/2 cups.*

To prepare the Corn, Jicama and Pineapple Salsa, combine the jicama, pineapple, corn, chili, cilantro, lime juice and garlic in a mixing bowl, season with salt and pepper, if desired, and toss. Cover and refrigerate for at least 1 hour to allow the flavors to blend. *Makes 2 cups.*

When you are ready to cook the salmon, preheat a grill, stovetop grill or broiler. Season the salmon fillets with the salt, black pepper and thyme; grill or broil for 3 to 5 minutes on each side for medium doneness. (The cooking time will vary with the thickness of the fillets.) If you are grilling, turn to make diamond-shaped grill marks. Remove from the heat and keep warm.

To serve, spoon 2 tablespoons of each salsa on each warm plate, forming a triangle by placing the salsas at opposing points along the outer edge of the plate. Place a salmon fillet in the center of each dish, garnish by crisscrossing 3 chives on top of each and serve immediately.

Gingered Cranberry-Cherry Salsa can be kept in the refrigerator, covered, for 2 to 3 days. Papaya-Kiwi Salsa and Corn, Jicama and Pineapple Salsa can be kept in the refrigerator, covered, for 2 days.

FISH ON THE BARBIE

When choosing fish to be grilled, remember that the fillets should be at least 3/4 inch thick. The thinner, more fragile fillets of sole and flounder won't work — they'll fall apart. What will work? Salmon, tuna and mahi mahi, to name a few. Halibut also works, but it is a very delicate fish, and should be dressed only with a sprinkle of seasoning and a mist of olive oil. Avoid other liquids such as lemon juice or vinegar, which will make the halibut stick to the grill.

POACHED SALMON ON MIXED GREENS WITH WILD RICE MÉLANGE

MAKES 4 SERVINGS

Moist, tender poached salmon on salad greens and wild rice studded with almonds makes for an appealing and nutritious meal. Serve with sliced Garlic-Herb Baguette (page 216) and Herbed Tofu Mayonnaise (page 207).

For the salmon:
4 cups Court Bouillon (page 203)
4 (4-ounce) salmon fillets

For the rice:
1 cup Steamed Fluffy Wild Rice (page 223)
$^1\!/_4$ cup thinly sliced scallions
$^1\!/_4$ cup toasted slivered almonds
$^1\!/_4$ cup finely cubed carrots
1 teaspoon balsamic vinegar
1 tablespoon olive oil

For the salad:
4 cups salad greens (such as baby arugula, frisée, romaine or red leaf lettuce), washed and patted dry
Herbed Tofu Mayonnaise (page 207)
12 slices Garlic-Herb Baguette (page 216)
4 sprigs lavender blossoms, optional

To poach the salmon, bring the bouillon to a simmer in a large, deep pan set over medium heat. Gently place the salmon fillets into the pan and simmer for 8 to 10 minutes, or until opaque. (The cooking time will vary with the thickness of the fillets.) Carefully remove the poached fillets and place them on a dry clean towel to remove any excess water. Transfer the salmon to a plate; cover and refrigerate until ready to serve.

To prepare the Wild Rice Mélange, combine the cooked wild rice, scallions, almonds, carrots, balsamic vinegar and olive oil in a bowl; mix well.

To serve, place equal portions of mixed greens on chilled plates and mound $^1\!/_3$ cup of the Wild Rice Mélange in the center of each. Top with a cold poached salmon fillet and garnish each plate with 3 slices Garlic-Herb Baguette, a dollop of Herbed Tofu Mayonnaise, and a sprig of lavender, if desired.

SEARED ONAGA WITH CUCUMBER, JICAMA AND HERB SALSA

MAKES 4 SERVINGS

This dish exemplifies "clean" eating: fresh fish so flavorful it needs only a quick sear and a simple accompaniment of crisp cucumbers and crunchy jicama tossed with herbs. I like to make this dish with onaga, a delectable fish from Hawaii. If it's not available in your area, Mexican cabrilla or farmed hybrid striped bass are two good choices. Edible flowers make a colorful garnish; add them just before serving to keep them from wilting.

For the salsa:

1 small English cucumber, peeled, seeded and diced

1 medium jicama, peeled and diced (about 1 cup)

2 tablespoons fresh lemon juice

1 teaspoon minced fresh thyme

1 tablespoon minced fresh tarragon

1 teaspoon kosher salt, optional

$^1/_2$ teaspoon freshly ground black pepper

$^1/_4$ cup edible flowers such as garlic or nasturtium, petals only, optional

For the onaga:

Plain Easy Quinoa (page 224)

16 pattypan squash or baby yellow squash

4 (4-ounce) onaga fillets

Canola oil in a spray bottle, or 1 teaspoon canola oil

To make the salsa, place the cucumber and jicama into a mixing bowl. Stir in lemon juice, thyme and tarragon; toss gently. Season with salt, if desired, and black pepper. Set aside. *Makes 2$^1/_2$ cups.*

Prepare the Plain Easy Quinoa and keep warm until ready to serve.

Bring a pot of water fitted with a steamer basket to a simmer over medium-high heat. Place the pattypan squash into the steamer basket; steam for 4 to 5 minutes, until it just begins to soften. Drain and keep warm.

To prepare the fish, spray or grease a nonstick pan with canola oil, set over medium-high heat and add the fillets; sear for 3 to 5 minutes on each side, or until they are lightly browned. (The cooking time will vary with the thickness of the fillets.)

To serve, add the edible flower petals to the salsa, if using. Place the seared fillets on warm plates and top with the Cucumber, Jicama and Herb Salsa. Serve with quinoa and steamed squash. Cucumber, Jicama and Herb Salsa can be kept in the refrigerator, covered, for 2 to 3 days.

SOUTHWESTERN-STYLE ROASTED SEA BASS WITH SUMMER VEGETABLES

MAKES 4 SERVINGS

Sea bass is a delectable fish, not to be confused with another delicious, but overfished and therefore endangered species, the Chilean sea bass, also known as the Patagonian toothfish. Seek out true sea bass and you won't be disappointed. In this recipe, roasting dramatizes the flavor and fragrance of the chili, cumin and garlic rubbed all over the succulent fish. I serve this dish on a mixture of black beans, corn and tomatoes made piquant with vinegar-marinated onions. Or, if you wish, Tomatillo Salsa (page 213) is an excellent accompaniment, too. If you are pressed for time, a can of low-sodium black beans, drained and rinsed, can be substituted for the dried beans.

For the vegetables:
1 cup dried black beans, soaked for 2 hours or overnight and rinsed
3 cups water
Pinch of chili-pepper flakes
$\frac{1}{2}$ cup finely diced red onion
$\frac{1}{4}$ cup red wine vinegar
Vegetable oil in a spray bottle, or 1 teaspoon vegetable oil
1 cup corn kernels
2 medium tomatoes, seeded and diced
$\frac{1}{4}$ to $\frac{1}{2}$ cup or more Vegetable Broth (page 201) or water, if needed

For the sea bass:
Vegetable oil in a spray bottle, or 1 teaspoon vegetable oil
1 teaspoon chili powder
1 teaspoon ground cumin
$\frac{1}{2}$ teaspoon freshly ground black pepper
1 teaspoon minced garlic
$\frac{1}{2}$ teaspoon kosher salt, optional
4 (4-ounce) sea bass fillets
4 sprigs cilantro for garnish
1 lime, cut into 4 wedges

Place the rinsed beans into a saucepan, add the water and chili-pepper flakes, and set over medium-high heat. Bring to a simmer and cook for about 90 minutes, or until the beans are tender. Drain and set aside.

When the beans are almost ready, combine the red onion and red wine vinegar in a mixing bowl and marinate for 10 to 15 minutes.

Spray or grease a nonstick pan with vegetable oil, set over medium-high heat and add the corn; sauté, stirring, for 2 to 3 minutes, or until the corn begins to soften. Add the tomato and cooked black beans; sauté, stirring, for 5 minutes. Add vegetable broth or water if the mixture is too dry.

Preheat the oven to 375 degrees F. Spray or grease a baking sheet with vegetable oil and set aside.

Combine the chili powder, cumin, black pepper, garlic and salt, if using, in a small bowl; mix well. Sprinkle this spice mixture on both sides of the sea bass fillets and place them on the prepared baking sheet. Roast for 10 to 12 minutes, turning once, until the fish is lightly browned and its juices run clear. (The cooking time will vary with the thickness of the fillets.)

To serve, place equal portions of the Summer Vegetables onto warm plates. Top each with a sea bass fillet and scatter some marinated onions over each. Garnish with cilantro sprigs and lime wedges.

DIAMOND GRILL MARKS

Diamond grill markings make whatever's on the grill look beautiful and tasty. And they're easy to master. All you need are two spatulas, or a spatula and a long-handled fork. Place your fish fillet on the grill for about 2 minutes. Then, with a decisive motion, slip a spatula under the fillet and place the other spatula or fork firmly on top (but don't pierce it.) Lift the fish and rotate it—don't flip it yet—at a 45-degree angle. Remove both spatulas and let it cook for another 2 minutes. When it's time to flip the fish, use the same two-spatula approach. Let the fillet cook for 2 minutes, and then use your spatulas to rotate the fish at a 45-degree angle. If you are grilling outdoors, once your fish is marked, move it away from the direct heat of the coals and cook to desired doneness. (Cooking time will vary with the thickness of the fillet.) Properly done, the fish should be moist and succulent inside, with beautiful diamond markings on the outside.

MAHI MAHI VERACRUZANA

MAKES 6 SERVINGS

The unusual combination of cinnamon, oregano and orange zest in this sauce is inspired by the cuisine of Veracruz, Mexico, where the food is a glorious mix of Spanish, Mexican and Caribbean influences. Serve the fish with tortillas and lime wedges.

For the sauce:

Olive oil and canola oil in a spray bottle, or 1 teaspoon olive oil

1 large Anaheim chili

1 teaspoon olive oil

1 medium onion, halved and thinly sliced

3 cloves garlic, thinly sliced

4 plum tomatoes, seeded and cut into 1-inch strips

2 tablespoons capers, rinsed

1 teaspoon minced fresh oregano

1 large strip orange zest

1 stick cinnamon

$^3/_4$ cup Fish Stock (page 202)

2 tablespoons finely chopped fresh cilantro

For the mahi mahi:

4 (4-ounce) mahi mahi fillets

2 tablespoons fresh lime juice

$^1/_2$ teaspoon mild chili powder

Olive oil and canola oil in a spray bottle, or 1 teaspoon olive oil

2 tablespoons Fish Stock (page 202)

1 lime, cut into 4 wedges

4 corn tortillas, warmed

Fresh cilantro sprigs for garnish

Preheat a grill, stovetop grill or broiler. Lightly spray or brush the chili pepper with 1 teaspoon olive oil; grill or broil for 5 minutes, turning so that all sides are charred. Transfer to a plastic bag, seal and set aside for about 10 minutes, or until the pepper is cool enough to handle. Remove the skin and seeds; dice and set aside.

Place the mahi mahi fillets into a shallow glass or ceramic dish, drizzle with lime juice and chili powder and refrigerate for 15 minutes.

Meanwhile, to make the sauce, spray or grease a large nonstick saucepan with olive oil and set over medium-high heat. Add the onions, garlic and chili pepper; sauté, stirring, for 3 to 5 minutes, or until the onions are translucent. Stir in the tomatoes, capers, oregano, orange zest, cinnamon stick and $^3/_4$ cup stock; reduce the heat to medium and simmer for 15 minutes. Remove from the heat. Remove the orange zest and cinnamon and keep warm.

Spray or grease a separate nonstick pan with olive oil and set over medium-high heat. Remove the mahi mahi from the marinade; discard the marinade. Place the fish into the pan in a single layer; sear for 3 to 4 minutes on each side, or until opaque. Add 2 tablespoons of fish stock and cover; simmer for 2 to 3 minutes, or until the fish is cooked through. (The cooking time will vary with the thickness of the fillets.)

To serve, stir the chopped cilantro into the sauce. Place the fish on warmed plates and ladle the Veracruzana Sauce over the top. Garnish with lime wedges, tortillas and cilantro sprigs.

TASTY MARINADES FOR GRILLING OR BROILING FISH

Marinades infuse fish with flavor. Make sure you choose a firm-fleshed fish that is appropriate for grilling or broiling, such as salmon, tuna or mahi mahi. Recall that the proteins in fish are more delicate than in meat and poultry, so you don't need to marinate the fish as long—10 minutes to an hour should do it (as opposed to 2 hours to overnight for meat and poultry). Here are a couple of ideas:

For 4 (4-ounce) fish fillets:

Dill and Lemon: Juice of 1 lemon and $\frac{1}{4}$ cup minced fresh dill. Combine and pour over the fillets; marinate in the refrigerator for 10 to 15 minutes before grilling or broiling. Mist the fish with a little olive oil just before grilling or broiling.

Mustard-Garlic: 4 tablespoons whole-grain mustard, 1 teaspoon olive oil, 1 teaspoon minced garlic. Brush the mustard mixture on the fillets just before grilling or broiling.

GRILLED MAHI MAHI WITH STIR-FRIED VEGETABLES AND WOOD EAR MUSHROOM SAUCE WITH FIVE-SPICE POWDER

MAKES 4 SERVINGS

I love the combination of textures in this dish—tender spinach, crisp snow peas, crunchy water chestnuts and feathery pea shoots. The dish gets a rich, nutty note from the dark sesame oil used as a sauté medium and from the wood ear mushrooms in the sauce. Wood ear mushrooms, sometimes called cloud ear mushrooms, have a crunchy texture and must be sliced very thinly. Trim the stems away completely (and, if you wish, save them for a delicious soup base), as they are too tough to add to the sauce. Wood ear mushrooms can be found in Asian markets and some supermarkets, most often in dried form. When rehydrated, they become very large. (You can save the soaking water, strain it well and use it for soup, also.) Wood Ear Mushroom Sauce is also delicious on any grilled fish, chicken or turkey breast.

For the sauce:

4 ounces fresh wood ear mushrooms, stemmed and finely sliced (about ⅓ cup), or 1 ounce dried wood ear mushrooms, or equivalent amounts of shiitake mushrooms

1 teaspoon canola oil

1 tablespoon minced ginger or galangal

1 tablespoon minced garlic

½ teaspoon five-spice powder

1¼ cups Chicken Stock (page 200) or more as needed

2 tablespoons low-sodium soy sauce, or to taste

2 teaspoons dark sesame oil

2 teaspoons arrowroot powder, dissolved in 2 tablespoons water

2 tablespoons minced scallions

For the mahi mahi:

4 (4-ounce) mahi mahi fillets

Olive oil and canola oil in a spray bottle, or 1 teaspoon olive oil

1 teaspoon mild chili powder

1 teaspoon kosher salt

2 teaspoons dark sesame oil

4 cups spinach, trimmed, washed and patted dry but slightly damp

1 cup snow peas

½ cup thinly sliced water chestnuts

1 cup pea shoot sprouts or bean sprouts

1 tablespoon low-sodium soy sauce

If you are using dried mushrooms, place them into a small bowl with enough warm water to cover; soak for 3 to 4 hours or overnight, until softened. When you are ready to cook, drain the mushrooms and slice them thinly.

To prepare the sauce, heat the canola oil in a small saucepan set over medium-high heat. Add the ginger and garlic; sauté, stirring, for 1 to 2 minutes, or until soft and fragrant. Add the five-spice powder and mushrooms; cook, stirring, for 2 to 3 minutes. Add the stock and soy sauce; cook for 8 to 10 minutes, or until the liquid reduces in volume to about 1 cup. Add the sesame oil. To thicken the sauce, add the dissolved arrowroot and simmer for 2 to 3 minutes. *Makes 1 cup.*

To prepare the fish, preheat a grill, stovetop grill or broiler. Spray or brush the mahi mahi with olive oil and season with the chili powder and salt. Grill or broil for 3 to 4 minutes on each side, or until opaque and cooked through. (The cooking time will vary with the thickness of the fillets.) If you are grilling, turn to make diamond-shaped grill marks. Remove from the heat, cover and keep warm.

Heat the sesame oil in a nonstick pan set over medium-high heat. Add the spinach, snow peas and water chestnuts; sauté, stirring, for 2 to 3 minutes, or until the spinach is wilted but still vibrant green. Add the sprouts and soy sauce; toss well.

Place equal portions of the stir-fried vegetables onto warm plates and top each with a mahi mahi fillet. Drizzle with Wood Ear Mushroom Sauce, sprinkle with scallions and serve. Wood Ear Mushroom Sauce can be kept in the refrigerator, covered, for 3 to 4 days.

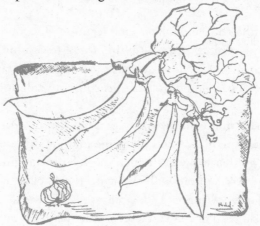

MAHI MAHI WITH GRAPEFRUIT, TARRAGON AND SHALLOT SAUCE AND HERBED QUINOA

MAKES 4 SERVINGS

Grapefruit endows this dish with both sweet and sour notes that contrast nicely with the richness of the mahi mahi. Use the sweetest variety of grapefruit available—I prefer ruby red, pomello fruit or even blood oranges. Don't forget the tarragon—it enhances whatever citrus fruit you choose.

For the quinoa:
Plain Easy Quinoa (page 224)
$^1/_2$ cup chopped fresh parsley
$^1/_2$ cup chopped fresh basil
1 tablespoon chopped fresh lemon
    thyme or common thyme
1 tablespoon chopped fresh tarragon

For the sauce:
1 tablespoon olive oil
1 tablespoon minced shallot
1 cup ruby red grapefruit juice
$^1/_2$ cup chardonnay
1 tablespoon chopped fresh tarragon

1 tablespoon sugar or fructose
$^1/_2$ teaspoon salt
$^1/_2$ teaspoon freshly ground black
    pepper

For the mahi mahi:
Olive oil and canola oil in a spray
    bottle, or 1 teaspoon olive oil
4 (4-ounce) mahi mahi fillets
4 cups watercress, washed and
    patted dry
1 grapefruit, peeled, pith removed and
    cut into thin slices for garnish
4 sprigs fresh tarragon, optional

Prepare Plain Easy Quinoa as directed on page 224. Remove from the heat and let stand for 10 minutes. Fluff with a fork, combine with the parsley, basil and thyme and toss until the herbs are thoroughly incorporated. Keep warm until ready to serve.

To make the sauce, heat 1 tablespoon olive oil in a saucepan set over medium-high heat and add the shallot; sauté, stirring, for 2 to 3 minutes, or until translucent and soft. Stir in the grapefruit juice, chardonnay, tarragon and sugar; cook until the liquid thickens and is reduced in volume by half. Season with salt and black pepper; set aside.

For the mahi mahi, spray or grease a nonstick pan with 1 teaspoon olive oil, set it over medium-high heat and place the mahi mahi into it; sear each side for 2 to 3 minutes, or until light golden brown. Reduce the heat to medium-low and cook for another 3 to 5 minutes. (The cooking time will vary with the thickness of the fillets.) To serve, place equal portions of Herbed Quinoa and watercress on warm plates and top with the grilled mahi mahi. Drizzle with grapefruit sauce. Garnish with grapefruit slices and tarragon sprigs, if desired.

PEPPERED AHI TUNA WITH CITRUS AND PEA SHOOT SALAD

MAKES 4 SERVINGS

Searing the seasoned ahi tuna quickly over high heat creates a paper-thin crust that seals in the juices of the tender ruby-fleshed fish. The pea shoots in the accompanying salad are generally available in the spring at Asian markets and farmers markets. If you can't find them, watercress is a great substitute.

For the salad:

1/4 cup fresh orange juice

2 tablespoons fresh lime juice

1 tablespoon Dijon mustard

2 tablespoons rice wine vinegar

1 teaspoon dark sesame oil

2 cups pea shoots or watercress, washed and patted dry

2 cups shredded napa cabbage

For the tuna:

4 (4-ounce) ahi or yellow-fin tuna fillets

1 teaspoon kosher salt

3 tablespoons freshly ground black pepper

1 teaspoon canola oil

1 orange, peeled, pith removed, and thinly sliced, for garnish

Combine the orange juice, lime juice, Dijon mustard, rice wine vinegar and sesame oil in a mixing bowl. Toss in the pea shoots or watercress and cabbage; mix well. Set aside.

Season the tuna fillets with salt and freshly ground black pepper.

Heat the canola oil in a nonstick pan set over medium-high heat. Place the tuna fillets into it in a single layer and sear for 2 to 3 minutes on each side for medium-rare or longer to taste. (The cooking time will vary with the thickness of the fillets.)

To serve, mound equal portions of salad on serving plates. Top each with a seared tuna fillet. Garnish with fresh orange slices.

GRILLED HALIBUT FLORENTINE WITH WARM TEQUILA-TOMATO VINAIGRETTE

MAKES 4 SERVINGS

This dish was inspired by the Florentine style of serving eggs or fish on a bed of spinach, topped with a super-rich Mornay sauce. I've made it much lighter by dropping the Mornay and substituting a Warm Tequila-Tomato Vinaigrette, a recipe from the Boulders Resort and Golden Door Spa in Carefree, Arizona. I like to season the spinach with a little nutmeg; it reinforces the earthy flavor of the greens. If you're in a hurry, frozen spinach will work instead of fresh. Just be sure to press out as much excess liquid as you can after thawing.

For the vinaigrette:
2 1/2 tablespoons olive oil
1 small onion, diced
1 tablespoon diced shallot
1 tablespoon minced garlic
3 tomatoes, diced
6 fresh basil leaves
1/4 cup tequila
Salt to taste
Freshly ground black pepper to taste
1/4 cup rice vinegar
2 tablespoons water

For the spinach:
Olive oil and canola oil in a spray bottle, or 1 teaspoon olive oil
4 cups fresh spinach, trimmed, washed and patted dry but slightly damp, or 1 (10-ounce) package frozen spinach, thawed and drained well
2 teaspoons olive oil
1/2 teaspoon kosher salt
1/4 teaspoon freshly ground black pepper
1/8 teaspoon grated nutmeg

For the halibut:
4 (4-ounce) halibut fillets
1/4 cup finely chopped fresh parsley

To prepare the vinaigrette, heat 1/2 tablespoon olive oil in a heavy skillet set over medium heat. Add the onion, shallot and garlic; cook, stirring often, for 3 to 4 minutes, or until the vegetables are softened and lightly browned. Add the tomatoes and basil and stir well; simmer 8 to 10 minutes.

Stir in the tequila and season lightly with salt and black pepper. Remove from the heat and let cool. Transfer to a blender or food processor fitted with a metal blade and process until smooth. Strain through a fine-mesh sieve. Add the vinegar, water and remaining 2 tablespoons of oil; whisk, then set aside until ready to serve. *Makes 1 1/2 cups.*

If you are using fresh spinach, spray or grease a nonstick pan with 1 teaspoon olive oil, set over medium heat and add the spinach; cook, stirring, for 1 to 2 minutes, until it wilts but is still a vivid green color. Drain and press any excess liquid from the spinach, then chop coarsely. (If you are using frozen spinach, press it to remove any excess liquid, then chop.) Wipe the pan with a paper towel and return it to the stove. Add the 2 teaspoons olive oil and heat over medium-high heat. Add the chopped spinach and season with salt, black pepper and nutmeg; cook, stirring, for 2 to 3 minutes. Keep warm until ready to serve.

To prepare the halibut, preheat a grill, stovetop grill or broiler. Grill or broil the halibut fillets for 4 to 5 minutes on each side, or until opaque but not overdone. (The cooking time will vary with the thickness of the fillets.) If you are grilling, turn to make diamond-shaped grill marks. Remove from the grill or broiler and keep warm.

Place equal portions of spinach onto warm plates and top each with a halibut fillet. Spoon $1\frac{1}{2}$ tablespoons of Warm Tequila-Tomato Vinaigrette over each and garnish with parsley. Warm Tequila-Tomato Vinaigrette can be kept in the refrigerator, covered, for 3 days.

BUYING FISH

All chefs will tell you that the best fish dishes begin in the fish market. The fresher the fish, the better the dish. But how do you know if what you're getting is fresh? Shop where you can buy fish with the skin on—and the head, too, if possible. I'm not advocating that you trim and scale your own fish; have the fish-monger do that for you once you've made your selection. But examining a fish with the skin on will help you choose the freshest fish. The skin should glisten and shine. The scales should be bright. The edges should not be dried out or yellow. The blood line in the center should be bright red. And, of course, fresh fish never smells fishy.

CITRUS-BROILED SEA SCALLOPS

MAKES 4 SERVINGS

Juicy sea scallops are broiled atop slender orange slices, which keep the tender chunks of shellfish moist and succulent. Crispy Asian Cole Slaw provides a contrast in texture and flavor. Look for sea scallops that glisten; if they are coated in a sticky film, they're old.

12 large sea scallops

1 teaspoon kosher salt

2 oranges, peeled, pith removed and cut into 12 ($^1/_4$-inch) rounds

$^1/_2$ cup Citrus Vinaigrette (page 208)

2 tablespoons finely chopped chives

1 teaspoon freshly ground black pepper

Crispy Asian Coleslaw (page 225)

Preheat the broiler.

Season the sea scallops with salt. Place the orange rounds onto a large piece of aluminum foil and place a scallop on each. Broil 4 to 6 inches away from the heating element for 3 to 4 minutes. Remove the scallops from the broiler just before they are cooked through; drizzle each with 2 tablespoons Citrus Vinaigrette and sprinkle with chives and black pepper. Return to the broiler for 1 minute longer.

Place equal portions of Crispy Asian Coleslaw on serving plates. Use a spatula to lift 3 scallop-topped orange rounds, intact, onto each plate. Serve immediately.

FIRECRACKER SHRIMP WITH FIVE-SPICE ACORN SQUASH

MAKES 4 SERVINGS

Shrimp and squash? Acorn squash is the perfect vessel for serving these spiced shrimp. Chili paste gives this soy-lime marinade a wonderful blast of heat. Adjust the amount to suit your taste.

2 small acorn squash, ends trimmed

1 teaspoon five-spice powder

20 large shrimp, shelled and deveined, tails intact

Olive oil and canola oil in a spray bottle, or 2 teaspoons olive oil

1 teaspoon fennel seeds, crushed

1 teaspoon Vietnamese chili paste

2 tablespoons fresh lime juice

1 tablespoon mirin (sweet rice wine)

2 tablespoons low-sodium soy sauce

2 teaspoons minced garlic

20 snow peas, ends trimmed

2 tablespoons chopped fresh chives

Ginger, Peanut and Cilantro Sauce and Dressing (page 210), optional

Preheat the oven to 375 degrees F. Cut the trimmed acorn squash in half, and scoop out and discard the seeds. Season the squash with five-spice powder and place the halves, flesh-side up, into a shallow baking pan. Pour in about $\frac{1}{2}$ inch of water and cover with aluminum foil; bake for 45 minutes, or until fork-tender. Keep warm.

Spray or brush the shrimp with 1 teaspoon olive oil. Combine the fennel seeds, chili paste, lime juice, mirin, soy sauce and garlic in a shallow glass or ceramic dish; mix well. Add the shrimp and toss to coat all sides. Cover and refrigerate for 35 to 45 minutes.

When the squash are cooked, bring a pot of water fitted with a steamer basket to a simmer over medium heat.

Meanwhile, spray or grease a large nonstick pan with olive oil and set over medium heat. Remove the shrimp from the marinade, reserving the liquid. Place the shrimp into the pan in a single layer; sauté, stirring, for 2 to 3 minutes on each side. Add the marinade; sauté, stirring, for another 2 minutes, or until the shrimp are completely pink and firm to the touch.

While the shrimp are cooking, add the snow peas to the steamer set over the simmering water; steam for 2 to 3 minutes, until they are tender-crisp and take on a vivid green color.

To serve, place 1 acorn squash half in the center of each warm plate. Nestle 5 shrimp inside each, letting their tails hang over the sides of the squash. Place the snow peas in between the shrimp in an upright position. Sprinkle with chopped chives. Drizzle with Ginger, Peanut and Cilantro Sauce and Dressing, if desired.

Hot Soba Noodles with Shrimp and Shiitake Mushrooms

MAKES 4 SERVINGS

What could be more soothing than a bowl of noodles and broth, piping hot? Add succulent shrimp and aromatic ginger, and you have a meal that nourishes both body and soul. To make fast work of this soup, buy shrimp that are already shelled and deveined or ask your fishmonger to do it for you.

16 large shrimp, shelled and deveined

1 tablespoon minced garlic

2 teaspoons dark sesame oil

3 tablespoons low-sodium soy sauce

1 ($\frac{3}{4}$-inch) piece gingerroot

4 ounces soba noodles

1 cup Chicken Stock (page 200)

Vegetable oil in a spray bottle, or
    1 teaspoon vegetable oil

4 cups spinach, trimmed, washed and
    patted dry but slightly damp

8 shiitake mushrooms, stemmed and
    quartered

4 teaspoons fresh lime juice

$\frac{1}{4}$ cup diagonally sliced scallions

Place the shrimp and garlic into a glass or ceramic dish, and pour in the sesame oil and soy sauce; toss to coat. Cover and refrigerate for 30 minutes.

Using a cheese grater, coarsely grate the gingerroot. Then, working over a small bowl, squeeze the grated gingerroot with your hands to extract the juice until you have 1 teaspoon. Reserve the juice and discard the ginger pulp.

Bring a medium-size pot of lightly salted water to a boil and add the soba noodles; simmer for 5 minutes, or until soft. Drain and return to the pot; pour in $\frac{1}{2}$ cup stock and keep warm.

Spray or grease another nonstick pan with vegetable oil, set it over medium heat and add the spinach; cook, stirring often, for 2 to 3 minutes, or until it just begins to wilt but is still a vivid green. Remove from the heat and keep warm.

Spray or grease a nonstick pan with vegetable oil and set over medium-high heat. Add the shrimp, shiitake mushrooms and any remaining marinade; sauté, stirring, for 3 to 5 minutes. Pour in the remaining $\frac{1}{2}$ cup stock and ginger juice; bring to a simmer. Cook for 1 to 2 minutes, or until the shrimp are pink and firm to the touch.

Place equal portions of the spinach into warm soup bowls. Spoon the hot soba noodles and stock over the spinach and top with the shrimp and shiitake mushrooms. Drizzle 1 teaspoon lime juice into each bowl, garnish with scallions and serve.

ITALIAN-STYLE CANNELLINI BEANS WITH SHRIMP

MAKES 6 SERVINGS

I make "food friends" wherever I go. When I was vacationing in San Francisco, an Italian-American fisherman shared his recipe for beans and shrimp with me. I've lightened it up a bit. To bring out the full flavor of the dish, make sure that the beans don't dry out—keep an eye on the pot and add more stock if necessary. You can also make this dish with any fresh fish that comes off the boat.

1 cup cannellini beans, soaked for 2 hours or overnight and rinsed

3 1/2 cups Chicken Stock (page 200) or water, or more as needed

1 medium onion, finely diced

1 large carrot, finely diced

2 celery ribs, finely diced

1 bay leaf

3 sprigs fresh thyme

1 cup finely diced plum tomatoes

1/4 cup canned tomato purée

18 large shrimp, shelled, deveined and butterflied

1/4 cup finely chopped fresh basil

1 tablespoon olive oil

1/2 teaspoon freshly ground black pepper

4 tablespoons chopped parsley

1 lemon, cut into 6 wedges

Drain the beans and place into a large pot. Add the stock, onion, carrot, celery, bay leaf and thyme; set the pot over medium heat and bring to a simmer. Cook for 45 minutes to 1 hour, or until the beans are tender. Add more broth if the beans become dry.

Preheat the oven to 350 degrees F. Transfer the contents of the pot to a casserole dish. Stir in the tomatoes and tomato purée. Bake for 15 to 20 minutes, or until the beans begin to bubble.

Meanwhile, in a small bowl, toss the shrimp with the basil, olive oil and black pepper. Remove the casserole from the oven; carefully remove the bay leaf and thyme sprigs. Arrange the butterflied shrimp on top of the beans; bake, covered, for another 20 minutes. Garnish with parsley and lemon wedges; serve hot.

Lobster and Butternut Squash Ravioli

MAKES 6 SERVINGS

Wonton wrappers are a staple of the spa kitchen—they can be filled with just about anything. Here, lobster and squash are bound with low-fat ricotta cheese seasoned with fresh herbs. This filling is particularly rich and creamy, a quality that comes from the ingredients themselves, and not from added fats. It's best to let the ravioli dry, uncovered, for 1 to 2 hours before cooking. They can be made a day in advance and refrigerated or frozen in a tightly sealed container for about 1 month.

Olive and canola oil in a spray bottle, or 1 teaspoon olive oil

1 medium butternut squash (about 10 ounces)

Vine-Ripened Tomato Coulis (page 205)

$\frac{1}{4}$ cup low-fat ricotta cheese

4 ounces cooked lobster meat (1 medium lobster tail)

2 tablespoons drained, chopped, oil-cured, sun-dried tomatoes

2 tablespoons chopped fresh basil

1 teaspoon chopped fresh thyme

$\frac{1}{2}$ teaspoon kosher salt

$\frac{1}{2}$ teaspoon freshly ground black pepper

2 teaspoons grated Meyer lemon zest or lemon zest

1 egg white, lightly beaten

Semolina flour for dusting

60 wonton wrappers

Basil leaves for garnish

Preheat the oven to 375 degrees F. Spray or brush the squash with olive oil. Place it on a baking sheet and bake for 1 hour, or until fork-tender.

Meanwhile, prepare the Vine-Ripened Tomato Coulis as directed on page 205; set aside.

Remove the squash from the oven and set aside until cool enough to handle. When cool, cut into the neck of the squash and scoop out 1 cup of the cooked flesh. (Reserve the remainder for another use.) Chop coarsely and transfer to a mixing bowl. Stir in the ricotta cheese, lobster, sun-dried tomatoes, basil, thyme, salt, black pepper and lemon zest.

Dust a baking sheet with semolina flour; set aside. Place 2 wonton wrappers on a work surface and brush with beaten egg white. Place 1 tablespoon of the squash-lobster filling in the center of one of the wrappers, then place the second wrapper on top, with the egg-brushed side facing down. Using your fingers, gently press the edges of the ravioli, releasing any air pockets. Repeat the process with the remaining filling and wonton wrappers. Transfer the ravioli to the prepared baking sheet and set aside to dry, uncovered, for 1 to 2 hours, or up to one day, refrigerated.

Bring a large pot of lightly salted water to a boil and immerse the ravioli in the water; simmer for 3 to 4 minutes, or until the ravioli are al dente.

To serve, spoon a little tomato coulis into warm bowls, use a slotted spoon to remove the ravioli from the pot, and place 5 each into the bowls. If you wish, you can spray or brush them with a little olive oil to keep them from sticking. Ladle the Vine-Ripened Tomato Coulis over them immediately and garnish with basil leaves.

Mexican-Style Crab Tostada

MAKES 4 SERVINGS

A classic tostada is deep-fried, then topped with vegetables and lots of sour cream, cheese and guacamole. This lighter recipe uses baked flour tortillas topped with ample amounts of lettuce, onion and tomatoes along with rich, succulent chunks of crab or your favorite seafood. Once the tortillas are baked and the ingredients are prepared, assembly takes no time at all. To save time, you can use canned low-fat refried black beans.

$\frac{1}{2}$ cup dried black beans, soaked for 2 hours or overnight and rinsed

1 teaspoon chili-pepper flakes

1 bay leaf

3 cups water

1 teaspoon kosher salt, optional

Vegetable oil in a spray bottle, or 1 teaspoon vegetable oil

4 whole-wheat flour tortillas

1 egg white, lightly beaten

Chili powder to taste, optional

4 cups shredded romaine lettuce

$\frac{1}{4}$ cup minced red onion

2 large tomatoes, finely diced

8 ounces cooked crabmeat

$\frac{1}{4}$ cup Salsa Mexicana (page 212), optional

$\frac{1}{4}$ cup Asparagus Guacamole (page 32), optional

2 tablespoons fresh cilantro leaves

1 lime, cut into 4 wedges

Place the dried black beans into a small pot with the chili-pepper flakes and bay leaf, pour in the water, set over medium-high heat and bring to a simmer; cook for $1\frac{1}{4}$ hours, or until the beans are soft, adding more water if necessary. Remove the beans from the heat and let cool. Remove and discard the bay leaf, and transfer the beans and any remaining liquid to a blender or food processor fitted with a metal blade; process until smooth. (If you are using canned black beans, place them into a blender or food processor fitted with a metal blade; process until smooth.) Season with salt, if desired.

Preheat the oven to 375 degrees F. Spray or grease a baking sheet with vegetable oil.

Brush the whole-wheat tortillas with the lightly beaten egg white, place on the prepared baking sheet, and sprinkle with chili powder, if desired. Bake for 10 to 15 minutes, turning once, or until the tortillas are golden brown and crisp. Remove from the oven and let cool.

Place 1 tortilla on each plate. Spread 3 tablespoons of the black bean purée on each. Scatter the lettuce, red onion, tomato, and crabmeat on top of the purée. If desired, dress each tostada with 2 tablespoons Salsa Mexicana and 2 tablespoons Asparagus Guacamole, if desired; garnish with cilantro and lime wedges.

GOLDEN DOOR BENTO BOX

The Golden Door spa is fashioned after a Japanese *Honjin* inn. It was designed as a sanctuary to rekindle vitality and spirituality. In the kitchen, we often look to Japan for inspiration. Every Thursday, we serve a Golden Door Bento Box lunch that has been very popular with the guests. Traditionally, bento boxes were a way for farmers and soldiers to bring meager provisions into the field or on the road. Today, bento boxes are fancy, elaborate box lunches for picnics, special celebrations and business luncheons. They are usually composed of four compartments that hold a variety of lunch items. Ours contains a Golden Door California Roll, Shrimp Nigiri Sushi, Blanched Vegetables, Seared Sea Bass, Soba Noodle–Crab Salad, Sweet and Sour Cucumber Salad and fruit for dessert. The Golden Door Bento Box can be a bit labor-intensive, but for a special luncheon it is a delicious and healthful treat that is well worth the time it takes to assemble. If you don't have an actual bento box, you can still enjoy the dish. Just place the components in separate bowls and serve family style. You will, however, need a sushi mat to roll the sushi.

For the cucumber salad:

1 English cucumber, thinly sliced

$1/2$ teaspoon sea salt

2 tablespoons mirin (sweet rice wine)

1 tablespoon rice vinegar

For the soba noodle–crab salad:

4 ounces soba noodles

4 ounces cooked crabmeat

$1/2$ cup diagonally sliced scallions

1 teaspoon dark sesame oil

2 cups shredded napa or Savoy cabbage

For the rice:

$3/4$ cup water

$1/2$ cup uncooked sushi rice, rinsed and drained

2 tablespoons chopped pickled ginger

$1/3$ cup rice vinegar

For the seared sea bass:

2 (4-ounce pieces) sea bass fillets, cut in half

1 teaspoon low-sodium soy sauce

1 teaspoon sesame oil

Canola oil in a spray bottle, or 1 teaspoon canola oil

For the blanched vegetables:

12 snow peas, trimmed

12 asparagus spears, tips only

$1 1/4$ teaspoons black sesame seeds

4 medium shiitake mushrooms, stems removed

1 cup Vegetable Broth (page 201)

1 tablespoon low-sodium soy sauce

1 teaspoon sesame oil

For the California roll:

1 medium carrot, cut into thin strips

¼ cup mirin (sweet rice wine)

1 small yam (about 4 ounces), baked and peeled

1 sheet nori seaweed

½ English cucumber, cut into thin strips

½ avocado, peeled, pitted and cut into thin slices

For the shrimp nigiri sushi:

4 medium shrimp, shell on

1 teaspoon wasabi paste, or 1 teaspoon wasabi powder dissolved in 1 teaspoon water

1 sheet nori, cut into ¼ x 2-inch strips

For the fruit salad:

½ honeydew melon, seeded, rind removed, and sliced

1 papaya, peeled, seeded and thinly sliced

½ cup fresh blueberries, washed and dried

4 sprigs fresh mint

1 tablespoon plum wine, optional

Condiments:

3 tablespoons wasabi paste, or 3 tablespoons wasabi powder dissolved in 3 tablespoons water

Pickled ginger

Low-sodium soy sauce

Lime-Miso Dipping Sauce and Dressing (page 211)

To prepare the cucumber salad, salt the cucumber lightly and toss it with the mirin and 1 tablespoon rice vinegar in a mixing bowl; cover and refrigerate for 1 hour.

Bring a medium-size pot of lightly salted water to a boil and add the soba noodles; simmer for 3 to 5 minutes, or until the noodles are just tender. Drain the noodles in a fine-mesh sieve, rinse under cold running water and transfer to a mixing bowl; stir in the crabmeat, scallions and sesame oil. Mix well, cover and refrigerate for 1 hour.

Wash, peel and slice the fruit for the fruit salad and set aside.

To prepare the rice, bring the water to a simmer in a small saucepan set over medium heat. Add the rice and reduce the heat to low; cook, covered, for 15 minutes. Remove from the heat and let stand for 10 minutes. Transfer the rice to a bowl and toss in the pickled ginger and 3 tablespoons rice vinegar, reserving the rest for assembling the sushi.

To prepare the sea bass, place the bass into a shallow glass or ceramic dish, pour in the soy sauce and sesame oil, toss to coat and refrigerate for 15 minutes. Spray or grease a nonstick pan with canola oil and set over medium-high heat. Remove the bass from the marinade, discarding the liquid. Place the bass into the pan in a single layer, working in batches if necessary. Sear on each side for 2 to 3 minutes, or until lightly browned. (The cooking time will vary with the thickness of the fillets.) Remove from the pan and let cool.

To prepare the blanched vegetables, bring a pot of water to a boil and prepare a bowl of ice water. Immerse the snow peas in the boiling water for 2 to 3 minutes, drain and plunge them into the ice water for 30 seconds to stop the cooking process. Drain again. Repeat the process with the asparagus tips. Sprinkle with black sesame seeds and set aside.

Combine the shiitake mushrooms, broth, soy sauce and sesame oil in a small saucepan set over medium heat and bring to a simmer; cook for 3 to 5 minutes, or until the mushrooms begin to soften. Remove from the heat and, using a slotted spoon, remove them from the broth; let cool.

To make the California roll, boil a pot of water and prepare a bowl of ice water. Immerse the carrots in the boiling water for 2 minutes, drain and plunge into the ice water for 30 seconds to stop the cooking process. Drain and toss with the mirin to coat.

Cut the baked and peeled yam lengthwise into $\frac{1}{2}$-inch slices.

Place the nori, smooth side down, on a sushi mat. Dampen your fingers with rice vinegar and spread half the rice over the nori, leaving a 1-inch border at the far edge of the nori sheet. Press gently so that the rice forms an even layer. Place the mirin-coated carrot, cucumber, avocado and yam strips in the middle of the rice. Lift the sushi mat from the edge nearest you and roll away from you to form a log shape. Use enough pressure to create a tight roll. Moisten the far end with a bit of rice vinegar and seal. With a sharp knife, cut the sushi roll into 8 equal-size pieces. Cover with a damp cloth and set aside in a cool place.

To make the shrimp nigiri sushi, bring a pot of water to a boil and prepare a bowl of ice water. Skewer several shrimp, working on the underside from head to tail to prevent curling. Immerse the shrimp in the boiling water for 3 minutes. Lift out the shrimp with their skewers and plunge into the ice water for 30 seconds to stop the cooking process. Remove the shrimp from the skewers. Shell and devein them, leaving the tails intact.

Moisten your hands with the remaining vinegar. Take $1\frac{1}{2}$ tablespoons of the remaining sushi rice and cradle it in your left hand. Crimp your hand to form an oblong mound of rice. Smear a dab of wasabi on this mound and place a shrimp flat on top. Press the shrimp to conform to the shape of the rice and wrap a nori strip around the middle. Repeat the process with the remaining shrimp and rice to make 3 more nigiri sushi pieces. Cover with a damp cloth and set aside in a cool place.

To serve, place $\frac{1}{2}$ cup napa or Savoy cabbage into one compartment of each bento box. Top with $\frac{1}{4}$ of the Sweet and Sour Cucumber Salad and $\frac{1}{4}$ of the Soba Noodle–Crab Salad. Place $\frac{1}{4}$ of the sushi, sea bass, steamed vegetables and fruit into individual compartments in each box, or place each component in its own bowl and serve family style. Drizzle the fruit with the plum wine, if desired. Serve with wasabi, pickled ginger, soy sauce and Lime-Miso Dipping Sauce and Dressing in individual sake cups or small bowls.

Picture forty famished people arriving in your dining room en masse. Some of them have been on the go since 6 A.M. — in an unhurried but purposeful way — but active just the same. While this is a serene place, many guests look at the wide variety of instruction and activities offered each day (several choices every hour) and can't resist filling their schedules to the maximum. The Golden Door urges a balance between exercise, learning and rest, but "rest" to a guest often means taking a quieter, more contemplative class such as T'ai Chi, or an afternoon massage or beauty treatment. Although naps are encouraged, quite a few guests do not take naps — if anything, they seem to devour the day.

By dinner they're ready to devour something more substantial than time well spent. They want a main dish with plenty of eye appeal, gusto and fuel. I always offer a vegetarian dish on my lunch and dinner menus, and I've found that despite being inherently light, they are among the most popular, not only with those who follow a strict vegetarian diet but with the "accidental vegetarian" type — you know, the ones who just don't seem to eat meat much anymore despite not being adamantly against it.

MEATLESS MAIN COURSES

I've gathered an eclectic collection of recipes for this chapter in much the same way that I like to keep the guests guessing what sort of sleight-of-hand I might pull in the kitchen that night. Will the vegetarian dish be informal, like Angel Hair Pasta with Diced Tomatoes, Edamame Beans, Basil and Virgin Olive Oil? Or will it be more formal, like Red Lentil Roulade with Spinach and Crimini Mushrooms? Will we go with real comfort food, like Vegan Irish Stew with Potato Gratinée? Or something light and exotic, such as a Thai Vegetable Medley with Coconut Milk and Cilantro?

They're all here, and more; my current favorites, as well as a few old-timers, like the Open-Faced Tempeh Sandwich with Pickled Red Cabbage on Old-Fashioned Tecate Bread that has been featured on our menu for years. This is great food without guilt — so filling that there's little need for portion control. I hope you'll sample your way through a good many of these dishes, noting how the recipes mirror my efforts to develop the flavors of each ingredient to the fullest.

ASPARAGUS AND SPA PESTO RISOTTO

MAKES 6 SERVINGS

Though not technically risotto (which is traditionally made with arborio rice and stirred constantly from start to finish), this rice borrows the Italian classic's final steps: vegetables and herbs are stirred into it at the end, and it gets a final flourish of rich nutty cheese.

Steamed Fluffy Brown Basmati Rice (page 223)

Olive oil and canola oil in a spray bottle, or 1 teaspoon olive oil

8 medium asparagus spears (about $3\frac{1}{2}$ ounces), trimmed, peeled and sliced into thin rounds

$\frac{1}{3}$ cup finely chopped fresh parsley

1 tablespoon grated Asiago cheese

$\frac{1}{4}$ cup Spa Pesto (page 214)

Salt and freshly ground black pepper to taste

Prepare the rice as directed on page 223, using brown basmati rice. Keep warm.

When the rice is done, spray or grease a small sauté pan with olive oil and set over medium heat. Add the asparagus; sauté for 2 to 3 minutes, or until it just begins to soften. Mix the asparagus into the warm rice and stir in the parsley, Asiago cheese and Spa Pesto. Season with salt and pepper to taste; serve immediately.

GREAT GRAINS

Some calorie counters will urge limiting consumption of grain and the carbohydrate foods that they produce, but the truth is that grains are the staple food of most of the world and have been so since the dawn of humanity. Eaten in moderation, they are part of a well-balanced diet. There are many varieties of grains, which are either cooked and eaten as they are or milled into flours for breads, pastas and other food products. If you buy grains in bulk, check their odor and color for rancidity, mildew or other contaminants. In this country, wheat is the predominant grain; its flour is used for everything from breads to pastas to sweets. But there are other grains. Here are some that I like to incorporate into my menus:

Barley: Barley has been cultivated since ancient times; the Egyptians used it as currency as well as food. Pearl (refined) barley is the most commonly used variety in this country. It must be rinsed and drained to remove its powdery coating. If overcooked, pearl barley can become gluey. Cooked for the right amount of time, this quality makes barley a good thickener for soups and stews.

Bulgur (Cracked Wheat): Bulgur is the product that results when wheat berries are steamed, dried and cracked. A Middle Eastern favorite, it is delicious as tabouleh salad, and it makes an excellent addition to stuffings, casseroles, breads and breakfast cereals.

Millet: One of the oldest grains under cultivation, millet is still a major nutrition source for millions of people all over Asia and North Africa. The bright yellow grain has a sweet, nutty flavor that intensifies if you sauté it lightly or toast it in a hot dry skillet before cooking it in water or broth.

Quinoa: Quinoa, often called the "super grain," was cultivated by the peoples of South America long before Columbus arrived in the New World. The high-protein grain is loaded with nutrients—especially iron, magnesium and B vitamins—and it contains more calcium than milk! It must be rinsed and drained before cooking. It's delicious on its own and can be added to baked goods, salads and desserts.

Rice: Rice is the daily bread of much of the world. The many different species of this grain produce rice of varying sizes, colors and flavors. Rice is classified by size—long-grain, medium-grain and short-grain. Long-grain, or Indica, rice, is any rice that is four to five times as long as it is wide. Properly cooked, it is marked by dry separate grains. Aromatic rice varieties such as jasmine and basmati are long-grain rice. Medium-grain rice is two to three times as long as it is wide. Cooked, it is softer than long-grain rice and tends to absorb more flavors from other foods. Medium-grain varieties include arborio from Italy, valencia from Spain, and sushi rice from Japan. Short-grain rice is very nearly round. High in a starch called amylopectin, it becomes sticky and soft when cooked.

Asian-style rice refers to both medium- and short-grain rices from Asia, which generally have a high amylopectin content. You'll also find brown rice on the market; this term applies to any rice that is milled to leave the nutritious bran layer intact. It has a rich, nutty flavor and requires a longer cooking time than white rice. Wild rice is not truly a rice at all, but an aquatic grass seed that resembles rice grains. It has an intense earthy aroma and a slightly crunchy texture.

Red Lentil Roulade with Spinach and Crimini Mushrooms and Yogurt-Horseradish Sauce

MAKES 8 SERVINGS

A wonderful vegetarian alternative for the holidays, this dish combines red lentils and semolina flour to make a rich, nutritious dough that is wrapped around a spinach-mushroom filling studded with red peppers. It is as beautiful as it is healthful and delicious. The Yogurt-Horseradish Sauce gives the dish a little bite.

For the sauce:

1 cup nonfat plain yogurt

2 tablespoons horseradish

2 tablespoons finely chopped fresh parsley

1 teaspoon freshly ground black pepper

For the roulade:

1 $\frac{1}{4}$ cups red lentils, rinsed and drained

2 $\frac{3}{4}$ cups Vegetable Broth (page 201)

1 teaspoon kosher salt

1 bay leaf

$\frac{1}{2}$ cup plus 2 tablespoons semolina flour

$\frac{1}{4}$ teaspoon crushed saffron threads

1 large red bell pepper, or 1 cup canned roasted red bell peppers

Olive oil and canola oil in a spray bottle, or 2 teaspoons olive oil

6 cups fresh spinach, trimmed, washed, patted dry and chopped, or 1 (10-ounce) package frozen spinach, thawed, drained and chopped

1 $\frac{1}{2}$ cups sliced crimini mushrooms or white mushrooms

1 teaspoon minced fresh thyme

2 tablespoons chopped fresh basil

1 teaspoon grated lemon zest

$\frac{1}{2}$ teaspoon freshly ground black pepper, optional

$\frac{1}{4}$ cup crumbled feta cheese

$\frac{1}{4}$ cup chopped walnuts

Vegetable oil in a spray bottle, or 2 teaspoons vegetable oil

To prepare the sauce, combine the yogurt, horseradish, parsley and black pepper in a small mixing bowl; mix well. Cover and refrigerate until ready to use. *Makes 1 $\frac{1}{4}$ cups.*

To make the roulade, combine the lentils, broth, salt and bay leaf in a small pot set over medium heat. Bring to a simmer; cover and cook for 35 minutes, or until the lentils are soft and the broth has been absorbed. Transfer to a mixing bowl, discard the bay leaf and set aside until cool enough to handle. Stir in $\frac{1}{2}$ cup semolina flour and the saffron; mix until the ingredients are incorporated and take on a dough-like consistency. Set aside.

Meanwhile, if you are using a fresh red bell pepper, preheat a grill, stovetop grill or broiler. Lightly spray or brush the red bell pepper with 1 teaspoon olive oil; grill for 5 minutes, turning so that all sides are charred. Transfer to a plastic bag, seal and set aside for about 10 minutes, or until the peppers are cool enough to handle. Remove the skin and seeds from the pepper and cut into thin strips. Set aside.

Spray or grease a large nonstick pan with 1 teaspoon vegetable oil and set over medium heat. Add the spinach, mushrooms, thyme, basil, lemon zest and black pepper; sauté, stirring, for 2 to 3 minutes, or until the vegetables are soft and wilted. Transfer to a colander and drain. Chop coarsely and pour the mixture into a mixing bowl. Stir in the feta cheese and roasted red bell pepper; set aside.

Set a dry, small nonstick pan over high heat. Add the chopped walnuts and toast lightly, stirring often, for 3 minutes, or until the nuts are golden brown and fragrant.

Preheat the oven to 350 degrees F. Spray or grease a baking sheet with 1 teaspoon vegetable oil and set aside. Dust a large sheet of parchment paper with the remaining semolina flour and, with your hands, shape the lentil dough into a rectangle. Then, using a rolling pin, roll into an 8 x 10-inch rectangle. Spray or brush the dough with 1 teaspoon vegetable oil. Spread the spinach-mushroom mixture onto the dough and sprinkle with the toasted walnuts. Slowly roll the dough into a log-shaped roulade, rolling the parchment paper along with the dough. Pinch the ends of the parchment and place the log onto the prepared baking sheet, seam-side down; spray or brush it with vegetable oil. Bake for 1 hour and 15 minutes, or until lightly crisp. Remove from the oven; let rest for 15 minutes.

Carefully remove the parchment paper and, using a sharp knife, cut the roulade into 8 rounds. Place 2 rounds each onto 4 warm plates; drizzle with Yogurt-Horseradish Sauce. Yogurt-Horseradish Sauce can be kept in the refrigerator, covered, for 2 to 3 days.

SAVOY CABBAGE WITH TOFU, LENTILS, SWEET CORN AND SHALLOT SAUCE

MAKES 4 SERVINGS

These savory stuffed cabbage leaves—my version of vegan burritos—make an excellent main course. The cabbage leaves can dry out easily, so bake them in a dish in which they fit snugly and add a little broth or water to keep them moist. I like to use black lentils here, but French du Puy lentils or regular green lentils work, too. Browning the shallots for the sauce brings out their sweetness and adds depth and complexity.

For the sauce:

1 teaspoon olive oil

$^1/_2$ cup thinly sliced shallots

1 teaspoon dried tarragon

$^1/_2$ teaspoon freshly ground black pepper

$^1/_3$ cup balsamic vinegar

1 $^1/_4$ cups Vegetable Broth (page 201)

1 tablespoon arrowroot dissolved in 3 tablespoons water

4 teaspoons chopped fresh parsley

For the cabbage:

$^3/_4$ cup black lentils, rinsed and drained

1 tablespoon minced shallot

$^1/_2$ teaspoon dried thyme

2 $^3/_4$ cups Vegetable Broth (page 201) or water

4 ounces firm tofu, drained

1 teaspoon peeled, minced fresh gingerroot

1 teaspoon minced garlic

1 tablespoon balsamic vinegar

1 tablespoon low-sodium soy sauce

8 Savoy cabbage leaves, center ribs and stems removed, washed and patted dry

Vegetable oil in a spray bottle, or 1 teaspoon vegetable oil

$^1/_2$ cup fresh corn kernels

1 celery rib, finely diced

3 tablespoons thinly sliced scallions, including tops

To prepare the sauce, heat the olive oil in a saucepan set over medium-high heat. Add the shallots; sauté, stirring often, for 3 to 4 minutes, or until the shallots begin to brown. Stir in the tarragon, black pepper and vinegar; cook for about 5 minutes, or until the liquid reduces in volume by half. Add the broth; cook for 8 to 10 minutes more, or until the liquid reduces to about 1 cup. To thicken the sauce, add the dissolved arrowroot and simmer for 2 minutes. Stir in the parsley. *Makes 1 cup.*

For the cabbage, combine the lentils, shallot, thyme and broth or water in a small pot set over medium heat; bring to a simmer. Cover and simmer for 35 to 40 minutes, or until the lentils are tender and all the liquid has been absorbed.

Meanwhile, wrap the tofu in a clean kitchen towel and cover with a heavy plate for 30 minutes.

Combine the gingerroot, garlic, balsamic vinegar and soy sauce in a small mixing bowl; mix well. Unwrap and dice the tofu, stir it into the liquid and toss to coat. Cover and marinate for 30 minutes.

Bring a pot of water to a boil. Prepare a bowl of ice water. Immerse the cabbage leaves in the boiling water for 1 to 2 minutes. Gently remove them with a slotted spoon; plunge into the ice water for 30 seconds to stop the cooking process. Pat the cabbage leaves dry with a clean towel; set aside.

Spray or grease a nonstick pan with vegetable oil and set over medium-high heat. Add the marinated tofu, corn and celery; sauté for 3 to 5 minutes, or until the vegetables just begin to soften. Drain the lentils, discarding the cooking liquid, and add them to the tofu mixture. Add the scallions; continue to sauté, stirring, for another 3 to 4 minutes, or until the mixture is well blended and heated through.

Preheat the oven to 350 degrees F. Place 2 cabbage leaves on a work surface so that the ends overlap slightly. Place $\frac{1}{2}$ cup of the lentil-tofu mixture in the center of the 2 overlapping leaves. Starting from the side nearest you, roll the cabbage over the stuffing, folding in the sides as you roll. Place the cabbage roll into a small baking dish, seam-side down. Repeat the process with the remaining cabbage leaves and stuffing to make 3 more rolls. Cover and bake for 5 to 10 minutes, or until thoroughly warm. Remove from the oven; place 1 stuffed cabbage onto each warm plate. Drizzle with the Shallot Sauce and serve immediately. Shallot Sauce can be kept in the refrigerator, covered, for 3 to 4 days.

Soy, Oh Soy

The soybean is a nutrient-rich bean that has been a staple for millions of people all over the world. It is rich in vitamins, minerals and fiber, but low in saturated fat and cholesterol. Its protein content makes it a good substitute for meat, and the variety of soy-based foods available today makes it appealing to vegetarians and meat-eaters alike.

In the past, such foods were hard to find and harder to cook. Today, there are literally hundreds of soy products on the market. Here are a few of my favorites:

Tofu: Tofu is made from a ground soybean liquid that undergoes a process similar to simple cheese-making, whereby the liquid becomes solid. Tofu is porous and absorbs the flavors of marinades and dressings or whatever it is cooked with. Don't freeze tofu or the consistency will be ruined. There are different styles of tofu. Firm tofu comes in water and should be stored that way. It is good in stir-fries and curries and is best when marinated before cooking. Silken tofu is a smooth-textured tofu that is ideal for creamy dressings, "mayonnaise," soups and salads.

Tempeh: Tempeh is a fermented soybean cake; the white or blue mold on the outside is perfectly okay to eat, but you can cut it off if you wish. Tempeh has a flavor redolent of earthy mushrooms and nuts, and its texture is quite meaty. It's perfect in soups, stews, casseroles and sandwiches.

Soy Flour and Protein Powder: These products can be blended with other flours to make muffins, pancakes, cookies and cakes. Soy powder can be added to fruit smoothies for added nutrition.

Soy "Milk," Soy "Cheese" and Soy "Yogurt": These nondairy versions of dairy products are a boon to those who are lactose intolerant. Innovative food manufacturers are turning out products that can be incorporated into a wide variety of recipes and are so tasty that they can be eaten on their own.

Soy Vegetables: Soybeans (often sold as edamame beans), soy sprouts and soy nuts are all loaded with protein and make great additions to salads and other dishes.

Soy Pasta: High in protein and nutrients, this pasta is a blend of soy and durum wheat flours. It comes in most pasta shapes and sizes, and tastes just like wheat-based pasta. It's perfect for al dente cooking.

Tofu Burgers, Soy Sausage and Soy Deli "Meats": Food manufacturers are producing all kinds of soy products, often seasoned to taste like meat products. They make for easy healthful meals.

Condiments: The versatile soybean also yields a variety of condiments. Made from fermented soybeans, soy sauce and its variants are the "salt" of choice for much of eastern Asia, added during cooking or at the table. I like to use low-sodium soy sauce; the full-strength sauce is too salty. Tamari is the Japanese version; it contains no wheat. Miso, another Japanese soy-based condiment, is made of fermented soy paste and barley or rice. Best known in this country as the basis of miso soup, it can also be used for stews, dressings and sauces. It, too, is high in sodium and should be used in small quantities. A little ginger juice (squeezed by hand from freshly grated ginger) will enhance the flavor of a miso broth.

SPICY TOFU AND LEMONGRASS STIR-FRY

MAKES 4 SERVINGS

We grow many of the herbs that we use in the Golden Door kitchen in our own organic garden. Lemongrass, in particular, grows in lush stalks that we harvest daily. The citrusy fragrance and flavor of the lemongrass really enhance this stir-fry recipe.

1 ½ cups Steamed Fluffy Long-Grain Brown Rice (page 223)

8 ounces firm tofu, diced

2 stalks lemongrass, trimmed, outer leaves removed, minced

1 tablespoon minced gingerroot

1 teaspoon minced garlic

1 teaspoon Vietnamese chili paste, or to taste

1 tablespoon fresh lime juice

1 tablespoon mirin (sweet rice wine)

½ cup low-fat coconut milk

¼ cup Vegetable Broth (page 201)

1 tablespoon low-sodium soy sauce

1 teaspoon dark sesame oil

Canola oil in a spray bottle, or 1 teaspoon canola oil

4 medium carrots, cut into thin strips

8 medium shiitake mushrooms, thinly sliced

1 cup broccoli florets

½ cup diagonally sliced scallions

Fresh chives for garnish

Edible flowers for garnish, optional

Prepare the rice as directed on page 223, using long-grain brown rice. Keep warm.

Combine the tofu, lemongrass, ginger, garlic, chili paste, lime juice and mirin in a small bowl; toss to coat. Cover with plastic wrap and refrigerate for 30 minutes.

Combine the coconut milk, broth, soy sauce and sesame oil in a bowl; set aside.

Heat the canola oil in a large pan set over medium-high heat. Add the tofu and marinade; sauté, stirring, for 2 to 3 minutes. Add the carrots, mushrooms and broccoli; sauté, still stirring, for another 2 to 3 minutes. Stir in the coconut milk mixture and scallions; cook for 4 to 5 minutes, or until the vegetables are just tender.

Place equal portions of cooked brown rice on each warmed plate and top with the tofu stir-fry. Garnish the dish with fresh chives and, if desired, edible flowers.

Baked Acorn Squash with Curried Tofu, Lentils, Spinach and Spiced Pecans

MAKES 4 SERVINGS

This is the ideal meatless dinner-party entrée. The components can be done ahead and the final dish assembled at the last minute. Acorn squash are high in calcium and fiber—and while they're low in calories, they don't taste like it. Here, their rich near-sweetness is balanced by curried tofu, spinach and spiced nuts. Look for small squash that are free of bruises or blemishes. Store them in a cool dry spot.

For the squash:
2 small acorn squash (about 3 pounds)
1 teaspoon five-spice powder

For the tofu:
8 ounces firm tofu, drained
1 teaspoon low-sodium soy sauce
2 teaspoons Madras curry powder
$\frac{1}{2}$ teaspoon dried oregano
Canola oil in a spray bottle, or
    1 teaspoon canola oil
2 tablespoons currants soaked in
    3 tablespoons water until plump

For the lentils:
$\frac{3}{4}$ cup black lentils, rinsed and drained
2 cups Vegetable Broth (page 201) or
    water
$\frac{1}{2}$ teaspoon dried basil
$\frac{1}{4}$ teaspoon chili-pepper flakes
$\frac{1}{4}$ cup chopped scallions

For the pecans:
1 tablespoon honey
1 tablespoon water
$\frac{1}{4}$ cup pecans or walnuts
$\frac{1}{4}$ teaspoon cayenne pepper

For the spinach:
Olive oil and canola oil in a spray
    bottle, or 1 teaspoon olive oil
4 cups fresh spinach, trimmed, washed
    and patted dry but still damp
Kosher salt to taste, optional

Preheat the oven to 375 degrees F. With a sharp knife, cut the squash in half lengthwise and remove the seeds. Trim the base so that the squash will lie flat; sprinkle the flesh with the five-spice powder. Place the squash halves into a shallow pan with $\frac{1}{2}$ inch of water; cover and bake for 45 to 55 minutes, or until fork-tender.

Meanwhile, wrap the tofu in a clean kitchen towel and cover with a heavy plate for 30 minutes.

Combine the lentils, broth, basil and chili-pepper flakes in a small pot set over medium heat. Cover and simmer for 20 to 30 minutes, or until all the liquid has been absorbed. Remove from the heat and mix in the scallions; set aside and keep warm.

Combine the honey and water in a small bowl; stir until dissolved. Scatter the pecans or walnuts on a baking sheet, brush with the dissolved honey and sprinkle with the cayenne. Bake for 15 minutes; remove from the oven and let cool.

Dice the pressed tofu; then place it into a small bowl and toss with the soy sauce, curry powder and oregano. Spray or grease a nonstick pan with canola oil and set it over medium-high heat. Add the tofu; sauté, shaking the pan gently, for 3 to 5 minutes, or until lightly browned. Drain the soaked currants and stir them into the tofu mixture. Remove from the heat and keep warm.

Wipe the pan with a towel, spray or grease it with olive oil and set it over medium-high heat. Add the spinach; sauté, stirring, for 2 to 3 minutes, or until the spinach is wilted. Season with salt if desired. Remove from the pan, drain any excess liquid and keep warm.

Place 1 baked squash half on each warmed plate. Spoon equal portions of the lentils, curried tofu and spinach into each. Scatter the spiced nuts on top; serve immediately.

REALLY MEATLESS

Meatless selections are among the most popular menu items at the Golden Door. Some of our guests choose them because they like to vary their diets between meat and vegetarian fare. Other guests are vegetarians, and among the vegetarians, the strictest are the vegans. I always instruct my staff to be extremely careful when cooking for vegetarians and vegans: no chicken-, fish- or meat-based broth of any kind. For the vegans, no dairy—only soy-based cheese and milk. But meatless eating is not only about what one can't eat; it's also about what one *can* eat. Few foods other than meat contain complete protein, but you can combine legumes, grains and (except for vegans) dairy to create complete proteins. Meatless eating is also about flavor: bold spices and seasonings, fresh luscious sun-ripened fruits and vegetables, fragrant olive oil and nutty satisfying grains lightened up with flavorful greens or scallion tops. Meatless eating should never be bland.

VEGAN IRISH STEW WITH POTATO GRATINÉE AND WILD MUSHROOM SAUCE

MAKES 6 SERVINGS

Don't let the long list of ingredients turn you off, as this is a straightforward stew. It's a great dish to make after you've made a few other dishes that call for wild mushrooms. That's because most recipes calling for wild mushrooms suggest discarding their tough fibrous stems. Instead, save them for this Wild Mushroom Sauce, which they infuse with a fresh-from-the-earth flavor. (They are strained out before serving.) One note of caution: Use only the wild or exotic mushrooms you can buy in the store; don't try to forage for mushrooms on your own. If you're not a vegan, you can substitute buttermilk for the soy milk. Depending on the occasion, you can spread the layer of mashed potatoes on top of the vegetables with a spoon, or pipe them on for a more formal meal.

For the sauce:

2 teaspoons olive oil

4 medium shallots, diced

2 celery ribs, diced

1 $\frac{1}{2}$ pounds crimini, oak and/or shiitake mushrooms, or stems and trimmings

2 small carrots, diced

3 to 4 sprigs fresh parsley

3 sprigs fresh thyme

1 teaspoon dried tarragon

1 bay leaf

1 clove

2 teaspoons freshly ground black pepper

2 tablespoons unbleached flour

2 tablespoons canned tomato purée

5 cups Vegetable Broth (page 201)

$\frac{1}{4}$ cup low-sodium soy sauce

3 tablespoons balsamic vinegar

For the stew and gratinée:

Vegetable oil in a spray bottle, or 2 teaspoons vegetable oil

2 pounds Yukon Gold potatoes (about 5), diced

$\frac{1}{3}$ cup soy milk

$\frac{1}{8}$ teaspoon freshly grated nutmeg

2 medium leeks, washed well, trimmed and diced

2 small shallots, minced

2 medium carrots, diced

2 medium portobello mushrooms, stems removed and diced

5 ounces commercial vegetable patty

1 teaspoon minced fresh thyme

1 bay leaf

$\frac{1}{2}$ teaspoon freshly ground black pepper

1 tablespoon balsamic vinegar

1 cup frozen peas, thawed

2 tablespoons toasted bread crumbs

2 tablespoons tofu mozzarella or almond (tofu) mozzarella, optional

To prepare the sauce, preheat the oven to 375 degrees F.

Heat the olive oil in a large, ovenproof saucepan set over medium heat. Add the shallots and celery; sauté, stirring, for 2 to 3 minutes, or until the shallots are translucent. Add the mushrooms; sauté, stirring frequently, until lightly browned. Stir in the carrots, parsley, thyme, tarragon, bay leaf, clove and black pepper; continue to sauté, stirring, for 15 minutes. The mixture should start to stick to the bottom of the saucepan just slightly.

Remove the pan from the heat, discard the bay leaf, and stir in the flour and tomato purée; bake for 15 to 20 minutes, or until the mushroom mixture is browned and well caramelized. Carefully remove the saucepan from the oven; deglaze it by adding the broth and scraping the bottom and sides of the pan to loosen any flavorful browned bits. Stir in the soy sauce and balsamic vinegar; simmer until reduced in volume to approximately 2 cups. Strain the mixture through a fine-mesh sieve and discard the solids. Transfer the mushroom sauce to another saucepan; keep warm until ready to serve. *Makes 2 cups.*

To make the stew, adjust the oven heat to 350 degrees F. Spray or grease an 8-inch pan with vegetable oil; set aside.

Place the potatoes into a pot and add enough water to cover. Bring to a boil and reduce the heat to medium; simmer for 20 minutes, or until the potatoes are fork-tender. When the potatoes are done, drain them immediately; while they are still steaming hot, mash by hand or with an electric mixer. (Do not overmix or they will become gluey.) Stir in the soy milk and nutmeg; fluff with a fork until light and fluffy.

Meanwhile, spray or grease a large nonstick pan and set over medium-high heat. Add the leeks, shallots and carrots; sauté, stirring, for 3 to 4 minutes, or until the vegetables begin to soften. Stir in the mushrooms, vegetable patty, thyme, bay leaf and black pepper; continue to sauté for 5 to 7 minutes, or until the vegetables are tender. Discard the bay leaf, then pour in the Wild Mushroom Sauce, balsamic vinegar and peas; simmer for 5 minutes. Transfer to the prepared baking pan. Spread the mashed potatoes on top, or if you wish, transfer the mashed potatoes into a pastry bag fitted with a star tip and pipe over the cooked vegetables. Sprinkle the bread crumbs and mozzarella, if using, on top. Bake for 20 to 25 minutes, or until the top is golden brown and the edges bubble. Serve hot. Wild Mushroom Sauce can be kept in the refrigerator, covered, for 4 to 5 days.

SHALLOT-HERB STUFFED POTATOES

MAKES 4 SERVINGS

A Golden Door favorite, these are great for family dinners—kids just love them. The rich flavor of the sautéed shallots makes these potatoes an instant hit. If you are vegan, you can substitute soy milk and rennet-free cheese for the dairy items. Be careful not to overmix the potatoes or they will become gluey rather than light and fluffy.

4 medium potatoes	1 tablespoon balsamic vinegar
1 teaspoon canola oil	1/4 cup Vegetable Broth (page 201)
2 teaspoons olive oil	1/2 cup low-fat cottage cheese
1 1/4 cups sliced shallots	1 tablespoon whole-grain mustard
2 teaspoons fresh thyme leaves	2 tablespoons grated Parmesan or Asiago cheese
1 teaspoon freshly ground black pepper	2 tablespoons chopped fresh parsley

Preheat the oven to 375 degrees F. Brush the potatoes with canola oil and place on a baking sheet. Bake the potatoes for 1 hour, or until fork-tender. Remove from the oven; set aside until they are just cool enough to handle.

Meanwhile, heat the olive oil in a nonstick pan set over medium-high heat. Add the shallots; sauté, stirring, for about 5 minutes, or until golden brown. Stir in the thyme and black pepper; cook for another 2 minutes. Deglaze the pan by adding the balsamic vinegar and broth, stirring with a wooden spoon to loosen any flavorful browned bits. Reduce the heat to medium; simmer for 2 to 3 minutes. Set aside.

When the potatoes are cool enough to handle but still warm, cut a thin layer off the top of each (holding it horizontally, as you would serve a baked potato); scoop out the flesh, leaving a 1/2-inch-thick shell.

Combine the scooped out potato, cottage cheese, mustard and caramelized shallots in a mixing bowl; mix well with a spatula. Spoon the mixture back into the potato shells, mounding it so that the potatoes are well rounded. Sprinkle with the grated cheese; return the stuffed potatoes and their tops to the oven for 15 minutes, or until the cheese is golden brown and the tops are crispy. Place a potato on each warmed plate, prop the top at a diagonal so that the stuffing can be seen, sprinkle with parsley and serve immediately.

Apple and Gruyère Sandwich on Wild Rice and Orange-Walnut Bread with Tarragon, Fennel and Blood Orange Mayonnaise

MAKES 4 SANDWICHES

If they are available, use just-picked apples for this sandwich. Otherwise, caramelize the apples by sautéing them for 5 to 10 minutes in a very hot nonstick pan sprayed with just a little vegetable oil. Toasting the bread releases the fragrance of the nuts and citrus, adding yet another layer of texture to this hearty meal. The Tarragon, Fennel and Blood Orange Mayonnaise that dresses the sandwich brings sweet aromas and delicate flavors to contrast with the yeasty bread and robust cheese. When you've gotten enough juice out of the blood orange to make the mayonnaise, you can cut the leftover orange in wedges and serve them on the side.

For the mayonnaise:
1 cup Silken Tofu Mayonnaise
    (page 206)
1/4 cup fresh blood orange juice
1 teaspoon minced fresh thyme
1 tablespoon chopped fresh tarragon
1/2 teaspoon crushed fennel seed
1 teaspoon grated orange zest

For the sandwich:
2 small Granny Smith apples, peeled
    and cored

2 tablespoons fresh lemon juice
4 slices Wild Rice and Orange-
    Walnut Bread (page 218) or other
    multigrain bread
1 cup grated Gruyere cheese
    (about 2 ounces)
1 cup sunflower, radish or bean
    sprouts
1 cup arugula leaves, washed and
    patted dry
Blood orange wedges

Combine the Silken Tofu Mayonnaise, blood orange juice, thyme, tarragon and fennel seed in a blender or small food processor fitted with a metal blade; pulse to incorporate. Transfer to a mixing bowl and stir in the orange zest. Set aside until ready to use. *Makes 1 cup.*

Slice the apples thinly and immediately toss them with lemon juice to prevent browning. Toast the Wild Rice and Orange-Walnut Bread lightly and spread each slice with 1 tablespoon of the Tarragon, Fennel and Blood Orange Mayonnaise. Top with equal portions of apple slices, Gruyere cheese, sprouts and arugula leaves. Garnish with blood orange wedges. Serve with the Vegetable, Chicken and Barley Soup (page 43), or Arugula, Grapefruit and Shaved Parmesan Salad (page 55), or the soup and salad of your choice. Tarragon, Fennel and Blood Orange Mayonnaise can be kept in the refrigerator, covered, for 4 to 5 days.

Open-Faced Tempeh Sandwich with Pickled Red Cabbage on Old-Fashioned Tecate Bread

MAKES 4 SERVINGS

Best known to vegetarians as a substitute for meat, tempeh can be a revelation to the non-vegetarian. Ground soybeans are mixed with grain, then fermented and pressed into a cake, which is often marinated before it is cooked. A fresh cake will be white with only a few black spots; do not buy it if the surface is covered with black spots.

1 (2-inch piece) gingerroot (about 2 ounces), peeled

2 tablespoons low-sodium soy sauce

2 tablespoons balsamic vinegar

$\frac{1}{4}$ cup apple juice

2 tablespoons finely chopped fresh parsley

8 ounces tempeh

Canola oil in a spray bottle, or 1 teaspoon canola oil

2 cups shredded red cabbage

$\frac{1}{4}$ cup red wine vinegar

$\frac{1}{2}$ teaspoon fructose or sugar, or to taste

$\frac{1}{4}$ cup Vegetable Broth (page 201) or water

4 slices Old-Fashioned Tecate Bread (page 217), or commercial whole-wheat bread

2 tablespoons whole-grain mustard

Shredded lettuce

Kosher dill pickles

8 slices tomato

Preheat the oven to 375 degrees F.

Using a cheese grater, grate the gingerroot coarsely. Then, working over a small bowl, squeeze the grated gingerroot with your hands to extract the juice until you have 1 tablespoon. Reserve the juice and discard the ginger pulp.

Combine the ginger juice, soy sauce, balsamic vinegar, apple juice and parsley in a mixing bowl; stir to mix well.

Place the tempeh into a glass or ceramic dish and pour the marinade on top; cover and refrigerate for 1 hour, turning once or twice.

Spray or grease a nonstick ovenproof pan with canola oil and set over medium-high heat. Remove the tempeh from the marinade and reserve the liquid. Place the tempeh into the pan and sear it for 3 to 4 minutes on each side, or until lightly browned. Add the marinade to the pan, cover and transfer to the oven; bake for 15 minutes, or until the tempeh is thoroughly cooked.

While the tempeh is baking, combine the shredded cabbage, red wine vinegar and fructose or sugar; stir well, and marinate for 15 minutes.

Remove the tempeh from the oven and let it cool slightly. Then, using a spatula, remove the tempeh from the pan, reserving the pan and its contents intact. Slice the tempeh diagonally; set aside.

Pour the broth into the tempeh pan and stir to loosen any flavorful browned bits and pan juices.

Toast the bread and spread each slice with $\frac{1}{2}$ tablespoon mustard. Spoon equal portions of pickled red cabbage onto each and top with a slice of tempeh. Spoon the pan juices over the tempeh. Garnish with lettuce, pickle and tomato; serve.

Anasazi Beans with Quinoa, Corn and Salsa Mexicana

MAKES 4 SERVINGS

This is a vegan recipe that will appeal to all categories of eaters. Most of the ingredients—Anasazi beans, corn, quinoa, hot chili peppers and tomato salsa—have been enjoyed in the Americas since well before the arrival of Columbus—and they are just as appealing and delicious today as they were then. The beans can be cooked ahead of time and stored in a plastic container with their broth, either in the freezer or the refrigerator. If you are a vegan, you can substitute soy cheese for the Asiago.

For the beans:

$^3/_4$ cup Anasazi beans, soaked for 2 hours or overnight, drained and rinsed

3 cups Vegetable Broth (page 201) or water

1 teaspoon chili-pepper flakes

1 teaspoon salt

1 bay leaf

For the quinoa:

1 tablespoon plus 2 teaspoons olive oil

1 tablespoon shallots

$^3/_4$ cup quinoa

2 teaspoons dried basil

$1^1/_2$ cups Vegetable Broth (page 201) or water

1 cup corn kernels

$^3/_4$ cup Salsa Mexicana (page 212)

$^1/_4$ cup grated Asiago cheese

4 sprigs fresh cilantro

To prepare the beans, place them in a saucepan, add the broth or water, chili-pepper flakes, salt and bay leaf and set over medium heat. Bring to a simmer, cover and simmer for about 90 minutes, or until tender. Set aside, reserving the cooking liquid. Remove the bay leaf.

Meanwhile, heat 1 tablespoon olive oil in a medium saucepan set over medium heat. Add the shallots; sauté, stirring, for 2 to 3 minutes, or until they are softened. Add the quinoa and stir in the basil and broth or water. Simmer, covered, for 20 minutes. Remove from the heat and keep warm.

Heat the remaining 2 teaspoons olive oil in a separate nonstick pan set over medium heat. Add the corn; sauté, stirring, for 4 to 5 minutes, or until softened. Add to the cooked quinoa; mix to incorporate.

To serve, spoon equal portions of the beans and their cooking liquid into 4 warmed bowls. Top with the quinoa and corn. Spoon 2 tablespoons Salsa Mexicana on the side of each bowl and sprinkle each with 1 tablespoon grated cheese. Garnish each with a cilantro sprig; serve.

THE MUSICAL FRUIT

Beans, beans, the musical fruit; the more you eat, the more you toot," or so says the old song. Beans do tend to cause gas, and that's because they contain sugars that are difficult for humans to digest. Soaking beans before cooking them is thought to lessen this quality because some of the indigestible sugars in the beans leach into the soaking water and are then discarded. There are other reasons to soak beans, as well. Soaking makes them softer and reduces cooking time. The traditional rule of thumb is to soak the beans for at least two hours or overnight, drain and discard the soaking water and cook in fresh water (or, if you wish, broth). If you are pressed for time, another method, known as the quick-soaking method, calls for boiling the beans for 2 to 3 minutes, and removing them from the heat. Cover and let soak for at least one hour, preferably 4 hours. And if you're really pressed for time, put the beans into a pot, cover them with water and kombu seaweed and simmer for 10 to 15 minutes. Rinse and cook. Finally, I always prefer dried beans, but if you like, you can use canned beans, which require no soaking at all. You will lose some of the fresh bean flavor, but you'll still have a nutritious, delicious dish.

Angel Hair Pasta with Diced Tomatoes, Edamame Beans, Basil and Virgin Olive Oil

MAKES 4 SERVINGS

I created this nutritious pasta recipe for the Golden Door's sister resort at Las Casitas in Puerto Rico. Not only is the pasta soy-based, but the topping is edamame beans—a form of soybean. I like this soy pasta because it cooks al dente and stays firm. If you can't find soy pasta, durum wheat pasta works just as well.

8 ounces soy angel-hair pasta

1 cup edamame beans

Olive oil and canola oil in a spray bottle, or 1 teaspoon olive oil

2 teaspoons minced garlic

4 vine-ripened tomatoes, seeded and finely diced

2 tablespoons extra-virgin olive oil

$\frac{1}{3}$ cup thinly sliced fresh basil

6 tablespoons grated Asiago or imported Pecorino cheese

4 fresh basil leaves for garnish

Boil a large pot of water and add the pasta, stirring it once with a fork to prevent sticking. Cook for 8 to 10 minutes, or until al dente. Transfer to a colander, drain and set aside.

Meanwhile, bring a small pot of water to a simmer over medium-high heat. Add the edamame beans; cook for 3 to 4 minutes. The beans should still be firm and a vivid green color. Drain and set aside.

Spray or grease a skillet with 1 teaspoon olive oil and set over medium heat. Add the garlic; stir for 1 to 2 minutes, or until softened. Add the tomatoes; cook for 1 minute, just to heat through. Add the cooked pasta, edamame beans and the 2 tablespoons extra-virgin olive oil; cook, tossing, for 2 to 3 minutes longer, to heat through. Stir in the basil.

Place equal portions of the hot pasta into warm bowls and sprinkle each with cheese. Garnish with a basil leaf and serve.

THAI VEGETABLE MEDLEY WITH COCONUT MILK AND CILANTRO

MAKES 4 SERVINGS

This curry dish is dedicated to Deborah Szekely, the founder of the Golden Door and my mentor and supporter, who has guided me through many years of culinary adventures. Deborah loves bold flavorful dishes, and curry is one of her favorites.

2 cups Steamed Fluffy Brown Rice (page 223)

1 tablespoon canola oil

1 teaspoon minced gingerroot

1 medium onion, cut in half and sliced

1 teaspoon kosher salt, or to taste

Neck of 1 butternut squash, cut into 1-inch cubes (about $1\frac{1}{2}$ cups)

2 medium turnips, trimmed and cut into 8 wedges each

2 medium carrots, cut into 1-inch pieces

4 medium red or fingerling potatoes, cut into 1-inch pieces

2 medium zucchini, cut into 1-inch pieces

2 plum tomatoes, seeded and diced

$2\frac{1}{2}$ cups hot Vegetable Broth (page 201), or more as needed

1 teaspoon red or yellow Thai curry paste, or more to taste

1 cup low-fat coconut milk

$1\frac{1}{2}$ tablespoons fresh lime juice

$\frac{1}{4}$ cup cilantro leaves

Cook the brown rice as directed on page 223; keep warm.

Meanwhile, heat the canola oil in a large nonstick pan set over medium-high heat. Add the ginger, onions and salt; cook 4 to 5 minutes, or until the onions begin to soften. Reduce the heat to low and, in separate sections of the saucepan, add the butternut squash, turnips, carrots, potatoes and zucchini. Scatter the tomatoes over the other vegetables; simmer gently.

In a separate saucepan set over medium heat, whisk the hot broth with the curry paste until the paste dissolves. Pour just enough of the curried broth over the vegetables to cover them; simmer over medium heat, covered, for 20 to 25 minutes, or until the vegetables are tender but not overcooked.

In a separate pan set over medium-high heat, boil the coconut milk until it reduces in volume by half. Pour over the vegetables; simmer gently for 5 minutes.

When you are ready to serve, stir in the lime juice. Spoon equal portions of cooked brown rice into warmed bowls and top with the curry. Scatter cilantro leaves on top for garnish.

LEBANESE-STYLE LENTILS AND RICE WITH SPINACH

MAKES 4 SERVINGS

Some years ago I had the pleasure of working for race car driver Andy Granatelli and his wife, Dolly. Dolly, who is of Lebanese descent, introduced me to the flavorful cuisine of her family's homeland, and this wonderful combination of lentils, rice and spinach was among the dishes she taught me. The easy-to-make dish is a meal in itself, or you can pair it with grilled fish or chicken.

$\frac{1}{2}$ cup lentils, preferably du Puy or green, rinsed and drained

$\frac{1}{2}$ cup uncooked short-grain brown rice

$3\frac{1}{2}$ cups Vegetable Broth (page 201)

1 bay leaf

1 teaspoon salt

1 tablespoon olive oil

1 medium onion, finely diced

$\frac{1}{8}$ teaspoon ground allspice

6 cups spinach leaves, trimmed, washed and patted dry but still damp, or 1 (10-ounce) package frozen spinach, thawed and drained

$\frac{1}{4}$ cup plain low-fat yogurt

Combine the lentils, rice, broth, bay leaf and salt in a medium-size pot set over medium heat; bring to a simmer. Cook, partially covered, for 40 to 45 minutes, or until all the liquid has been absorbed and the lentils and rice are tender. Discard the bay leaf.

Meanwhile, heat the olive oil in a nonstick pan set over medium-high heat. Add the onions; sauté, stirring, for 5 to 8 minutes, or until golden brown. Spoon the onions into the lentils and rice; stir to blend. Stir in the allspice. Remove from the heat, cover and keep warm.

Once you have finished the onions, place the spinach into the same pan and set it over medium-high heat. Cook, stirring, for about 2 to 3 minutes, or until the spinach is wilted. The spinach should be bright green and slightly moist. Drain off any excess liquid.

Place equal portions of lentils and brown rice into warmed bowls. Top each with sautéed spinach and a dollop of yogurt. Serve immediately.

A Hill of . . . Legumes

Legumes—the seeds of plants that have pods—are among the stars of spa cooking. They contain no cholesterol, little or no fat (depending on the variety) and are loaded with protein, cholesterol-lowering fiber and other nutrients. They're also a delicious, versatile food group that encompasses beans (usually kidney-shaped or oval), split peas (usually round) and lentils (usually shaped like flat disks). The term dry beans refers to varieties of beans other than soybeans and green beans.

With my European roots, I generally cook my beans in vegetable broth or water, and I add a bay leaf, some thyme, and an onion spiked with 4 to 5 cloves. Cook until the liquid is just absorbed and the beans are softened; don't drain the beans or their skin will dry out.

Here are some of the legumes I like to use:

Adzuki Bean: A small red bean with a slightly bitter aftertaste that is used in Asian cookery.

Anasazi Bean: Named for the Native American people who cultivated them in the American Southwest a thousand years ago, these burgundy-colored beans turn deep pink when cooked.

Black Bean (Turtle Bean): A native of the Americas, this earthy sweetish black bean soaks up the flavor of its cooking liquid and seasonings. They are often used in Mexican, Caribbean and South American cooking and are great in salads, chili, dips, soups and stews.

Cannellini Bean: A large white bean used in many Italian dishes. It has a sweet, earthy flavor and a creamy texture that is lovely in soups, casseroles or salads.

Chickpea (Garbanzo Bean): A Mediterranean bean with a rich nutty quality. Middle Eastern cooks use it in a variety of dishes—most famously in the garlicky dip, hummus, and ground as falafel.

Flageolet: Immature kidney beans, flageolets are white or pale green in color, with a delicate flavor. They are favored for the French cassoulet, and do nicely in salads.

Lentils: These flat oval-shaped legumes come in a variety of colors. They make great soups and salads, side dishes and meatless main courses. In India, they are a staple protein source known as _dal_. They do not require soaking.

Pinto Bean: Uncooked, pinto beans are mottled beige; when cooked they turn brown. Their earthy flavor and powdery texture are ideal for Mexican and Tex-Mex dishes.

Split Pea: Split peas are dried peas that have been steamed to loosen their skins, then peeled and split. Because they have been prepared this way, they don't require soaking. Green or yellow, they make a wonderful soup, sauce or side dish.

Many first-time visitors to the Golden Door arrive believing that by forgoing dessert they will be healthier. But most health regimens fail because of this kind of deprivation. One of the principles we strive to teach our guests is that only with an increasingly robust enjoyment of life can one keep going. And dessert only makes life more enjoyable!

What's more, everyone will always want it. But because most desserts traditionally rely heavily on rich ingredients, they are the first things banished from a healthy eating regime. I have a few simple techniques and creative substitutions for high-fat ingredients so that you can eat dessert with pleasure and without guilt. In this chapter, you'll learn how to replace high-fat ingredients with high-flavor, low-fat, puréed fruits; how to use whole grains to give

DESSERTS

baked goods toothsome texture and how to make silky chocolate frosting using creamy tofu.

Of course, there's nothing more wonderful to round out a meal than a piece of fresh seasonal fruit eaten out of hand. Fruit provides great inspiration, too, for the simple cobblers, crisps and *clafoutis* I love to serve at the Door and in my own home. For something different, try the Fruited Couscous with Mint. What could be more healthful and delicious than tiny morsels of this North African pasta tossed with fruit and seasoned with fragrant mint? Among my favorite desserts, and a Golden Door specialty, is the Blueberry Crisp. Whatever you choose, this chapter gives you plenty of reasons to serve desserts with a flourish. Eat them with joy.

ROSEMARY-INFUSED CHOCOLATE FUDGE CAKE WITH CHOCOLATE-TOFU FROSTING

MAKES 1 (6-INCH) ROUND CAKE

Coffee infused with fresh rosemary and cocoa give this luscious fudge cake its distinctive character. A mashed banana keeps the cake moist without adding more fat. The cake will serve 6 people.

For the cake:

Vegetable oil in a spray bottle, or 1 teaspoon vegetable oil

4 sprigs fresh rosemary

$\frac{1}{2}$ cup hot, strong, freshly brewed coffee

1 teaspoon pure vanilla extract

1 teaspoon Kahlua or coffee brandy, optional

1 large ripe banana

$\frac{1}{2}$ cup packed brown sugar

1 cup unbleached flour, sifted

$\frac{3}{4}$ cup cocoa powder, sifted

1 teaspoon baking powder

$\frac{1}{2}$ teaspoon baking soda

$\frac{1}{4}$ teaspoon ground cinnamon

4 egg whites, at room temperature

$\frac{1}{4}$ teaspoon kosher salt

For the frosting:

$\frac{1}{2}$ cup firm silken tofu, drained

2 tablespoons pure maple syrup

2 tablespoons cocoa powder, sifted

2 tablespoons commercial chocolate-flavored soy milk

Preheat the oven to 375 degrees F. Spray or grease a 6-inch round baking pan with vegetable oil; set aside.

Steep the rosemary sprigs in the hot coffee for 15 minutes. Remove the sprigs, set aside and let cool.

Pour the cooled rosemary-infused coffee, vanilla extract and Kahlua or coffee brandy, if using, into a blender or food processor fitted with a metal blade. Add the banana; process until smooth. Transfer to a mixing bowl and stir in the brown sugar.

In another large mixing bowl, combine the flour, cocoa powder, baking powder, baking soda and cinnamon. Stir in the mixture of coffee, banana and brown sugar; mix well.

Using an eggbeater or electric mixer fitted with a whip, beat the egg whites and salt at high speed until they form soft peaks. Gently fold the whipped egg whites into the batter until they are fully incorporated. Pour into the prepared pan; bake for 30 to 35 minutes, or until a toothpick inserted into the center of the cake comes out clean. Remove from the oven, turn out onto a rack and let cool for about 20 minutes.

Meanwhile, make the frosting by combining the tofu, maple syrup, cocoa powder and soy milk in a wide-based blender or a food processor fitted with a metal blade; process until smooth, then transfer to a bowl.

When the cake has cooled completely, use a spatula to frost the top and sides of the cake.

FLOWERS YOU CAN EAT

Edible flowers are among the most beautiful garnishes of all. Their brilliant colors light up whatever they're served with. I like to use edible flowers in salads and salsas—they're often an extension of the other ingredients (arugula flowers in arugula salad, for example). I also like to use them on desserts. I can't think of anything more exquisite than candied rose petals on a smoothly frosted cake. Just be sure to use flowers that have not been sprayed with pesticides or other chemicals; you can often find edible blooms in the farmers market or the produce section of a gourmet store. Once you get the flowers home, place them into a bowl of cold water and wash gently. Remove from the water and gently shake off the excess water just before serving. Here are some that I like to use:

Arugula: Besides its peppery green leaves, the arugula also produces tiny pastel yellow and white flowers. Serve them in soup, salad or salsa.

Borage: A tiny violet-colored edible flower that blooms in the spring, borage adds a distinctive peppery taste to salads and it's a beauty of a garnish for cakes. I also like to steep it in herbal tea.

Calendula: Bright orange and yellow, calendula flowers look like marigolds. They're mildly sweet.

Day Lily: Orange, yellow and burgundy day lily petals are crunchy and taste a little like lettuce.

Geranium: Scented geranium flowers and leaves add an exotic perfume to salads, soups and cakes. Try steeping two dozen leaves in one cup of boiling water and let the water stand for 1 to 2 hours. Strain and use the scented water for cakes or for cooking jasmine rice.

Lavender: These tiny fragrant purple blooms are often used for sachets and dried arrangements; in the Mediterranean countries and, increasingly, on the other side of the Atlantic, they have many culinary applications as well—in cakes, sauces, marinades, sorbets, beverages and as a garnish. Use the fresh or dried form.

Nasturtium: Tangy and peppery, brilliant in color, these flowers can be added to salads or soups.

Rose Petals: They come in a rainbow of colors, and their soft, velvety texture and sweet fragrance make for a luxurious garnish. You can also use rose petals in cakes and scented water.

Violet: These tiny bright purple flowers are perfect for garnishing fresh fruit, cookies or cakes. They can easily be candied: just rinse the flowers, shake them to dry a bit and while they are still damp, sprinkle with casting sugar (a very fine sugar). Let dry in a dry, warm spot.

LEMON POLENTA CAKE WITH MACERATED STRAWBERRIES

MAKES 1 (8-INCH) ROUND CAKE

Fine polenta, otherwise known as cornmeal, adds a rich texture and pale yellow color to this dense, moist cake. (Avoid the coarse-grained polenta.) The cake is delicious on its own, and when topped with strawberries that have been macerated (the term for marinating fruit) in Grand Marnier, it won't get soggy—and the flavor combination is sublime. It will keep, covered, for 2 to 3 days. With a hot cup of coffee or tea, it's the perfect afternoon treat.

For the cake:

Canola oil in a spray bottle, or 1 teaspoon canola oil

1 cup unbleached flour, sifted

$^1/_3$ cup cornmeal

1 teaspoon baking powder

1 tablespoon lemon zest

4 eggs, at room temperature, separated

1 teaspoon pure vanilla extract

$^3/_4$ cup low-fat buttermilk, at room temperature

$^1/_2$ cup sugar

$^1/_2$ teaspoon kosher salt

2 tablespoons canola oil

For the topping:

$1^1/_2$ cups strawberries, stems removed and quartered

2 tablespoons Grand Marnier or orange-flavored liqueur

6 sprigs fresh mint

Confectioners' sugar for dusting

Preheat the oven to 350 degrees F. Spray or grease an 8-inch round baking pan with canola oil; set aside.

Combine the flour, cornmeal, baking powder and lemon zest in a mixing bowl; mix until completely blended. Set aside.

Prepare a shallow pan of hot—but not boiling—water. Combine the egg yolks, vanilla, buttermilk and $^1/_4$ cup of sugar in a mixing bowl, and place the bowl into the pan of hot water; use an electric hand mixer to mix for 3 to 4 minutes, or until the mixture is light, creamy and pale yellow in color, and the beaters make "ribbons" in the batter.

Using an eggbeater or an electric mixer fitted with a whip, beat the egg whites and salt at medium-high speed until soft peaks form. Gradually add the remaining $\frac{1}{4}$ cup sugar; beat for 2 more minutes. Using a rubber spatula, gently fold the egg whites into the yolk mixture. Then gradually fold the flour-cornmeal mixture into the eggs, $\frac{1}{2}$ cup at a time. Gradually add the canola oil, blending until it is just incorporated.

Pour the cake batter into the prepared pan; bake for 30 to 35 minutes, or until the cake is a light golden brown color and a toothpick inserted into the center of the cake comes out clean. Remove from the oven, turn out onto a rack and let cool for about 20 minutes.

Meanwhile, while the cake is baking, place the strawberries into a separate bowl and pour the Grand Marnier over them; toss gently to coat. Cover and macerate for at least 30 minutes, or until you are ready to serve.

Just before serving, garnish the cake with the strawberries and mint sprigs and dust it lightly with confectioners' sugar.

THE VERY BEST DESSERT

There is no better dessert than fresh fruit—a ripe pear, a sweet summer melon, fresh berries bursting with flavor, sweet-tart kiwifruit full of vitamin C and potassium. I've cooked in many private homes and I can't tell you how many times I've seen a bowl of fruit in the kitchen, artfully arranged and hardly touched. To encourage young folks (and older folks) to eat more fruit, I'll cut it up, douse it with a little orange juice to keep it from turning brown, chill it for an hour or so and serve it for dessert. Somehow, when fruit is already cut up, we tend to eat more of it. Now, most of us crave something rich and chocolatey once in a while, and it's perfectly fine to satisfy that craving—my baking staff and I work long hours to create delicious and healthful confections to do just that. But when all is said and done, there's nothing quite like a perfect piece of fresh fruit, Mother Nature's gift to us all.

YAM-ORANGE PIE WITH BRAN CRUST

MAKES 1 (8-INCH) PIE

I prefer yam to pumpkin for my fall holiday pies. Yams have a lower water content and a creamy texture, are naturally sweet—and their rich orange color echoes the colors of the season. Here, orange juice binds the crust; notice that there are no egg yolks or heavy cream in the filling—its creaminess is achieved with the yams and bananas, while its feather-light texture owes to the egg whites that are gently folded into the spiced yams.

For the filling:

Vegetable oil in a spray bottle, or
   1 teaspoon vegetable oil

$1\frac{1}{2}$ pounds yams, scrubbed

3 tablespoons frozen orange juice
   concentrate

1 banana

$\frac{1}{2}$ cup low-fat ricotta cheese

$\frac{1}{4}$ cup packed brown sugar, optional

1 teaspoon ground cinnamon

$\frac{1}{4}$ teaspoon grated nutmeg

3 egg whites at room temperature

Pinch of salt

For the crust:

Vegetable oil in a spray bottle, or
   2 teaspoons vegetable oil

$1\frac{1}{4}$ cups All-Bran or 100 percent bran
   cereal

3 tablespoons frozen orange juice concentrate

Preheat the oven to 350 degrees F. Spray or grease an 8-inch pie tin with 1 teaspoon vegetable oil and set aside. Spray or brush the yams with 1 teaspoon vegetable oil and place on a baking sheet; bake for 45 minutes, or until they are fork-tender. Remove from the oven and let cool.

Meanwhile, to make the crust, pour the bran cereal into a blender or food processor fitted with a metal blade; pulse until the bran is crushed to coarse crumbs. Transfer to a bowl and add 3 tablespoons of orange juice concentrate; mix until incorporated. Press the mixture into the prepared pie tin and spray or brush with 1 teaspoon vegetable oil. Bake for 10 to 12 minutes, or until the crust sets. Remove from the oven and let cool.

When the yams are cool enough to handle, peel them. Measure $1\frac{1}{2}$ cups cooked yam and transfer to a blender or food processor fitted with a metal blade. Add 3 tablespoons orange juice concentrate, the banana, ricotta cheese, brown sugar, if using, cinnamon and nutmeg; process until smooth; then transfer to a mixing bowl.

Using an eggbeater or electric mixer, beat the egg whites and salt at high speed until soft peaks form. Gently fold into the yam-banana mixture until just incorporated. Spoon the yam filling into the piecrust and smooth the top with a spatula; bake for 45 minutes, or until the pie is lightly browned on top. Remove from the oven and let the pie cool before serving.

BLUEBERRY CRISP

This dessert could not be easier. It will be one that you want to make over and over again, using fresh seasonal fruit. I like to make it with fresh blueberries, but once, when I was running low on them, I tried it with equal parts of raspberries, blackberries and sliced straw-berries, and it worked just as well. You can make the crisps in individual ramekins or one big quiche pan. If you are only serving four, mix up the full amount of topping ingredients called for below; bake up half tonight and save the rest, covered in an airtight container, for another night. It will keep for 2 to 3 days.

Canola oil in spray bottle, or
    1 teaspoon canola oil
3 cups blueberries
2 teaspoons minced orange zest
2 teaspoons pure vanilla extract
$^1/_3$ cup whole-wheat flour, sifted

$^1/_3$ cup rolled oats
$^1/_4$ cup firmly packed brown sugar
2 tablespoons canola oil
1 tablespoon honey
2 teaspoons ground cinnamon
$^1/_8$ teaspoon grated nutmeg

Preheat the oven to 350 degrees F. Spray or grease 8 ($4^1/_2$-ounce) ramekins or 1 (9-inch) quiche dish or other baking dish with canola oil. Combine the blueberries, orange zest and vanilla in a mixing bowl; toss gently. If you are using ramekins, divide the blueberry mixture between them. If you are using a single baking dish, pour the mixture into it and smooth into an even layer.

Combine the whole-wheat flour, rolled oats, brown sugar, canola oil, honey, cinnamon and nutmeg in a medium-size bowl. Using your hands, mix the ingredients until they are incor-porated and uniformly crumbly. Scatter the mixture over the blueberries in an even layer; bake for 35 to 40 minutes, or until golden brown. Serve warm.

Summer Fruit Tart

MAKES 1 (4½ x 16-INCH) TART

The dough for this tart is a yeast-based dough that is rolled very thinly, creating a crisp crust on which any fresh fruit can be arranged. If you wish, make extra dough and freeze it, double-wrapped, for up to 1 week; or bake your extra dough as sweet rolls or bread.

For the crust:

Canola oil in a spray bottle, or
  2 teaspoons canola oil

1 tablespoon active dry yeast
  (1 envelope)

1 tablespoon sugar or honey

¾ cup lukewarm water

1 tablespoon canola oil

1¼ to 1½ cups semolina flour plus
  ¼ cup for dusting

⅓ cup sifted whole-wheat flour

½ teaspoon kosher salt

For the filling:

1 pint blueberries

2 Golden Delicious apples

2 teaspoons fresh lemon juice

5 apricots, pitted and thinly sliced

3 tablespoons sugar

1 teaspoon cinnamon

¼ cup apricot preserves

1 tablespoon apple juice or water

Preheat the oven to 375 degrees F. Line a large baking sheet with parchment paper, spray or brush with 1 teaspoon canola oil, and sprinkle it with a little semolina flour. Spray or grease a large mixing bowl with 1 teaspoon canola oil.

In the bowl of an electric mixer fitted with a dough hook, dissolve the yeast and sugar or honey in the lukewarm water.

Combine 1¼ cups semolina flour and the whole-wheat flour in a bowl; mix in the salt.

While the mixer is running at slow speed, pour in 1 tablespoon canola oil and add the flour mixture, 1 cup at a time; mix until the dough pulls away from the sides of the bowl. If the dough is too sticky, add the extra ¼ cup of flour. Continue mixing until the dough is smooth and elastic. Place it into the prepared mixing bowl, cover with a damp towel and place the bowl into a warm, draft-free spot. Let it rise for 15 to 20 minutes, or until it doubles in volume.

Place the dough on a floured work surface, sprinkle with the semolina flour, and knead well for 1 or 2 minutes; alternate pressing with the heel of your hand and folding the dough over. With a floured rolling pin, roll the dough into a rectangle about $4\frac{1}{2}$ x 16 inches in size and $\frac{3}{8}$ inch high. Transfer the dough to the prepared baking sheet; crimp the edges between your thumb and index finger to form a scalloped crust. With a fork, pierce the bottom of the dough several times to prevent it from rising unevenly. Set aside and let rise for 10 minutes.

When you are ready to bake, carefully arrange the blueberries in a long thin row extending lengthwise down the center of the crust, massing the berries so that there is no dough showing through the fruit.

Peel and core the apples and drizzle with lemon juice. Cut them in half lengthwise, then slice each half crosswise into thin crescent-shaped slices. Place the slices on the dough next to the blueberries, overlapping them so that no dough is exposed.

Arrange the apricot slices in a row on the other side of the berries, side by side, as tightly as possible, so that no dough is exposed. Sprinkle the fruit with the sugar and cinnamon. Bake for 30 minutes, or until the dough is light brown and crisp.

Meanwhile, combine the apricot preserves and apple juice in a small saucepan set over medium heat. Bring the mixture to a simmer, stirring constantly. Remove from the heat and strain through a fine-mesh sieve. Remove the tart from the oven, brush with the strained apricot glaze, and let cool. If the tart is completely cooled when you are ready to serve, reheat it in the oven at 350 degrees F for 5 to 7 minutes before serving.

APPLE-CRANBERRY CLAFOUTIS

MAKES 8 SERVINGS

I love warm desserts. Heat seems to enhance whatever flavors and textures you are working with so that every bite is a treat for the taste buds. Serve this variation on the classic French clafoutis hot out of the oven and enjoy any leftovers the next day. You'll feel virtuous when you see my spa version of the topping (which resembles a slightly thickened crepe); the original is made with three times the amount of eggs.

Vegetable oil in a spray bottle, or
    1 teaspoon vegetable oil
2 Granny Smith apples
2 teaspoons fresh lemon juice
1 tablespoon canola oil
1/4 cup dehydrated cranberries
1/4 cup packed brown sugar
1 tablespoon Grand Marnier or orange
    liqueur, optional
1/2 teaspoon ground cinnamon

2 eggs
1 egg white
1/2 cup 1 percent low-fat milk
1/4 cup unbleached flour
1 teaspoon baking powder
2 tablespoons cornmeal
1/8 teaspoon grated nutmeg
8 fresh mint sprigs for garnish,
    optional

Preheat the oven to 375 degrees F. Spray or grease a 6-inch round, nonstick baking dish with vegetable oil and set aside.

Peel and core the apples, slice them thinly and drizzle with the lemon juice. Heat the canola oil in a nonstick pan set over medium-high heat. Add the apples and cranberries; sauté, stirring, for 3 to 5 minutes, or until the fruit is softened. Stir in the brown sugar, Grand Marnier or orange liqueur, if using, and cinnamon; cook, stirring, for another 3 to 5 minutes, or until the apples begin to caramelize. Transfer the apple mixture to the prepared baking dish and let cool.

Combine the eggs, egg white and milk in a blender; process until smooth. (Or, place the eggs, egg white and milk into a mixing bowl; using a whisk, beat until smooth.) Transfer to a mixing bowl and whisk in the flour, baking powder, cornmeal and nutmeg. Pour the batter over the apples and cranberries; bake for 40 to 45 minutes, or until the crust is golden brown. Let cool just slightly. Garnish with fresh mint sprigs just before serving.

Apricot Yogurt Parfait

Yogurt cheese, sweetened with a little confectioners' sugar, makes a delicious velvety dessert. I flavor it with stewed dried apricots, but prunes or frozen peaches can be used in the same way. Yogurt cheese is also an excellent fat-free alternative to crème fraiche or cream cheese. It can be flavored with your favorite herbs and spices.

1 quart plain nonfat yogurt	$^3/_4$ cup diced pineapple
3 tablespoons confectioners' sugar, sifted	2 kiwifruit, peeled and finely diced
$^1/_4$ teaspoon pure vanilla extract	1 small mango, peeled, pitted and diced
$^1/_2$ cup dried apricots	1 cup blueberries
$^1/_2$ cup apple juice	Fresh mint sprigs for garnish, optional

Line a sieve or colander with 2 layers of cheesecloth and place it into a slightly larger pot. Combine the yogurt, confectioners' sugar and vanilla in a mixing bowl; mix well. Transfer the mixture to the prepared sieve or colander. Cover and transfer the sieve or colander in its pot to the refrigerator and chill for 3 to 4 hours. The yogurt will drain quite a bit of liquid, so it's important to keep your sieve or colander in the pot.

Combine the dried apricots and apple juice in a small saucepan set over medium heat. Bring to a simmer, cover and simmer for 15 minutes, or until softened. Transfer to a blender or food processor fitted with a metal blade; process until smooth. With a rubber spatula, scrape the apricot purée into a large mixing bowl and let cool. Pour the drained yogurt into the apricot purée; mix well.

Gently toss the pineapple and kiwi in a small mixing bowl. Gently toss the mango and blueberries in another small bowl.

To assemble the dessert, spoon about 4 tablespoons of the apricot yogurt cheese into a parfait dish or shallow champagne glass. Top with about 4 tablespoons of the pineapple-kiwi mixture, then 2 tablespoons of yogurt and 4 tablespoons of the mango-blueberry mixture. Top with a final dollop of apricot yogurt. Repeat the process to assemble 5 more parfaits. Garnish with fresh mint sprigs if desired.

CHOCOLATE-MOCHA FLAN

MAKES 10 SERVINGS

Cinnamon and chocolate are an authentic Mexican combination, one that gives this custardy dessert its rich flavor. A few simple ingredients are combined here to make the ultimate comfort-food dessert, which I learned while working at the Golden Door's sister spa, Rancho La Puerta, in Mexico. The flan can be made ahead of time. I like to serve it at room temperature to better appreciate the delicate flavors. Of course, it can be covered and refrigerated if any is left over.

1 $\frac{1}{2}$ ounces finely chopped bittersweet chocolate

2 $\frac{1}{2}$ cups 1 percent low-fat milk

5 tablespoons pure maple syrup

1 $\frac{1}{2}$ teaspoons ground cinnamon

2 teaspoons instant coffee or espresso granules

2 eggs

3 egg whites

2 teaspoons Kahlua or coffee brandy

Confectioners' sugar for garnish

Fresh mint sprigs for garnish

Preheat the oven to 350 degrees F.

Combine the chocolate, milk and maple syrup in a saucepan set over medium-low heat. Bring to a simmer, stirring constantly, until the chocolate has melted. Be careful not to boil the milk or it may scorch, giving the flan a burned bitter flavor. Remove from the heat and stir in the cinnamon and instant coffee. Set aside and let cool slightly.

Whisk the eggs, egg whites and Kahlua or coffee brandy in a mixing bowl. Slowly pour the warm milk mixture into the egg mixture in a thin stream, whisking constantly so the eggs do not scramble. Strain through a fine-mesh sieve to remove any milk solids and any remaining foam. (This is also the way to save the dish if the egg starts to scramble.)

Pour equal amounts of flan batter into 10 ramekins and place them into a large, deep pan. Fill the pan with enough water to come one-third of the way up the sides of the ramekins. Be careful not to get any water into the ramekins. Bake for 45 minutes to 1 hour, or until the flan is firm. Remove from the oven and let cool to room temperature. Garnish with confectioners' sugar and mint sprigs.

Golden Door Chocolate Chip Cookies

MAKES 24 COOKIES

Yes, we do make and eat chocolate chip cookies at the Golden Door. There is no such thing as forbidden food here—instead, we stress moderate portions and reinterpretation of traditionally high-fat foods. Using fruit purées (prune for these cookies) in place of butter and cream is an easy nutritious way to maintain texture and flavor and cut the fat. Leftover prune purée can be used for other baked goods; store it covered in the refrigerator for 4 to 5 days. Or, to save time, use packaged prune purée or baby-food prune purée.

For the prune purée:
1 ½ cups pitted prunes
2 cups water

For the cookies:
Vegetable oil in a spray bottle, or
    2 teaspoons vegetable oil
1 cup rolled oats
1 cup sifted unbleached flour

1 teaspoon baking soda
½ teaspoon kosher salt
½ cup packed brown sugar
2 eggs
2 egg whites
3 tablespoons canola oil
2 teaspoons pure vanilla extract
¼ cup buttermilk
¼ cup semisweet chocolate chips

Combine the prunes and water in a small pot set over medium heat and bring to a simmer. Simmer for 40 minutes, or until the prunes are very soft. Drain, then transfer to a blender or food processor fitted with a metal blade; process until smooth. Strain the prune purée through a fine-mesh sieve and set aside to cool. *Makes 1 ¼ cups.*

Preheat the oven to 375 degrees F. Line two baking sheets with parchment paper or waxed paper and spray or brush with 1 teaspoon vegetable oil each.

Place the oats into a dry skillet set over medium heat; toast, shaking the pan lightly, for 3 to 4 minutes, or until lightly browned. Combine the toasted oats, flour, baking soda and salt in a large mixing bowl; mix well.

In the bowl of an electric mixer fitted with a whip, beat the brown sugar, eggs and egg whites at high speed, until the eggs are frothy and double in volume. Add the canola oil, vanilla, buttermilk and ⅔ cup of the prune purée; mix well. With the mixer on low speed, gradually add the flour mixture, and blend well. Using a rubber spatula, stir in the chocolate chips. Spoon heaping tablespoons of dough about 1 inch apart on the prepared baking sheets; bake for 15 minutes, or until the cookies are golden brown. Serve immediately or store in an airtight container for up to 1 week.

ALMOND LACE COOKIES

MAKES 36 COOKIES

These attractive cookies are crisp, light and slightly buttery. Make a batch and keep them in your cookie jar. They're also the basis of a luscious "sandwich" with Mango-Banana-Orange Sorbet (see page 182).

$\frac{1}{2}$ cup chopped almonds

1 cup whole-wheat flour

$\frac{1}{2}$ cup quick-cooking oats

$\frac{1}{2}$ cup corn syrup or pure maple syrup

$\frac{1}{2}$ cup firmly packed dark-brown sugar

$\frac{1}{4}$ cup unsalted butter, softened

$\frac{1}{4}$ cup canola oil

1 teaspoon pure vanilla extract

Preheat oven to 375 degrees F. Line two baking sheets with parchment paper and set aside.

Toast the almonds in a hot, dry skillet set over medium-high heat, stirring once or twice, for 3 to 4 minutes, until they are golden brown. Remove from the heat and set aside to cool.

Combine the flour, oats and toasted almonds in a small bowl and set aside. Combine the corn syrup or maple syrup, brown sugar, butter and oil in a nonstick saucepan set over medium heat. Cook, stirring, until the mixture comes to a boil. Remove from the heat. Stir in the vanilla. Add the flour mixture and blend thoroughly.

Drop by tablespoons onto the prepared baking sheets, leaving at least 2 inches between cookies. Bake for 8 to 9 minutes, or until golden brown. Remove from oven and cool completely. Peel carefully from the parchment paper. Serve immediately or store in an airtight container.

SPA TRUFFLES WITH CRANBERRIES, WALNUTS AND CHOCOLATE CHIPS

MAKES 20 TRUFFLES

There's a little bit of everything delicious in these "truffles." Smooth cream cheese sweetened with confectioners' sugar is studded with fragrant toasted walnuts, tart dried cranberries and chocolate chips. Make these for holiday giving and eating—but don't try to make them in advance; when covered, they keep only for a day in the refrigerator.

2 tablespoons chopped walnuts

8 ounces low-fat cream cheese

$\frac{1}{4}$ cup confectioners' sugar, sifted

$\frac{1}{4}$ cup dehydrated cranberries

2 teaspoons minced orange zest

$\frac{1}{4}$ cup bittersweet chocolate chips

$\frac{1}{4}$ cup sifted unsweetened cocoa powder

Toast the walnuts in a hot, dry skillet set over medium-high heat for 3 to 4 minutes, stirring once or twice, until they are light brown in color. Remove from the heat and set aside to cool.

Combine the cream cheese and confectioners' sugar in a small mixing bowl; mix well with a spatula until the cheese has softened. Add the dried cranberries, orange zest, toasted walnuts and chocolate chips; stir gently until incorporated. Refrigerate for 1 hour.

Take about 1 tablespoon of the mixture in your hand and roll it into a ball. Repeat the process to make a total of 20 balls. Roll the balls in the cocoa powder to coat lightly. Place the truffles on a plate and refrigerate for 30 minutes.

WHEN A COOKIE ISN'T JUST A COOKIE

At the Golden Door, we take our cookies seriously. After all, if you're going to indulge in a cookie, it might as well be a great one. In fact, we like ours so much, we serve them as a formal dessert—and we think that this is a great idea for home entertaining: a do-ahead dessert that keeps beautifully and always gets raves. The key to elevating the humble cookie to a fancy dessert is in the presentation. Slice a strawberry and fan the slices around the cookie. Cut a blood orange into wedges (removing all the unattractive pith and the membrane around the wedges) and use them as a garnish. Slice up a starfruit. When pomegranates are in season, scatter the red seeds around the plate. Dust the edges of the plate with cocoa powder or cinnamon. You'll have the most glamorous cookie on the block.

CINNAMON-SUGAR NACHOS WITH PINEAPPLE-CRANBERRY SALSA AND MANGO-LIME COULIS

MAKES 6 SERVINGS

This is the Golden Door version of that old-fashioned comfort food, cinnamon toast. These crunchy sweet tortilla chips are an unusual yet very popular dessert among our guests. Serve them family style with a bowl of Pineapple-Cranberry Salsa for dipping and a drizzle of Mango-Lime Coulis. You'll find the salsa to be quite a chameleon; it changes with every bite.

For the salsa:

1 $^3/_4$ to 2 cups finely diced fresh pineapple or canned crushed pineapple, drained

$^1/_4$ cup dried cranberries

2 tablespoons thinly sliced fresh mint leaves

For the coulis:

1 ripe mango, peeled, pitted and diced

3 tablespoons fresh orange juice

2 tablespoons fresh lime juice

For the nachos:

Vegetable oil in a spray bottle, or 1 teaspoon vegetable oil

2 teaspoons ground cinnamon

$^1/_4$ cup granulated sugar

2 (7-inch) nonfat whole-wheat tortillas

2 egg whites, lightly beaten with 1 tablespoon water

Fresh mint sprigs for garnish

To make the salsa, combine the pineapple, cranberries and mint in a small mixing bowl; mix well, cover and refrigerate until ready to use. *Makes 2 cups.*

To prepare the coulis, combine the mango chunks, orange juice and lime juice in a blender; process until smooth. Refrigerate until ready to serve. *Makes 1 cup.*

Preheat the oven to 350 degrees F. Line a baking sheet with parchment or waxed paper, spray with vegetable oil and set aside.

Combine the cinnamon and sugar in a small cup; mix well and set aside. Brush the tortillas with the beaten egg white and cut each tortilla into 12 wedges. Dredge the tortilla chips in the cinnamon-sugar and place them onto the prepared baking sheet in a single layer. Bake for 10 minutes, or until golden brown and crisp. Remove from the oven and let cool.

Spoon equal portions of the salsa into 4 ramekins and place each ramekin on a dessert plate. Arrange the cinnamon-sugar chips around each ramekin and drizzle the mango coulis around the chips. Garnish with mint sprigs and serve. Pineapple-Cranberry Salsa can be kept for 2 days and Mango-Lime Coulis for 2 to 3 days, covered, in the refrigerator.

GREEN APPLE AND MOROCCAN MINT TEA SORBET

MAKES 8 SERVINGS

For strong mint flavor, I like to use Moroccan mint tea here; regular mint tea will give this tart sorbet a more mellow mint flavor. Once this sorbet is made, you can return it to the freezer for about 1 hour. Any longer and it will become too hard.

2 tea bags Moroccan mint tea or
    other mint tea
1 cup boiling water
3 Granny Smith apples, peeled, cored
    and sliced
1 tablespoon fresh lemon juice

$1/4$ cup minced fresh mint leaves
Fresh mint sprigs for garnish
Fresh strawberries or raspberries
    for garnish
Citrus-Almond Tuiles (page 222)
    for garnish, optional

Steep the tea bags in the hot water to brew a strong tea. Refrigerate until cool.

Toss the apples in the lemon juice to prevent browning and arrange them in an even layer in a glass or ceramic dish. Pour the cooled mint tea over it. Cover and freeze for 3 to 4 hours, or until the fruit is frozen solid.

Thaw the fruit for 10 to 15 minutes. Break the apples into small pieces, transfer to a wide-based blender or food processor fitted with a metal blade, and add the minced mint; pulse until it is evenly incorporated.

Serve immediately in chilled dessert cups or return to the freezer, covered, for up to 1 hour. Garnish with mint sprigs, fresh berries and Citrus-Almond Tuiles, if desired.

VOILÀ, SORBET

When the weather is hot, sorbet is the dessert of choice. And once you taste homemade sorbet, you'll never go back to store-bought. Lighter than ice cream and dairy free, it's ideal for those on restricted diets. And the flavor combinations are endless: peach-apricot sorbet with banana, raspberries with banana, watermelon with cranberry, beet with cranberry—use your imagination. The basic method for making sorbet couldn't be simpler: freeze the fruit. A little while before serving, let it thaw and then give it a spin in the food processor for 3 to 4 minutes—just until creamy.

Mango-Banana-Orange Sorbet

MAKES 8 SERVINGS

The key to a great sorbet is juicy, ripe fruit. If mangoes aren't available, use peaches, apricots or nectarines. The one constant should be the banana, which adds smoothness and creaminess to this flavorful sorbet. Don't leave it in the freezer for more than 1 hour or it will become solid again and require another spin in the food processor.

1 medium ripe mango, peeled and diced

2 large ripe bananas, peeled and thinly sliced

$\frac{1}{2}$ cup fresh orange juice

$\frac{1}{4}$ cup fresh lime juice

Citrus-Almond Tuiles (page 222), optional

Combine the mango, banana, orange juice and lime juice in a glass or ceramic pan. Spread the fruit evenly over the bottom of the dish; cover and freeze for 3 to 4 hours, or until the fruit is frozen solid.

Remove from the freezer and let thaw for 10 minutes. Break the fruit into small pieces, then transfer it to a wide-based blender or food processor fitted with a metal blade; process until smooth and creamy. Serve immediately in chilled dessert cups or return to the freezer, covered, for up to 1 hour. Garnish with Citrus-Almond Tuiles, if desired.

Serving Suggestion: Almond Lace Cookie Sandwich
Makes 4 servings

8 Almond Lace Cookies (page 178)
2 cups Mango-Banana-Orange Sorbet

Bake the cookies as directed on page 178. Prepare the sorbet as directed above.

To assemble the sandwich, place 1 cookie, textured side down, on a plate so that the flat smooth side will be on the inside of the sandwich. With a medium-size ice-cream scoop, place a well-rounded portion of sorbet onto the cookie. Place another cookie on top, textured side out and smooth side in, and press lightly. Repeat the process to make 3 more sandwiches. Serve immediately or freeze for up to 1 hour before serving.

FRUITED COUSCOUS WITH MINT

MAKES 6 SERVINGS

Couscous—the tiny North African pasta—is a fabulously versatile food, as is evident from this recipe. I like to use whole-wheat couscous, both for its nutritional value and its more complex texture. Here it is sweetened with orange juice, spiced, and tossed with plump currants for a warm home-style dessert.

1 ripe pineapple, trimmed and finely diced (about 1 3/4 cup)

1 Gala, Golden Delicious or Fuji apple, peeled, cored and finely diced

1 orange, peeled, pith removed and cut into segments

2 teaspoons minced candied ginger

1 tablespoon Kirsch liqueur, optional

1/4 cup dried currants

2 tablespoons apple juice

1/2 cup whole-wheat couscous

2 herbal tea bags (cinnamon-apple or cardamom spice)

1/2 cup boiling water

1 teaspoon grated orange zest

6 fresh mint sprigs for garnish, optional

With a spatula, combine the pineapple, apple, orange and candied ginger in a mixing bowl. Stir in the Kirsch, if using. Cover and refrigerate for 1 hour or more, until chilled.

Combine the currants and apple juice in a small saucepan set over medium heat and bring to a simmer. Simmer for 1 to 2 minutes; remove from the heat and let stand for 10 minutes, or until the currants are plump and juicy. Set aside until ready to use.

Place the couscous and tea bags into a small pot or bowl, pour in the boiling water, stir quickly, cover and let stand for 5 minutes. Remove the tea bags and fluff the couscous with a fork. Mix in the plumped currants with their marinade and the orange zest; stir gently to blend.

Place equal portions of the fruit mixture into 6 wineglasses or dessert cups. Spoon equal portions of the couscous over the fruit and garnish with fresh mint sprigs.

ALMOND CREPES WITH
SPICED PINEAPPLE AND KIWIFRUIT

MAKES 8 SERVINGS

Learn how to make these crepes and you will have a no-fail dessert for any occasion. These are filled with pineapple and kiwifruit, but crepes make a great base for all kinds of dessert fillings. Letting the batter rest for 20 to 30 minutes after it is mixed, which allows the flour to develop, results in a better crepe. And remember that a good nonstick pan is essential for crepe-making.

For the crepes:

$\frac{1}{4}$ cup sliced almonds

$\frac{3}{4}$ cup 1 percent low-fat milk

1 egg

$\frac{1}{2}$ teaspoon salt, optional

1 teaspoon canola oil

$\frac{1}{2}$ teaspoon almond extract

$\frac{1}{4}$ cup unbleached white flour

$\frac{1}{4}$ cup whole-wheat flour

Vegetable oil in a spray bottle, or
   1 teaspoon vegetable oil

For the filling:

16 ounces canned unsweetened
   crushed pineapple in juice

$\frac{1}{4}$ teaspoon ground allspice

1 tablespoon brown sugar

2 kiwifruit, peeled and sliced into
   8 thin slices each

2 tablespoons confectioners' sugar,
   optional

8 fresh mint sprigs, optional

Place the almonds into a food mill or food processor fitted with a metal blade; process briefly to make a coarse meal. Be careful not to overprocess or the almonds will become paste. Or, if you wish, place the almonds on a work surface, cover with a sheet of wax paper and use a rolling pin to crush them. Set aside.

Combine the milk, egg, salt (if using), canola oil, almond extract, ground almonds and flours in a blender; process until smooth. (Or whisk by hand in a bowl.) Set aside and let the batter rest for about 20 to 30 minutes.

Meanwhile, prepare the fruit filling. Combine the crushed pineapple and juice in a small saucepan set over medium heat and bring to a simmer. Stir in the allspice and brown sugar; simmer for another 8 to 10 minutes, or until lightly caramelized and syrupy. Remove from the heat and keep warm.

When you are ready to cook, spray or grease a 6-inch nonstick pan or crepe pan with vegetable oil and set it over medium-high heat. Carefully wipe any excess oil from the pan with a paper towel. Ladle about $1\frac{1}{2}$ tablespoons of batter into the pan. Lift the pan and tip it gently in all directions to spread a thin, even layer of batter over the bottom of the pan. Return the pan to the heat and let the crepe cook for about 1 minute, until one side is lightly browned. Then, gently shake the pan to loosen the crepe, and use a spatula to turn it over. Cook the other side of the crepe about 30 seconds and transfer it to a warmed plate. Repeat the process with the remaining batter for 7 more crepes, separating the stacked crepes with wax paper.

Place a crepe on a dessert plate and spoon 2 tablespoons of the warm pineapple mixture over it. Top with 2 slices of kiwifruit. Fold the crepe in half, dust with confectioners' sugar and garnish with a sprig of mint. Repeat the process with the remaining crepes; serve immediately.

CREPE EXPECTATIONS

Crepes make wonderful desserts; they welcome all kinds of fillings and they're fairly easy to make. For delicate crepes, the batter must be allowed to rest for 20 to 30 minutes between mixing and cooking, during which the flour develops. This is ideal for entertaining, as the batter can be made ahead of time and then cooked up just before serving, as the appreciative guests salivate! And don't worry if the flour develops too much and the batter becomes too thick—just add 2 to 3 tablespoons of low-fat milk. Once you start to cook, spoon the batter into the pan and tilt the pan to spread the batter evenly. The heat should be set at medium. Keep the pan on the heat source for even cooking and turn once so that both sides are a beautiful light brown. Turn the finished crepe out onto a serving plate, spoon your filling—cooked apple and raisins, pineapple, or kiwi—on top and fold over. Dust with confectioners' sugar and you have a very elegant dessert.

POACHED SECKEL PEARS WITH
STILTON CHEESE AND LEMON-SPICE SAUCE

MAKES 6 SERVINGS

Seckel pears are tasty and small—the perfect size for holding just enough Stilton to satisfy. Buy them only if they are ripe; otherwise, use Bosc or Bartlett. For Golden Door guests, I pipe the cheese mixture into the pear with a pastry bag, but at home, I spoon it into the fruit. If you can't find Stilton cheese, use another variety of bleu cheese.

6 Seckel pears

1 ½ cups pear juice or apple juice

1 tablespoon fresh lemon juice

1 clove

1 small stick cinnamon

1 teaspoon arrowroot powder dissolved in 2 tablespoons water

3 ounces grated Stilton cheese

2 ounces low-fat cream cheese

½ cup fresh raspberries

6 sprigs fresh mint

Peel the pears, starting ¼ inch from the stem, leaving the top ¼ inch unpeeled with the stem attached.

Using a small melon-baller or sharp knife, carefully core the pear from the bottom, making a small hollow area for the cheese.

Combine the pear juice or apple juice, lemon juice, clove and cinnamon stick in a deep ceramic saucepan with a cover. Place the pears, stem up, into the saucepan, set the pan over medium heat, cover and simmer for 8 to 10 minutes. Carefully remove the pears from the pan, reserving the poaching liquid, and let cool.

Strain the poaching liquid into a small saucepan and set it over medium-high heat. Cook for 20 minutes, or until the liquid reduces in volume by one-third. To thicken the sauce, stir in the dissolved arrowroot and simmer for 1 to 2 minutes. Remove from the heat and keep warm.

Combine the grated Stilton and cream cheese in a small mixing bowl; mix until the cheeses take on a creamy consistency. Spoon about 2 to 3 teaspoons of the mixture into the hollow in the bottom of each pear. (Or, if you wish, transfer the cheese mousse to a pastry bag fitted with a star tip. Pipe the cheese into the hollow in the bottom of each pear.) Place a filled pear on each dessert plate. Ladle the sauce around the pear and garnish with fresh raspberries and mint sprigs.

BUTTERNUT SQUASH AND ORANGE CRÈME

MAKES 6 SERVINGS

Here's a dessert to satisfy your cravings for something smooth, creamy and sweet. And you'll never guess you're eating tofu! I developed it in December 2001, when I was invited, along with a group of renowned chefs, to the Culinary Institute of America at Greystone to devise recipes based on soy products. This is the kind of healthful snack that I like to serve to Golden Door guests who are craving something sweet after heavy exercise. If your butternut squash has green streaks on the outside, the crème will not be as sweet, so look for an unblemished squash that is the color of butterscotch, with a smooth, hard skin.

1 small butternut squash
 (about 2 1/2 pounds)

1 tablespoon canola oil

1 cup diced silken tofu

1/4 cup pure maple syrup or honey

1/2 cup fresh orange juice

1/2 cup commercial vanilla-flavored soy milk

2 tablespoons grated orange zest

1/2 cup blueberries, raspberries or seasonal fruit

1/8 tablespoon grated nutmeg

Preheat the oven to 350 degrees F. Brush the squash with the canola oil; bake for 1 hour and 20 minutes, or until fork-tender. Let cool.

Cut the squash in half. Remove the seeds and discard or save for another use. Scoop out 1 cup of the flesh and transfer it to a blender or food processor fitted with a metal blade. Add the silken tofu, maple syrup or honey, orange juice, soy milk and orange zest; process until smooth.

Spoon equal portions of berries or other fruit into chilled wineglasses or dessert cups. Pour the crème over the fruit and grate a little nutmeg over the top. Chill for 30 minutes. Serve chilled.

What can be more satisfying on a cool morning than cupping your hands around a rustic mug of hot tea and feeling the warmth seep through the clay? Or reaching for a tall, moisture-covered glass of ruby red Iced Watermelon-Cranberry Drink after a hot afternoon spent in the garden?

At the Golden Door, we advocate drinking at least eight glasses of water a day, and to do this guests usually have a classic squeeze-type exercise bottle full of pure water close at hand. Thirst is a sensation you lose somewhat as you age, so it's important to be almost ritualistic about rehydration.

But the pleasure in taking a good, long drink of a cool, delicious beverage is lost in this modern-day ritual. I believe it's important to take a few moments several times each day—and not just at meals—to sit down with a drink that doesn't come straight from a bottle. Why not reward yourself, while you're sitting in a favorite chair, with something you can easily concoct yourself?

BEVERAGES

Herbal teas are infusions of hot water and various kinds of dried herbs, aromatic roots, barks, spices or flowers that have an array of flavors and medicinal properties. At the Door we serve them frequently, hot or cold. We're all familiar with the store-bought bagged varieties of teas, but what about livening them up a bit with a simple addition or two, such as our Rose Hip and Cranberry Tea? The acidity of this vitamin C–rich booster cuts thirst and cleans the palate in a way that a canned diet drink never can, and it has become a favorite with many of the guests.

Sometimes in the early evening at the end of a warm day, I'll serve a Sparkling Lavender Lemonade. And then there's the kick of a Carrot, Apple and Gingerroot Juice. If these don't convert you to the fun of mixing your own drinks, then I don't know what will.

CARROT, APPLE AND GINGERROOT JUICE

MAKES 2 CUPS

A juicer is an essential tool in the Golden Door kitchen. I highly recommend having one at home, too. Whenever possible, use organic fruits and vegetables for juices such as this one; organics are always a healthful choice, but that's particularly true for juices, as the whole fruit—skin and all—is processed through the juicer. (With a juicer, you don't cut away outer layers that have been exposed to pesticides and such.)

5 medium carrots, scrubbed
    and trimmed
4 medium Fuji, Gala or Golden
    Delicious apples, quartered, cored
    and seeded

1 (1-inch) piece gingerroot
    (about 1 ounce), peeled

Using a juicer, process the carrots, apples and gingerroot until smooth. Serve immediately.

GOT FRUIT?

If you've got an abundance of fruit in the house and know you'll never be able to eat it all, don't wait for it to go bad; make a fruit drink! Just process it in the blender with a bit of fresh lemon or lime juice and some ice and you've got a refreshing drink. You can combine fruits or keep them separate. If you want a smooth creamy drink, add half of a banana. Bottoms up!

ICED WATERMELON-CRANBERRY DRINK

MAKES 4 SERVINGS

This makes a wonderful nonalcoholic party punch. Multiply the ingredients according to the number of guests you expect. Use 100 percent cranberry juice.

> 4 cups seeded, diced watermelon
>   (about 1 pound)
> 1 cup cranberry juice
> 2 cups ice cubes
> 4 fresh mint sprigs, optional

Combine the watermelon and cranberry juice in a food processor fitted with a metal blade; pulse to combine. Transfer juices and pulp to a fine-mesh sieve and strain; discard the pulp. Divide the ice equally between 4 tall glasses, pour in the juice and garnish with fresh mint sprigs if desired.

HAPPY HOUR

Every evening when the day's activities are done, Golden Door guests gather for a cocktail hour—or rather, a mocktail hour. They nibble at the hors d'oeuvres we pass around and they drink exotic drinks. The combinations are different every night, but they all have one thing in common: there's not a trace of alcohol in any of them. And nobody misses it. It's the gathering together that they enjoy, the pause before dinner. It's a time to relax. Not that we're against drinking alcohol completely. After all, the scientific evidence suggests that wine in moderation protects against heart disease. At the Golden Door on Saturday nights, when the week-long spa program is done, guests gather for a farewell dinner. On that night, we always offer everyone a glass of wine. Everything in moderation.

Rose Hip and Cranberry Tea

MAKES 2 SERVINGS

Rose hip tea is high in vitamin C. I like to use a rose hip and hibiscus flower tea blend (available at specialty tea shops and health food stores) but any rose hip tea will do. Look for a cranberry juice that is 100 percent juice.

2 cups water

1 $\frac{1}{2}$ cups cranberry juice

1 clove

2 rose hip tea bags,
   or 2 rose hip–blend tea bags

2 tablespoons clover honey

2 orange slices for garnish

Combine the water, cranberry juice and clove in a medium-size pot set over medium heat. Bring to a simmer.

Using a spoon, remove the clove from the cranberry juice. Place the rose hip tea bags into a warmed teapot, pour in the hot cranberry-water mixture, stir in the honey, and steep for 5 to 7 minutes. Pour into mugs, garnish with orange slices and serve.

A Proper Cup of (Herbal) Tea

Tea devotees will tell you that there's a right way and a wrong way to brew tea. At the Golden Door, we favor herbal tea, and we believe that for it, too, there's a right and wrong way to brew. If you use tea bags, steep them for 3 to 10 minutes in hot water. Just be aware that the bags, though convenient, lose some of their volatile oils when stored for long periods of time. So buy the bags in small quantities and restock when you need them. And by all means, add a kick to your herbal tea with other ingredients. For a stimulating pick-me-up, try a cinnamon stick, 1 tablespoon of grated or sliced fresh ginger, an aromatic star anise, 3 or 4 crushed cardamom pods, or 1 or 2 cloves (never more—they become overpowering!). For a calming brew, try chamomile. If you want to intensify the flavor of your tea, layer the flavors. For example, while your mint tea bag is steeping, add a few fresh mint leaves. You won't believe the difference!

SPARKLING LAVENDER LEMONADE

MAKES 6 SERVINGS

What's more refreshing than a sparkling drink on a hot summer day? This lavender-infused lemonade soothes unlike any other. It's a great offering for an intimate lunch or for a midday pick-me-up.

2 cups water

$\frac{1}{2}$ cup lavender flowers, stripped from the stem

$\frac{1}{3}$ cup lavender or clover honey

$\frac{1}{2}$ cup fresh lemon juice

4 cups sparkling water or sparkling mineral water

1 cup ice cubes

6 sprigs lavender blossoms, optional

Bring the water to a boil in a small pot. Remove from the heat; add the lavender flowers and let steep for 10 minutes. Strain. Add the honey and stir until it has dissolved. Cover and refrigerate until well chilled.

When you are ready to serve, pour the chilled lavender infusion into a large pitcher, and stir in the lemon juice and sparkling water. Divide the ice equally between 6 tall glasses, pour in the Sparkling Lavender Lemonade and garnish with lavender blossoms if desired.

HOT MINTED APPLE JUICE

MAKES 6 SERVINGS

I like to use unsweetened, unfiltered apple juice for this warming tonic. The clear apple juices on the market are typically made from concentrate and are usually quite sweet. The unsweetened, unfiltered juice is less sweet and, when heated, makes for a milder drink.

1 Delicious or Pippin apple, quartered and seeded

2 $\frac{1}{2}$ cups unsweetened, unfiltered apple juice

2 $\frac{1}{2}$ cups water

2 peppermint tea bags

2 sprigs fresh mint

Combine the apple, apple juice and water in a small saucepan set over medium heat; simmer for 5 minutes, and remove from the heat. Add the tea bags and mint sprigs; steep for 10 minutes. Strain through a fine-mesh sieve, pour into 6 mugs and serve hot.

GOOD OLD H$_2$O

I love to concoct tantalizing drinks for my guests at the Golden Door, but pure fresh water is hard to beat. Your body is 70 percent water, so you owe it to yourself to replenish it frequently. At the Golden Door, we encourage guests to drink water throughout the day, and most carry water bottles around with them as they go from activity to activity. If water is not your favorite drink, you needn't fall back on beverages made with too much sugar or artificial sweeteners. Try fresh lemonade. We add a teaspoon of fresh lemon juice to 8 ounces of water and just a touch of the sweetener of your choice. I always tell our guests that nature makes us thirsty so that we'll be motivated to keep replenishing fluids and maintain the body's water balance.

BANANA-STRAWBERRY SMOOTHIE

MAKES 4 SERVINGS

Let your imagination and your local produce market be your guide when you make smoothies. Peaches, plums, raspberries—all sorts of fruits and berries—can be substituted for the strawberries here. Ripe banana is the essential ingredient; it gives the smoothie its creamy mouth-feel, and its sweet flavor eliminates the need to add sugar, even if your berries are a little tart.

$1\frac{1}{2}$ **cups hulled strawberries**

2 medium bananas

2 cups plain nonfat yogurt

Place the strawberries, bananas and yogurt into a blender or food processor fitted with a metal blade; process until smooth and creamy. Pour into 4 glasses and serve immediately.

As a young culinary student at the Centre d' Enseignements et de Recherches des Industries Alimentaires in Belgium, I—like most other culinary students of that time—learned what are called the *fonds de cuisine:* the basic recipes that were then considered the building blocks of all other dishes. (Indeed, in some quarters, they are still considered to be so.)

These fonds, or foundations, included stocks, sauces, stuffings, marinades, simple potato and vegetable preparations, thickeners and other basics. The same recipes had been passed from generation to generation from the time of Escoffier—in some cases, before the time of Escoffier—with very little change. Many called for generous measures of oil, butter, eggs and cream.

When I began cooking at the Golden Door, I realized I would have to expand my concept of what constitutes the basics. I adapted many of the old faithfuls to my new lighter style of cooking. And I added others along the way. Salsas are a good example of the latter category. Very soon after its introduction to the U.S. mainstream a few decades ago, tomato salsa became a wildly popular condiment, outpacing even ketchup. And no wonder—salsa is light, consisting of fruits and/or vegetables, but oh so flavorful and infinitely variable. It has earned its place in my collection of Golden Door Basics. I use salsas not just as appetizers, but

GOLDEN DOOR BASICS

as accompaniments to all kinds of dishes. I can't imagine cooking without them.

This chapter is full of these indispensable foundation recipes that I use again and again with all kinds of culinary creations, and all meet our healthful standard. There are stocks, of course, pretty much the same as when I was a student. For another basic—mayonnaise— I've lightened up the recipe by using tofu instead of eggs and oil. Vinaigrettes, dressings and sauces have likewise been lightened up, often flavored with citrus and tropical fruits as well as ethnic flavoring agents.

In this chapter, I've also included a few simple breads (such as a versatile Semolina Dough that will make Focaccia, Garlic-Herb Baguette and Pizza Crust), some rice and grain cooking fundamentals, and a flavorful Crispy Asian Coleslaw. In these pages, too, is the secret behind our baked chips, a favorite with guests who love to use them as dipping tools for our mock guacamole.

As you can see, this is a diverse chapter, one that I hope will serve you well in your own efforts at healthful cooking. Master these and you'll have a set of contemporary fonds de cuisine that you can build on.

THE WELL-STOCKED PANTRY

Once upon a time, when everybody cooked at home almost every night, a well-stocked pantry was something you could take for granted. Today, with family members running in different directions on any given night, everyone's plans are subject to change at a moment's notice; with effortless but calorie-laden take-out foods beckoning from every storefront, a well-stocked pantry is our first line of defense for healthful eating. Are you inviting guests for an impromptu Sunday supper? The quinoa in your pantry will make a delectable centerpiece for the meal. Or maybe you were planning on pasta and fresh tomato sauce again, but when you got to the market you found so-so tomatoes but marvelous napa cabbage. If so, the wild rice in the pantry will serve as the basis for a wonderful stuffing. Or perhaps you got home late to find nothing in the fridge except onions, bell peppers and some leftover cooked chicken. The soy sauce, chili paste, sesame oil and Asian herbs and spices in your pantry will help you transform those humble ingredients into a delicious stir-fry. A well-stocked pantry filled with an assortment of diverse ingredients can raise your everyday cooking to new heights of nutrition and flavor. In this day and age, when I speak of the pantry, I include the freezer and the refrigerator—all places where you can keep staples. Here are some of the things I always have on hand, both in my spa kitchen and my home kitchen.

High-quality organic canned
    chicken stock and vegetable broth
    (or frozen homemade)
Extra-virgin olive oil
Aged balsamic vinegar
Rice wine vinegar
Mirin (sweet rice wine)
Low-sodium soy sauce
Dark sesame oil
Vietnamese chili paste
Wasabi
Tamarind paste
Miso
Tahini
Whole-grain mustard
Unbleached flour
Whole-wheat flour
Semolina flour
Cornmeal
Frozen whole-wheat and/or
    corn tortillas
Soba noodles
Quinoa
Brown basmati rice
White jasmine rice
Wild rice

Couscous
Pasta (whole-wheat, soy or quinoa)
Dried or canned beans, lentils
    and split peas
Potatoes
Onions
Garlic
Ginger
Canned tomatoes
Canned tomato purée
Dried herbs and spices including
    thyme, basil, oregano, cumin,
    nutmeg, cinnamon, chili powder,
    chili-pepper flakes, coriander, Madras
    curry powder (Yes, I prefer fresh herbs,
    but dried will do in a pinch if you can't
    get to the store for fresh. I never use
    dried parsley, however.)
Arrowroot powder
Kosher salt
Black peppercorns
Pink peppercorns
Capers
Cornichons

GEARING UP

The choices in kitchen equipment on the market today are staggering. Some of what's out there is the sort of thing only a gadget collector could love. It works, but you don't really need it to do the job. But basic equipment of good solid quality is essential. Here is what I recommend:

Knives: Good knives are the cook's best friend. An 8-inch stainless- or carbon-steel chef's knife will be among your most often-used tools. So will a good paring knife and a serrated knife (good for cutting bread or slicing tomatoes and other odd jobs). A boning knife is useful in the spa kitchen. True, most home cooks won't bone their own poultry and meats, but the boning knife is excellent for trimming fat, and that's something all spa cooks do. Don't forget a sharpener of some kind. A dull knife will slow you down and make your food look sloppy.

Pots and Pans: Your choice of pots and pans for your spa kitchen is important. Nonstick sauté pans—an 8-inch and a 12-inch—make it possible for you to use less oil in your cooking. You'll need a good, solid stockpot with a heavy bottom, a 2-quart and a 4-quart saucepan. A stainless steel pot-and-steamer or a steamer insert that will fit into one of your other pots is indispensable for steaming vegetables. I also like a cast-iron pan for browning meats and poultry. The heat is always nice and even, and it adds a bit of iron to your diet. (If your grandmother had one and it has somehow come into your possession, hold on to it! Just remember to wash and dry it thoroughly after using and then put it on the heat and give it a coat of cooking oil before you put it away. This prevents rust.) I avoid aluminum cooking surfaces; they make the food taste metallic and can discolor it as well, especially foods that contain folic acid, such as spinach, broccoli and other greens.

Gadgets: Your kitchen should be equipped with both a food processor and a blender. Each is suited for different tasks (see "Blend or Process?" on page 203). I also like to have a small coffee grinder in which I grind, not coffee beans, but spices. Freshly ground spices have a stronger aroma and flavor—and that's important in the spa kitchen, where we use less salt and fat, and other ingredients have to work a little harder.

Utensils and Miscellaneous: If you have nonstick pots and pans, wooden spoons are a must for stirring soup, and scraping the nonstick surface. You'll want a whole set of these, as you'll use more than one at a time. You can also use a heat-resistant plastic spatula. Curved spatulas are useful for folding eggs into batter. A wire whisk is necessary for beating egg whites and whisking dressings. Buy good-quality stainless steel and it won't rust. You'll want a set of stainless-steel mixing bowls and a stainless-steel grater for grating ginger and potatoes. A stainless-steel colander and a wire-mesh sieve are essential for washing produce as well as straining stocks and certain cooked foods. A salad spinner makes washing and drying greens a breeze. Add a ladle, a slotted spoon, a set of measuring cups and spoons, a swivel-design vegetable peeler (it peels the thinnest possible layers), a wooden rolling pin, and you'll be well-equipped in the utensil department. Plastic cutting boards are easy to clean and will stand up to lots of use. Mine are color-coded: green for vegetables, red for meats and poultry, and white for other tasks such as slicing bread. You will need two spray bottles, one for vegetable oil and one for an olive oil-canola oil blend (see "About Oil in a Spray Bottle" on page xxii). Spraying pots, pans, grills and the food itself enables you to use less oil, yet coat surfaces evenly. Finally, don't forget a good supply of kitchen towels and some heat-proof oven mitts.

CHICKEN STOCK

MAKES 2 QUARTS

Chicken stock is one of the things that transfers seamlessly from haute cuisine to the spa kitchen. Years ago, when I was a freshman in spa cuisine, I quickly learned the need for stock—especially chicken stock—in this style of cooking. It is the basis for many a luscious soup, sauce or stew, and it can add body and flavor and much-needed moisture when used as a cooking medium. You'll see chicken stock pop up over and over again in this book—indeed, in most any cookbook. Make a large quantity and freeze it in individual containers, so it will always be on hand. And do make a point to buy organic chickens.

$1\frac{1}{2}$ pounds chicken bones, rinsed and
    cut into 3-inch pieces

3 quarts cold water

1 medium onion, coarsely chopped

1 small carrot, coarsely chopped

1 celery rib, coarsely chopped

4 sprigs fresh parsley

1 clove garlic, crushed

1 bay leaf

$\frac{1}{3}$ teaspoon black peppercorns

2 sprigs fresh thyme

1 teaspoon salt, optional

Place the chicken bones in a large stockpot, add the water and set over medium-high heat. Bring to a simmer, skimming the surface to remove any fat and impurities. Add the onion, carrot, celery, parsley, garlic, bay leaf, peppercorns, thyme and salt, if using. Simmer, uncovered, for $1\frac{1}{2}$ hours, or until the liquid is reduced in volume by about $\frac{1}{3}$ and takes on a golden color. Using a fine-mesh sieve or colander lined with cheesecloth, strain into a large bowl or other container. Press gently on the solids to remove all the liquid; discard the solids and skim off any fat. Use immediately or refrigerate or freeze for later use. Chicken Stock can be kept in the refrigerator, covered, for 2 to 3 days or in the freezer for several weeks.

STOCK OPTIONS

In haute cuisine, stocks are the building blocks of sauces, soups, stews, braised meats and other dishes. In spa cuisine, they serve yet another purpose: they are essential moisteners of sautéed, pan-fried and stir-fried meats and fish. (Actually, they can serve this purpose in haute cuisine too, but in spa cookery, we don't use the fats and creams of haute cuisine, so they're even more important for us.) In a professional kitchen there are always big pots full of simmering stock; all the chef has to do is dip into one if a piece of chicken looks a little dry. For the home cook, I suggest keeping a small pot of stock simmering nearby when you do your stove-top cooking. (Cold stock will impede the cooking; besides, if you heat the stock, you prevent any bacterial contamination.)

VEGETABLE BROTH

MAKES 1¹⁄₂ QUARTS

If there are any vegetarians or vegans at your table, Vegetable Broth is yet another culinary must-have. This flavorful broth made only from vegetables can be used anywhere you'd use Chicken Stock—in soups, sauces, stews and as a cooking medium. Clear, devoid of fat and light in color, it's a vegetarian or vegan's secret weapon for boosting the flavor of a dish. Make it in quantity and freeze in small individual containers so it's always there when you need it.

1 medium leek, sliced and washed well	2 sprigs fresh basil
2 celery ribs, coarsely chopped	2 sprigs fresh thyme
1 large carrot, coarsely chopped	1 bay leaf
1 medium onion, coarsely chopped	1 teaspoon kosher salt, optional
3 large cabbage leaves	1 teaspoon freshly ground
5 cloves	black pepper
4 sprigs fresh parsley	1 quart water

Combine all ingredients in a large stockpot. Set the pot over medium-high heat and bring to a boil. Reduce the heat to medium-low and simmer, uncovered, for 1 hour, or until the liquid has reduced in volume by about a third.

Using a fine-mesh sieve or colander lined with cheesecloth, strain into a large bowl or other container. Press gently on the solids to remove all the liquid; discard the solids. Use immediately or refrigerate or freeze for later use. Vegetable Broth can be kept in the refrigerator, covered, for 3 to 4 days or in the freezer for up to 1 month.

Fish Stock

MAKES 1½ QUARTS

There are two secrets to making crystal clear, delicate fish stock. First, use fish bones from non-oily fish, such as sea bass, halibut or sole. Second, let the stock simmer without stirring or bringing it to a boil. Fish stock is used as the basis for fish soups, fish sauces and fish stews. Cook up a pot and freeze in small individual containers so it's always ready.

1 ¼ pounds fish bones, rinsed

2 celery ribs, coarsely chopped

1 medium carrot, coarsely chopped

1 medium leek, washed well and coarsely chopped

2 bay leaves

2 sprigs fresh thyme

4 sprigs fresh parsley

2 quarts water

1 cup white wine

Combine all ingredients in a nonaluminum stockpot. Set over medium-high heat. Bring to a near-boil and reduce the heat to medium-low; simmer, uncovered, for 45 minutes, or until the liquid reduces in volume by about a fourth. Skim the surface to remove any foam that forms, but do not stir while cooking or the stock will become cloudy.

Using a fine-mesh sieve or colander lined with cheesecloth, strain into a large bowl or other container. Press gently on the solids to remove all the liquid; discard the solids. Rinse the pot and return the clear fish stock to it. Skim off any foam that forms on the surface. Use immediately or refrigerate or freeze for later use. Fish Stock can be kept in the refrigerator, covered, for 3 to 4 days or in the freezer for 1 month.

COURT BOUILLON

MAKES 1$\frac{1}{2}$ QUARTS

Court bouillon is the French term for a basic poaching liquid. This aromatic liquid is usually used to impart delicate flavor and moisture to fish, seafood and vegetables. It is purely a cooking liquid; discard after using.

1 medium onion, coarsely chopped

1 small carrot, coarsely chopped

2 celery ribs, coarsely chopped

1 ($\frac{1}{2}$-inch) piece gingerroot
    (about 1 ounce), peeled and sliced

1 lemon, sliced

6 sprigs fresh parsley, crushed

1 teaspoon kosher salt

5 cups water

$\frac{1}{4}$ cup apple cider vinegar or
    white wine

Combine all ingredients in a large, shallow pan. Set over medium heat and bring to a simmer. Simmer for 15 to 20 minutes, or until the vegetables are soft and the broth is flavorful. Use the resulting broth immediately for poaching.

BLEND OR PROCESS?

Which is better? The food processor or the blender? Actually neither is better than the other. Each is good at different tasks. And it's worthwhile to know what those tasks are.

The food processor is better for thicker mixtures—puréed vegetables, dips, thick soups, drinks made with crushed ice and the like. It can be messy if you try to process very liquid soups or drinks. The blender is better for those liquidy items—thinner soups or blended drinks.

But that's not the end of it. The new-generation, more-powerful wide-based blenders work fine for thicker purées of the sort that used to go best in the food processor. Mini food processors and hand-held power mixers (some of which come with cup attachments that transform them into mini-processors) are good at blending thinner soups and drinks.

BALSAMIC SAUCE

MAKES ABOUT ⅓ CUP

This very versatile sauce is delicious with chicken or other meats, tossed with vegetables, mixed into grains or used to dress salads. It is also an example of a classic sauce-making technique—cooking a liquid until it reduces in volume, to intensify its flavor. But while classic reduction-style sauces often call for long lists of ingredients—including chicken or veal bones and stocks—and hours of cooking, this sauce has only two components, is completely vegan and cooks up fairly quickly. The result is a bright, flavorful sauce.

> 1 cup aged balsamic vinegar
> 2 tablespoons fructose or sugar

Combine the balsamic vinegar and fructose or sugar in a small saucepan. Set over medium heat and bring to a simmer. Simmer for about 20 to 25 minutes, or until the sauce is reduced in volume to about ⅓ cup. Remove from the heat and let cool slightly. Transfer to a serving container and set aside until ready to serve. Balsamic Sauce can be kept in the refrigerator, covered, for 1 week.

THE PLOT THICKENS

When it comes to thickening a sauce, classical cooking recognizes a few "usual suspects"—cream, eggs, butter, flour, butter mixed with flour, etc. But there are other lighter ways to thicken a sauce. One simple way is to dissolve a teaspoon of arrowroot powder in a tablespoon of water, mix it into the sauce and cook for 4 to 5 minutes. Arrowroot, available in the spice section of the supermarket, gives your sauce a nice silken quality.

You can also add 2 to 3 tablespoons of puréed cannellini beans and their cooking liquid. Puréed well-cooked carrots, onions, celery or baked yam can also be used in small quantities to thicken sauces.

Vine-Ripened Tomato Coulis

MAKES 1 ½ CUPS

This quick-cooking tomato sauce has a fresh-from-the-garden flavor. It's delightful on pasta, grilled vegetables or Turkey Rice Meatballs (page 102). Summertime, when tomatoes are at their peak, is the best time to make tomato coulis. In the winter, I use half fresh tomatoes and half canned plum tomatoes to achieve a summertime flavor. Be sure to use a good-quality non-aluminum pot with a heavy bottom to prevent the sauce from sticking and burning. And keep stirring as the sauce cooks.

1 teaspoon vegetable oil

8 vine-ripened tomatoes, quartered

1 celery rib, coarsely chopped

1 teaspoon minced garlic

1 bay leaf

2 tablespoons finely chopped fresh basil

½ teaspoon kosher salt

¼ teaspoon freshly ground black pepper

1 tablespoon olive oil

Heat the oil in a small pot set over medium heat. Add the tomatoes, celery, garlic and bay leaf; bring to a simmer. Simmer, stirring occasionally, for 25 to 30 minutes, or until the tomatoes soften and have released their juices and the mixture reduces in volume by a third. Remove the bay leaf and transfer to a blender or food processor fitted with a metal blade; pulse to incorporate. Do not overblend or the mixture will lose its vibrant red color. Strain through a fine-mesh sieve; stir in the basil, salt, black pepper and olive oil. Vine-Ripened Tomato Coulis can be kept in the refrigerator, covered, for 5 days or in the freezer for 1 month.

SILKEN TOFU MAYONNAISE

MAKES 1⅔ CUPS

Silken tofu, a creamy variety of tofu, is the perfect substitute for fat; it gives a wonderful mouth-feel and is packed with nutrition. The mayonnaise recipe below is a good example of the uses of this "wonder ingredient." It has only 9 calories and 1 gram of fat per tablespoon (unlike traditional mayonnaise made from egg yolks and oil, which contains a total of 12 grams of fat per tablespoon). Besides, it's easy to make. I use it alone as a mayonnaise and as a base for dips, dressings and sauces.

1 tablespoon minced shallots

1 tablespoon Dijon mustard

2½ tablespoons apple cider vinegar

¼ cup water

10 ounces silken tofu

1 teaspoon freshly ground black pepper

Combine all ingredients in a blender or food processor fitted with a metal blade; process until smooth and creamy. Silken Tofu Mayonnaise can be kept in the refrigerator, covered, for 3 to 4 days.

VARIATION: ROASTED RED PEPPER AND BASIL MAYONNAISE

MAKES 1½ CUPS

1 cup Silken Tofu Mayonnaise (see above)

Olive oil and canola oil in a spray bottle, or 1 teaspoon olive oil

2 medium red bell peppers

Pinch of cayenne pepper, optional

¼ cup finely chopped fresh basil

Prepare the Silken Tofu Mayonnaise as directed above and set aside.

Heat a grill, stovetop grill or broiler. Spray or brush the peppers with 1 teaspoon olive oil. Grill or broil the peppers for about 5 minutes, turning so that all sides are charred. Transfer to a plastic bag, seal, and set aside for about 10 minutes, or until the peppers are cool enough to handle. Remove the skin and seeds from the peppers and chop coarsely.

Combine the peppers, Silken Tofu Mayonnaise and cayenne pepper, if using, in a blender or food processor fitted with a metal blade. Pulse until the peppers are fully incorporated. Be careful not to overblend or the mayonnaise will lose its vibrant red color. Add the basil and pulse until incorporated. Roasted Red Pepper and Basil Mayonnaise can be kept in the refrigerator, covered, for 3 to 4 days.

VARIATION: HERBED TOFU MAYONNAISE

MAKES 1½ CUPS

1 cup Silken Tofu Mayonnaise (page 206)
⅓ cup chopped fresh parsley
⅓ chopped fresh basil
2 tablespoons chopped scallions
2 teaspoons fresh tarragon leaves

Prepare the Silken Tofu Mayonnaise as directed on page 206.

Combine the Silken Tofu Mayonnaise, parsley, basil, scallions and tarragon in a blender or food processor fitted with a metal blade; pulse until green in color and chunky in texture. Do not overblend. Herbed Tofu Mayonnaise can be kept in the refrigerator, covered, for 1 day.

Citrus Vinaigrette

MAKES 1 CUP

This Citrus Vinaigrette is a variation on the classic French vinaigrette. I've reduced the amount of oil called for and upped the flavor ante with the addition of such nontraditional ingredients as maple syrup, orange juice and orange zest. I like to use lemon thyme because of its wonderful fragrance, but if it's not available, regular thyme will work. Use this Citrus Vinaigrette on all kinds of salads and greens. Be sure to toss the entire salad with the vinaigrette before portioning it onto serving plates.

2 tablespoons water

1/3 cup fresh orange juice

2 tablespoons Champagne vinegar or chardonnay

2 tablespoons olive oil

1 tablespoon pure maple syrup

1 tablespoon Dijon mustard

1 teaspoon grated orange zest

1/2 teaspoon chopped fresh lemon thyme or common thyme

Salt and freshly ground black pepper to taste, optional

Combine the water, orange juice, vinegar or wine, olive oil, maple syrup and mustard in a blender; process until smooth. (Or place all ingredients into a bowl and, using a fork, beat until smooth.) Transfer to a mixing bowl and stir in the orange zest and thyme. Season with salt and black pepper if desired. Citrus Vinaigrette can be kept in the refrigerator, covered, for 2 to 3 days.

Mango-Tahini Dressing

MAKES 2 CUPS

Tart-sweet mangoes get a nutty infusion from tahini, the paste made from ground sesame seeds. The tahini is so rich you only need a tablespoon, which keeps the fat content of this dressing to a minimum. Use it to dress chicken salad, jicama salad or grilled fish or lamb.

1 ripe mango, peeled, pitted and diced

1 tablespoon minced shallot

1 tablespoon tahini

3 tablespoons fresh lime juice

1 teaspoon Champagne vinegar or white balsamic vinegar

$\frac{1}{2}$ cup water

1 teaspoon minced lime zest

Combine the mango, shallot, tahini, lime juice, vinegar and water in a blender or food processor fitted with a metal blade; process until smooth. Transfer to a bowl and stir in the minced lime zest. Mango-Tahini Dressing can be kept in the refrigerator, covered, for 4 to 5 days.

GINGER, PEANUT AND CILANTRO SAUCE AND DRESSING

MAKES 1 CUP

This dressing is one of the most popular at the Golden Door. It's one of those multitasking condiments that can be used as a dipping sauce for baked wontons or vegetables, as a sauce for grilled poultry, seafood or meat dishes, or as a dressing for all kinds of salads. Keep in mind that as ginger gets older, it tends to get stringy; if you can find it, you can substitute galangal, ginger's Southeast Asian cousin. Its texture is less stringy.

$1\frac{1}{2}$ tablespoons minced fresh
    gingerroot

1 tablespoon rice vinegar

$\frac{1}{4}$ cup fresh orange juice

1 tablespoon fresh lime juice

1 teaspoon Vietnamese chili sauce

2 tablespoons chunky peanut butter

1 tablespoon honey

2 tablespoons water

4 sprigs fresh cilantro

Combine the ginger, vinegar, orange juice, lime juice, chili sauce, peanut butter, honey and water in a blender or food processor fitted with a metal blade; process until smooth. Add the cilantro sprigs and pulse to combine. Ginger, Peanut and Cilantro Sauce and Dressing can be kept in the refrigerator, covered, for 5 days.

LIME-MISO DIPPING SAUCE AND DRESSING

MAKES 1 CUP

Miso, a pungent, salty paste made of fermented soybeans and rice, adds depth and flavor to sauces, dressings and soups. Here, a little lime juice gives the sauce an extra dimension. Use it as a dipping sauce for vegetables or any Asian-inspired dish, or to baste fish, shellfish, tofu or grilled chicken breast.

1 tablespoon *shiromiso* (white miso)	¹/₂ teaspoon Vietnamese chili paste
¹/₃ cup water	2 teaspoons dark sesame oil
2 tablespoons low-sodium soy sauce	1 teaspoon grated lemon zest
¹/₄ cup fresh lime juice	1 teaspoon minced garlic
1 tablespoon honey	3 tablespoons minced fresh cilantro

Combine the miso, water, soy sauce, lime juice, honey, chili paste, sesame oil, lemon zest and garlic in a mixing bowl; whisk until smooth and thoroughly blended. Stir in the fresh cilantro. Lime-Miso Dipping Sauce and Dressing can be kept in the refrigerator, covered, for up to 5 days.

SALSA MEXICANA

MAKES 2 CUPS

We call this classic salsa "Mexicana." In Mexico, where countless varieties of salsas are a hallmark of the cuisine, they call this one *salsa cruda*—that is, uncooked sauce. Whatever you call it, it's delicious. At the Golden Door, it is present on the table as a condiment with every meal. Serve it with chips or as a sauce for any dish that you want to infuse with a Mexican flare. A word of caution: the capsaicin (the hot note) in the chili pepper is intense and can be painful to the skin. When handling piquant peppers, always wear latex or synthetic gloves to protect your hands, and wash your hands before touching your face.

2 large tomatoes, finely chopped
$1/2$ small red onion, minced
2 jalapeño chilies, seeded and minced
$1/4$ cup finely chopped fresh cilantro
$1/4$ cup fresh lime juice

$1/2$ teaspoon kosher salt
$1/2$ teaspoon freshly ground
   black pepper

Combine all ingredients in a mixing bowl and mix well. Cover and refrigerate for 1 hour to let the flavors marry. Salsa Mexicana can be kept in the refrigerator, covered, for 2 days.

Tomatillo Salsa

The tomatillo is a tart citrus fruit that resembles a small green tomato, but it is actually a member of the gooseberry family. Its papery husk protects its smooth, sometimes sticky, skin. Loaded with vitamins C and K, tomatillos are a healthful addition to salsas, sauces, soups and dressings. Charring the tomatillos lightly adds a rich smoky flavor to their characteristic tartness. Serve it as a dip or with omelets, grilled chicken, veggie burgers or grilled salmon—anything that needs a little extra zing.

6 to 8 tomatillos (about 1 pound), peeled and rinsed

1 teaspoon canola oil

¼ medium onion, finely diced

2 teaspoons minced garlic

½ small carrot, finely diced

1 serrano chili, seeded and minced

1 tablespoon ground cumin

½ teaspoon kosher salt

2 tablespoons chopped fresh cilantro

2 to 3 tablespoons Vegetable Broth (page 201), or as needed

Heat a grill, stovetop grill or broiler. Grill or broil the tomatillos for about 5 minutes, or until they are lightly charred but still firm. Remove from the heat and set aside.

Heat the canola oil in a small saucepan set over medium-low heat. Add the onion, garlic, carrot and serrano chili; sauté, stirring, for 2 to 3 minutes, or until the vegetables begin to soften. Stir in the charred tomatillos, cumin and salt. Cover and simmer for 10 to 15 minutes, or until the tomatillos are soft and have opened and released their juices. (If the salsa begins to dry out before the tomatillos are softened, add 2 to 3 tablespoons broth.) Transfer to a blender or food processor fitted with a metal blade and add the cilantro; pulse until the salsa is coarsely chopped, so as not to crush the tomatillo seeds.

SPA PESTO

MAKES 1 CUP

Puréed white beans and yogurt give the Golden Door version of pesto the rich texture of the classic sauce—without all the fat that comes from the large amounts of cheese, olive oil and nuts called for in the traditional recipe. The secret to this recipe is to cook the beans until there is just barely enough liquid in the pot to cover them, and then to purée them with that liquid for a flavorful, moist, creamy pesto. If you're pressed for time, you can use canned beans. Serve the pesto with pasta, as a dip or on meat or fish.

$^1/_4$ cup dried white beans, soaked for 2 hours or overnight and rinsed	1 tablespoon olive oil
2 cups water	$^1/_3$ cup nonfat plain yogurt
1 teaspoon salt	$^1/_2$ cup finely chopped fresh basil
$^1/_4$ onion	$^1/_4$ cup finely chopped fresh parsley
1 bay leaf	1 tablespoon grated Parmesan cheese
2 tablespoons pine nuts (pignoli)	$^1/_2$ teaspoon freshly ground black pepper
3 cloves garlic, sliced	$^1/_2$ teaspoon kosher salt

To cook the dried beans, drain and place them in a small pot. Add the water, salt, onion and bay leaf, and set over medium heat; simmer for about 1 hour, or until the beans are tender. (Be sure to add more broth if the beans become dry during cooking.) Remove the beans from the heat and let cool in their cooking liquid. Remove the bay leaf.

Meanwhile, place the pine nuts into a small, dry pan set over medium-high heat; toast them, stirring often, for about 3 to 4 minutes, or until golden brown. Remove from the heat and transfer to a blender or food processor fitted with a metal blade. Add $^1/_4$ cup cooked beans and about 3 tablespoons of their cooking liquid, garlic, olive oil, yogurt, basil, parsley, Parmesan cheese, black pepper and salt; process until smooth. Spa Pesto can be kept in the refrigerator, covered, for up to 5 days.

VARIATION: SOUTHWESTERN SPA PESTO

To give this pesto a Southwestern twist, try substituting $^1/_2$ cup fresh watercress leaves or $^1/_4$ cup fresh cilantro for the basil; pair the resulting pesto with grilled fish.

SEMOLINA DOUGH

FOR FOCACCIA, GARLIC-HERB BAGUETTE AND PIZZA CRUST

Semolina Dough rates as a most valuable player in the Golden Door kitchen. I use it as the basis for our Focaccia, our Garlic-Herb Baguette, and our Pizza Crust, because I believe semolina makes a superior dough.

Semolina Dough:

1 tablespoon active dry yeast (1 envelope)

1 teaspoon sugar or honey

1 1/4 cups lukewarm water

1 3/4 to 2 cups semolina flour, plus more for dusting

3/4 cup whole-wheat flour

1 teaspoon kosher salt

1 tablespoon olive oil

Vegetable oil in a spray bottle, or 1 teaspoon vegetable oil

Rosemary-Garlic Seasoning (for Focaccia or Garlic-Herb Baguette; omit for Pizza Crust):

1 tablespoon olive oil

2 tablespoons minced fresh rosemary leaves

1 tablespoon minced fresh garlic

To make the seasoning for the Focaccia or Garlic-Herb Baguette, heat the olive oil in a small nonstick sauté pan set over medium heat. Add the rosemary and garlic; sauté, stirring occasionally, for 2 to 3 minutes, or until the garlic is soft and translucent. Remove from the heat and let cool.

To make Semolina Dough, in the bowl of an electric mixer fitted with a dough hook, dissolve the yeast and sugar or honey in the warm water. Add the Rosemary-Garlic Seasoning, if using. In a separate bowl, combine 1 3/4 cups semolina flour, the whole-wheat flour and salt. While the mixer is running at slow speed, pour in the olive oil and add the flour mixture, 1 cup at a time; mix until the dough pulls away from the sides of the bowl. If the dough is too sticky, add the extra 1/4 cup semolina flour. Continue mixing until the dough is smooth and elastic. Place it in a clean mixing bowl, cover with a damp towel, and place the bowl in a warm, draft-free spot. Let it rise for 25 to 45 minutes, or until it doubles in volume.

Preheat the oven to 350 degrees F. Spray or grease a baking sheet with vegetable oil and dust lightly with semolina flour. Transfer the dough to a floured work surface; knead well for 1 to 2 minutes, alternately pressing with the heel of your hand and folding the dough over.

At this point, select one of three options for finishing the dough:

FOCACCIA

MAKES 1 (10 x 12-INCH) SHEET FOCACCIA

Topping for Focaccia:
2 teaspoons salt
Olive oil and canola oil in a spray bottle, or 2 teaspoons olive oil

With a rolling pin, form the dough (which includes the Rosemary-Garlic Seasoning) into a rectangle about 10 x 12 inches. Place the rolled dough onto the prepared baking sheet, spray or brush it with 1 teaspoon olive oil and sprinkle with salt. Set aside to rise again for 15 to 20 minutes.

Bake for 20 to 25 minutes, or until the bread is crisp and golden brown. About 5 minutes before removing it from the oven, spray or brush again with the remaining teaspoon olive oil. Invert on a wire rack and let cool.

GARLIC-HERB BAGUETTE

MAKES 3 (10-INCH) BAGUETTE LOAVES

Divide the kneaded dough (which includes the Rosemary-Garlic Seasoning) into 3 pieces and place on a floured work surface. With the palm of your hand, roll one piece to form a 10-inch baguette loaf. Repeat with the other 2 pieces of dough. Place the loaves on the prepared baking sheet. Sprinkle with semolina flour and set aside to rise for 10 to 15 minutes, or until doubled in volume.

Bake for about 25 minutes, or until crisp and lightly browned. Cool on wire racks.

PIZZA CRUST

MAKES 1 (19-INCH) PIZZA CRUST OR 8 INDIVIDUAL PIZZA CRUSTS

Place the dough (minus the Rosemary-Garlic Seasoning) on a lightly floured work surface; knead well, alternately pressing with the heel of your hand and folding the dough over. If you are making 1 large pizza, use a rolling pin to roll the dough to fit the pan. If you are making 8 small pizzas, divide the dough into 8 equal portions and shape into small balls. With your fingertips, spread each ball into a 5-inch circle. Let the dough rise for 10 minutes.

Use your fingers to poke holes in the risen dough; bake for 15 minutes, or until the Pizza Crust is firm and begins to brown on the bottom. Remove from the oven. Spread and scatter the toppings of your choice on the crust. Spray lightly with olive oil and return to the oven; bake another 15 to 20 minutes.

OLD-FASHIONED TECATE BREAD

MAKES 2 (9 1/2 x 4 1/2-INCH) LOAVES

This recipe originated at our sister spa, Rancho La Puerta. When Ignacio Leon, the baker there, came to the Golden Door in the 1970s, he brought the recipe for this wonderful, complex bread with him. It's delicious toasted by itself for breakfast, or as a base for luncheon or supper sandwiches.

2 tablespoons active dry yeast
  (2 envelopes)
2 tablespoons honey
2 1/2 cups lukewarm water
1/4 cup canola oil

1/4 cup dark molasses
1 tablespoon salt
1 cup wheat bran
6 to 6 1/2 cups whole-wheat flour,
  plus more for dusting

In the bowl of an electric mixer fitted with a dough hook, dissolve the yeast and honey in the warm water. Add the oil and molasses. In a separate bowl, combine the salt, bran and 6 cups flour. While the mixer is running at slow speed, add the flour mixture, 1 cup at a time, and mix until the dough pulls away from the sides of the bowl. If the dough is too sticky, add the extra 1/2 cup flour. Continue mixing until the dough is smooth and elastic. Place it in a clean, lightly floured mixing bowl, cover with a damp towel and place the bowl in a warm, draft-free spot. Let it rise for 30 to 40 minutes, or until it doubles in volume.

Preheat the oven to 350 degrees F. Spray or grease 2 (9 1/2 x 4 1/2-inch) loaf pans lightly with vegetable oil.

Turn the dough onto a lightly floured work surface; knead well for 4 to 5 minutes until smooth, alternately pressing with the heel of your hand and folding the dough over. Form the dough into 2 loaves and place them in the prepared pans. Cover again with a towel and let rise for 20 to 30 minutes, or until nearly doubled in volume.

Bake 50 minutes, or until browned on top and firm on the bottom. Turn out of the pan onto a wire rack and let cool.

WILD RICE AND ORANGE-WALNUT BREAD

MAKES 2 (9½ x 4½-INCH) LOAVES

Golden Door guests just love to discuss recipes with me. This bread is the result of an inspiring conversation I had with guest Mia King, who suggested I try using wild rice to make bread. I combined it with walnuts and orange zest to make an excellent loaf, perfect for toasting. Be sure to allow enough time to cook the rice before you start to bake. Or make the rice ahead of time. You'll need precisely 1 cup of cooked rice for this recipe, which means that if you start with ½ cup of raw rice, you'll have a small amount of rice left over. Don't try to add it to the bread; save it for tomorrow's luncheon salad!

1 cup Steamed Fluffy Wild Rice
   (page 223)

2 tablespoons active dry yeast
   (2 envelopes)

2½ cups 1 percent low-fat milk, warm

⅜ cup honey

⅜ cup walnut oil or olive oil

½ cup chopped walnuts

4½ to 5 cups semolina flour, plus
   ½ cup for dusting

1 cup whole-wheat flour

1 teaspoon kosher salt

2 tablespoons grated orange zest

Vegetable oil in a spray bottle, or
   2 teaspoons vegetable oil

Prepare the wild rice as directed on page 223.

In the bowl of an electric mixer fitted with a dough hook, dissolve the yeast in the warm milk and stir in the honey and walnut oil or olive oil. In a separate bowl, combine the walnuts, 1 cup cooked wild rice, 4½ cups semolina flour, the whole-wheat flour, salt and orange zest. While the mixer is running at low speed, add the flour mixture, 1 cup at a time; mix until the dough pulls away from the sides of the bowl. If the dough is too sticky, add the extra ½ cup flour. Continue mixing until the dough is smooth and elastic. Place it in a clean, lightly floured mixing bowl, cover with a damp towel and place the bowl in a warm, draft-free spot. Let it rise for 30 minutes, or until it doubles in volume.

Preheat the oven to 350 degrees F. Spray or grease 2 (9½ x 4½-inch) loaf pans with vegetable oil and set aside.

Turn the dough out onto a lightly floured work surface; knead vigorously for 4 to 5 minutes, or until smooth. Form into 2 loaves and place in the prepared pans. Cover again with a towel and let rise for 20 to 30 minutes, until doubled in volume.

Bake 40 to 50 minutes, or until the bread is golden brown. Turn the bread out of the pan and let cool on a wire rack.

FLOUR POWER

All the bread recipes in this book call for an optional $\frac{1}{4}$ to $\frac{1}{2}$ cup flour. That's because it's rare for any two loaves to react the same way. It depends on where you live, how much humidity is in the air, and whether it's a rainy day or a clear day when you decide to bake bread. It depends on the flour itself, whether it was made from summer or winter wheat (difficult if not impossible for the consumer to ascertain), how coarsely it was ground, how much gluten it contains—and how all these variables work together. It depends on the yeast, which is, after all, a living organism and extremely variable. So the extra flour is an equalizer. If your dough is too soft or sticky, add a little more flour until you get a smooth, elastic dough. If the dough is too stiff, add a tablespoon or so of water and fold several times until you get—that's right—a smooth, elastic dough.

GOLDEN DOOR CHIPS

MAKES 32 CHIPS

I season these chips with a mixture of toasted cumin and cayenne, but use whatever dried herbs and spices you like. The egg whites promote even baking and keep the chips crispy. Serve with dips or as a garnish. Use either wheat or corn tortillas for these chips. Keep in mind that the corn tortillas tend to get crispier than the whole wheat. The whole-wheat tortillas are typically bigger than the corn; at the Golden Door, we trim them into 5-inch rounds before proceeding with the recipe. (If you don't mind irregular shapes, don't trim the whole-wheat tortillas—just cut them into 2-inch pieces before baking.) You can make a sweet version for garnishing sorbets and puddings by sprinkling a cinnamon-sugar mixture on the warm chips.

Vegetable oil in a spray bottle, or
  1 teaspoon vegetable oil

2 teaspoons cumin powder

4 soft corn tortillas, or 4 whole-wheat
  tortillas trimmed to 5-inch rounds,
  or 4 whole-wheat pita breads

1 egg white, lightly beaten with
  2 teaspoons water

$^1/_4$ teaspoon cayenne pepper, optional

Preheat the oven to 375 degrees F. Spray or grease a baking sheet with vegetable oil.

Pour the cumin powder into a dry frying pan set over medium heat; toast, shaking the pan frequently, for 2 to 3 minutes, or until the cumin is fragrant. Be careful; cumin smokes and burns easily.

Brush the tortillas on both sides with the egg white and cut each into 8 segments. Place the segments on the prepared baking sheet; bake for 10 to 15 minutes, or until the chips are golden brown and crisp. Turn the chips once during baking.

Remove from the oven and sprinkle the chips with the cumin and cayenne; let cool.

SAVORY FIVE-SPICE TUILES

MAKES 14 TUILES

Tuile is the French word for tile, the shape that these savory crackers take when they are cooled the traditional way, draped over a rolling pin. I usually make them in the shape of a cup or cone, which is easy to do using a muffin tin or ramekin as a mold. Serve these savory tuiles with salsas or dips, or fill them with salads. At the Golden Door, our guests are often watching their calories, so we make smaller tuiles than the 3½-inch tuiles described here; you can make them whatever size you like. They can also be made sweet with a few simple modifications (see Citrus-Almond Tuiles, page 222).

Vegetable oil in a spray bottle, or
    1 teaspoon vegetable oil
¼ cup slivered almonds
2 egg whites
2 tablespoons canola oil
1 teaspoon sesame oil
2 teaspoons low-sodium soy sauce

⅓ cup fresh orange juice
2 tablespoons grated lemon zest
2 tablespoons pure maple syrup
⅓ cup unbleached flour
½ teaspoon five-spice powder
2 tablespoons arrowroot powder

Preheat the oven to 375 degrees F. Line a baking sheet with parchment paper and spray or brush with vegetable oil.

Place the almonds into a food mill or food processor fitted with a metal blade; process briefly to make a coarse meal. Be careful not to overprocess or the almonds will become paste. Or, if you wish, place the almonds on a work surface, cover with wax paper and use a rolling pin to crush them. Set aside.

Combine the egg whites, canola oil, sesame oil, soy sauce, orange juice, lemon zest and maple syrup in a mixing bowl; whisk to blend. Whisk in the almonds, flour, five-spice powder and arrowroot; mix well.

Spoon 2 tablespoons of the batter onto the prepared baking sheet; using the back of a spoon, spread to it form a 3½-inch circle. The tuile should be very thin. Repeat the process with the remaining batter to make 13 more tuiles. Bake for 10 to 15 minutes, or until the tuiles are golden brown. Watch carefully, as tuiles can burn easily.

Working quickly, remove the tuiles from the baking sheet with a metal spatula and while they are hot, press them into a muffin tin or ramekin with your fingers to form a cup or cone shape. Or, if you prefer, drape the tuiles over a rolling pin to form the traditional tile shape. Let the tuiles cool; serve or store in an airtight container in a cool spot until ready to use.

CITRUS-ALMOND TUILES

MAKES 14 TUILES

In France, sweet tuiles are the traditional accompaniment to ice cream or sorbet. This recipe was developed to accommodate the many Golden Door guests who do not eat dairy but do eat dessert! *Tuiles*—French for "tiles"—are very versatile and can be molded into any shape you desire—drape them over a rolling pin to create the traditional shape, or tuck them into muffin tins or ramekins to make small cups or cone shapes. They are delicious on their own or as a garnish, but can also be filled with sorbet or fresh or stewed fruits.

Vegetable oil in a spray bottle, or
   1 teaspoon vegetable oil
$1/4$ cup slivered almonds
2 egg whites
$1/3$ cup pure maple syrup
2 tablespoons canola oil

2 tablespoons melted butter
$1/4$ cup fresh orange juice
1 teaspoon pure vanilla extract
$1/4$ cup packed brown sugar
1 tablespoon grated lemon zest
$1/2$ cup unbleached flour

Preheat the oven to 375 degrees F. Line a baking sheet with parchment or waxed paper; spray or brush with vegetable oil and set aside.

Place the almonds into a food mill or food processor fitted with a metal blade; process briefly to make a coarse meal. Be careful not to overprocess or the almonds will become paste. Or, if you wish, place the almonds on a work surface, cover with wax paper and use a rolling pin to crush them. Set aside.

Combine the egg whites, maple syrup, canola oil, butter, orange juice, vanilla, brown sugar and lemon zest in a mixing bowl; whisk to blend. Whisk in the flour and ground almonds; mix well.

Spoon 2 tablespoons of the batter onto the prepared baking sheet; using the back of a spoon, spread it to form a $3\frac{1}{2}$-inch circle. The tuile should be very thin. Repeat the process with the remaining batter to make 13 more tuiles. Bake for 10 to 15 minutes, or until the tuiles are golden brown. Watch carefully, as tuiles can burn easily.

Working quickly, remove the tuiles from the baking sheet with a metal spatula and while they are hot, press them into a muffin tin or ramekin with your fingers to form a cup or cone shape. Or, if you prefer, drape the tuiles over a rolling pin to form the traditional tile shape. Let the tuiles cool; serve or store in an airtight container in a cool spot until ready to use.

STEAMED FLUFFY RICE

MAKES 2 CUPS

Learn this recipe and you'll never need another. It works equally well with white or brown rice, jasmine or basmati. Just remember that brown rice takes longer to cook than white, so time your rice accordingly. Of the brown rice varieties, long-grain brown rice is easier to cook. The short-grain brown rice, also called California brown rice, has a tasty nutty flavor and a somewhat chewy texture as well as a longer cooking time: 30 minutes.

$^3/_4$ cup long-grain brown rice, brown jasmine rice, or white jasmine rice, brown basmati rice or short-grain brown rice, rinsed and drained

$1^1/_2$ cups Vegetable Broth (page 201) or water

1 bay leaf

Combine the rice, broth or water and bay leaf in a medium-size pot set over medium heat; simmer, covered, for 20 minutes for white jasmine rice, 25 minutes for brown basmati rice, 25 to 30 minutes for long-grain brown rice or brown jasmine rice, or 30 minutes for short-grain brown (California) rice, or until the liquid has been absorbed and the rice is tender. Remove from heat, discard the bay leaf and fluff with a fork; keep warm until ready to serve.

VARIATION: STEAMED FLUFFY WILD RICE

MAKES $1^3/_4$ CUPS

$2^1/_2$ cups Vegetable Broth (page 201) or water

$^1/_2$ cup wild rice, rinsed and drained

1 bay leaf

Heat the broth to a boil in a small pot set over medium heat. Add the rice and bay leaf and simmer, partially covered, for 35 to 45 minutes, or until all the liquid has been absorbed and the rice is tender. Remove from the heat, discard the bay leaf and fluff with a fork; keep warm until ready to serve.

PLAIN EASY QUINOA

MAKES ABOUT 2 ½ CUPS

Quinoa, the staple food of the Incas long before the Europeans set foot in the Americas, is often called the "super grain" because it is so nutritious. It has a wonderful nutty flavor and cooks easily. Just be sure to simmer it slowly and be exact when measuring the quinoa and the liquid. Quinoa has many applications—in salads, muffins, desserts, as a hot side dish mixed with various flavorings, or simply steamed, as in the recipe below. I make it at home at least once a week.

2 cups Vegetable Broth (page 201) or water

1 bay leaf

1 teaspoon kosher salt, optional

1 cup quinoa, rinsed in a fine-mesh strainer and drained

Pour the broth into a medium-size pot, add the bay leaf and salt, if using. Set over medium heat, bring to a boil, add the quinoa and reduce the heat; cover and simmer for 20 minutes. Remove from the heat and let stand for 10 minutes. Remove the bay leaf, fluff with a fork and serve, or use as an ingredient in another recipe.

THE FINAL TOUCH

Before you bring your finished dish to the table, give it one last touch—a sprinkling of chopped fresh herbs (maybe chives, parsley or cilantro, depending on what you're serving), an herb garnish (perhaps a sprig of rosemary or, for sweets, lavender or mint), a squeeze of fresh lemon or lime juice in a broth-based dish, or a wedge of blood orange to garnish a salad or dessert. That final touch wakes up your food, makes it come alive on the taste buds and gives it that element of extra flavor and aroma that is essential, not just in the spa kitchen, but in any kitchen.

CRISPY ASIAN COLESLAW

MAKES 4 SERVINGS

Texture is almost as important as flavor when it comes to lightening up our food. In this salad, wonton wrappers are baked into crunchy golden strips and tossed with crisp cabbage, radicchio and carrots. The crispy wontons on the top of the salad make you feel as though you're eating something that has a lot more calories than this actually does. The napa cabbage that I use here, also known as Chinese cabbage, is conical in shape, with milky white leaves that are tender, crisp and delicately flavored, making it an excellent choice for raw vegetable salads and slaws. Choose cabbage with tightly packed leaves and bright green tips. The salad is delicious on its own but can become a main course when tossed with shredded duck, chicken or chunks of seafood.

Vegetable oil in a spray bottle, or
1 tablespoon vegetable oil

1 cup shredded napa cabbage

$\frac{1}{2}$ cup shredded radicchio

$\frac{1}{2}$ cup thinly sliced carrots (cut matchstick style)

1 cup watercress or arugula, washed and patted dry

$\frac{1}{2}$ cup pea sprouts or bean sprouts

2 teaspoons sesame oil

2 tablespoons rice wine vinegar

2 tablespoons mirin (sweet sake)

2 tablespoons fresh lime juice

3 wonton wrappers

Preheat the oven to 325 degrees F. Spray or grease a baking sheet with 1 teaspoon vegetable oil and set aside.

Combine the cabbage, radicchio, carrots, watercress or arugula, sprouts, sesame oil, vinegar, mirin and lime juice in a bowl; toss to mix well. Cover and refrigerate for 15 to 30 minutes.

Meanwhile, cut the wonton wrappers into $\frac{1}{4}$-inch strips and place on the prepared baking sheet. Spray or brush with 1 teaspoon vegetable oil. Bake for 20 minutes, or until the wonton strips are crisp and golden brown. Spray or brush with the remaining oil and let cool.

When ready to serve, toss half of the wonton crisps into the salad. Place equal portions of salad on chilled plates and top with wonton crisps.